Bringing Your
Faith to Work

Bringing Your Faith to Work

Answers for Break-Room Skeptics

Norman L. Geisler
Randy Douglass

BakerBooks
Grand Rapids, Michigan

Published by Baker Books
a division of Baker Publishing Group
P.O. Box 6287, Grand Rapids, MI 49516-6287
www.bakerbooks.com

Printed in the United States of America

Library of Congress Cataloging-in-Publication Data
Geisler, Norman L.
    Bringing your faith to work : answers for break-room skeptics / Norman L.
      Geisler, Randy Douglass.
      p. cm.
    Includes bibliographical references (p.).
    ISBN 0-8010-6554-2 (pbk.)
    1. Employees—Religious life. 2. Apologetics. I. Douglass, Randy. II. Title.
BV4593.G54 2005
248'.5—dc22
                                                    2005013046

Contents

Acknowledgments

From Norm and Randy:
We would like to thank the staff at Baker for believing in the vision of this book. People like Cheryl Van Andel, Angela McKinney, Laura Weller, and Paul Brinkerhoff, our project editor, made writing this book a pleasure.

From Norm:
Special thanks go to Christina Woodside for her invaluable expertise in coordinating the communicational logistics of two authors in two different cities. Her professionalism, administrative skill, and pleasant spirit make her a rare gem indeed.

From Randy:
Thanks to my mother, Nita, whose prayers and encouragement were like rain to a dry and thirsty land.

Thanks to my daughters, Sarah and Laura, who always believed in me even when I didn't.

Thanks to my mentor, Norm, who believed in the importance of this book and gave me both the honor and privilege of writing it with him.

Special thanks to my wife Kristie, who for almost twenty-two years has endured the good times as well as the bad. Throughout it all, she has been my advisor, my confidante, my editor, and my best friend. This book would never have happened without her wisdom and sacrifice.

How can we thank God enough for you in return for all the joy we have in the presence of our God because of you?

2 Thessalonians 3:9

Part One

Salt and Light in the Workplace

1

Our Role

You are the salt of the earth. But if the salt loses its saltiness, how can it be made salty again? It is no longer good for anything, except to be thrown out and trampled by men.

Matthew 5:13

You are the light of the world. A city on a hill cannot be hidden.

Matthew 5:14

The silence at the lunch table was deafening. I (Randy) had been leading my Impact Your Marketplace seminar at a men's conference, in which I share how to be a witness for God at work and still be successful in your job. At the lunch break, a group of men sat down to eat with me and began asking questions about my seminar. I asked them, "What are the worst witnessing approaches you have seen in the workplace?" The answers came quickly, and each one brought groans: "Bringing your Bible to a staff meeting," "Putting tracts in the men's room," "Playing your Christian music louder than anyone else," "Sitting by yourself in the lunchroom reading the Bible while everyone else is eating," "Putting Scripture in a PowerPoint presentation to the sales staff when it is not allowed."

One man shared, "We have a Christian guy at work known as 'Preacher Joe.' The guys love to put a picture of a naked woman in his locker and wait for him to open it. As soon as he does and sees the picture, he starts to condemn them as sinners who deserve hell and quotes Bible verses. The guys just double over with laughter and think he and all Christians are jerks." Everyone at the table got quiet, for we all knew people like "Preacher Joe."

I then asked, "How do you think Jesus would witness in your work-place?" That's when the room went silent. "Do you think he would use any of the witnessing approaches you just shared?" Everyone agreed that Jesus would not use *any* of these witnessing approaches. "I agree with you, but how *would* Jesus witness on your job?" More silence. I replied, "I think Jesus would be salt and light on your job. That's how Jesus witnessed in his marketplace. He was salt and light." I then went on to explain how Jesus was salt and light.

Pass the Salt

> You are the salt of the earth.
>
> Matthew 5:13

Salt Is a Preservative

In Jesus's day, salt was used for taste, but its primary function was as a preservative. When the farmers and fishermen and housewives heard Jesus's words, they would have thought of how they used salt to preserve their meat and catch of fish. Preservation of meat and fish was one of the most extensive uses of salt in their day. Because there was no refrigeration in those days, meat and fish were packed in salt to draw blood and moisture from them. Bible teacher Haddon Robinson writes, "After catching fish in the Lake of Galilee, the fishermen sold them in the capital city of Jerusalem, many miles to the south. Transportation was slow and refrigeration non-existent, so they would salt down the catch. When a farmer killed a cow, he would salt the meat, the only method of preservation."[1]

Salt That Loses Its Preservative Qualities Is Useless

> You are the salt of the earth. But if the salt loses its saltiness, how can it be made salty again? It is no longer good for anything, except to be thrown out and trampled by men.
>
> Matthew 5:13

Now whoever heard of "unsalty salt"? When we buy table salt, sodium chloride, such as Morton's from the store, it is pure. But the Morton Salt Company didn't exist back in Jesus's day. A primary source of salt was the Dead Sea. Not much was known about refining salt in those days. Because telling the difference between the salt and the sand on the shores of the sea was difficult, this substance, which people called "salt," was sometimes really a mixture of more sand than salt. When it was more sand than salt, it had lost its savor and was therefore good for nothing. People would gather up the sand/salt mixture and cast it out in their fields to use as fertilizer. Some would throw it out the door to harden the pathway that led to their front porch.

As Salt, Jesus Was a Preservative in His World

Jesus was salt to the moral decay in his world. He lived a life of purity and integrity, and this convicted those who were in his presence. His integrity made his salt pure, and he shook this salt on the moral wounds he encountered. John 4 tells about Jesus's conversation with a Samaritan woman at a well. Things were going fine until he said, "Go, call your husband and come back" (v. 16). She responded, "I have no husband." Jesus said to her, "You are right when you say you have no husband. The fact is, you have had five husbands, and the man you now have is not your husband. What you have just said is quite true" (vv. 17–18). Now we would say to Jesus, "No, Lord. You blew it. You made her uncomfortable. Get her saved first and then address her sinful living conditions." But Jesus knew he had to expose the moral decay in her life. What was her response? "Sir," the woman said, "I can see that you are a prophet" (v. 19).

In John 8 when Jesus dealt with the woman caught in adultery, he asked her, "Woman, where are [your accusers]? Has no one condemned you?" (v. 10). "No one, sir," she said. "Then neither do I condemn you," Jesus declared. "Go now and leave your life of sin" (v. 11). Jesus did not just leave her with a warm, fuzzy glow of forgiveness. He also dealt with her sin issue and poured his salt in her sinful wound. In fact, he commanded her to leave her sinful lifestyle.

More often than not, Jesus was salt to the Pharisees, the religious leaders of the day—the ones who should not have needed his salt. He saw that their moral decay was not that of immorality but of a false morality. Full of pride and condemnation, the Pharisees were driving people away from God and not toward him. So Jesus confronted them. But note that he did this to their face and did it lovingly. He warned them of the results of their choices and offered them a chance to repent. He poured his salt into their sinful wound of pride.

The point is this: Jesus was salt, a preservative that worked against the moral decay he found in his world. He was salt by living a life of integrity, taking a stand against sin, and impacting the lives of the people he encountered.

In the next chapter, we will see how we are to be salt in our world.

Turn On the Light

> You are the light of the world.
>
> Matthew 5:14

Light Is Revealing

When my children were little, the power in our house went out one night. I had to feel my way across the room, stepping on or tripping over many toys along the way, then carefully grope my way down the basement stairs to get to the fuse box. Once I flipped the switch, the house was filled with light. Only then did I discover the obstacle course I had passed through! Spiritually, light functions in much the same way. Paul wrote to the Ephesians, "You were once darkness, but now you are light in the Lord. Live as children of light (for the fruit of the light consists in all goodness, righteousness and truth) and find out what pleases the Lord. Have nothing to do with the fruitless deeds of darkness, but rather expose them" (Eph. 5:8–11). Notice that as light we are not to ignore or imitate the "deeds of darkness" but rather "expose" or reveal them. Light reveals the truth of a person's situation. Light may reveal that the path a person is traveling is filled with dangers and ultimately will end in disaster.

Light Is Guiding

In Jesus's day when people ventured outside at night, they carried lanterns to guide them along the way. Today we use flashlights to help us see where we are going. Jesus said that whoever does not have his light walks in darkness (John 8:12). His point is that this world is in darkness and its people need his light to guide them along the way (John 1:5; 3:19; 12:46).

"When speaking of *salt*, Jesus implied the culture is rotting with moral decay. When speaking of *light*, He implied the world was covered with moral and spiritual darkness. The only way for people to see clearly what matters is for us to become light."[2] Light shows people the correct path to take to keep from walking off a spiritual cliff.

Light Is Not to Be Hidden

A city on a hill cannot be hidden. Neither do people light a lamp and put it under a bowl. Instead they put it on its stand, and it gives light to everyone in the house.

Matthew 5:14–15

Hill cities in the Holy Land glowed in the distance at night because of the lights in each house. In their houses, people would set a lantern on a table so everyone could see. Today we simply turn on the lights as we enter a dark room. We wouldn't think of covering the light in our houses unless we were trying to hide from people outside.

When we are the light of the world, everyone will know it. People will see the difference not only in our behavior but also in our path in life. We are not to hide Christ's light ("put it under a bowl") by living like everyone else around us and trying to fit in with the world. Paul warns us about trying to hide our light: "Do not conform any longer to the pattern of this world, but be transformed by the renewing of your mind. Then you will be able to test and approve what God's will is—his good, pleasing and perfect will" (Rom. 12:2). When we cover our light, we are simply trying to hide the fact that we are Christ-followers.

Jesus Was a Light to His World

Jesus declared, "I am the light of the world. Whoever follows me will never walk in darkness, but will have the light of life" (John 8:12). As light, Jesus revealed people's sin, as we have seen with the woman at the well and the Pharisees. But he also guided them to a better way. Jesus guided the woman at the well to see him as the one whom she should worship. He guided the adulterous woman of John 8 to her new path of living by telling her, "Go now and leave your life of sin" (v. 11). He guided the Pharisees time and time again to the path they should take. Sometimes they listened, as did Nicodemus (John 3). But most of the time they rejected the Light and his path (John 7:32; 11:57).

As light, Jesus was never hidden. When the chief priests and guards and Pharisees came to arrest Jesus in the Garden of Gethsemane, he said, "Every day I was with you in the temple courts, and you did not lay a hand on me. But this is your hour—when darkness reigns" (Luke 22:53). His point was that he was always in the open and never hid.

In the next chapter, we will see how we are to be a light in our world.

Not an Option

Being Salt and Light Is Our Responsibility

You may be thinking, *I don't want to be salt and light at work. It's too risky!* Yes, it is risky. But it is far riskier to be saltless or lightless. If you refuse to be salt and light, your place of impact, your workplace, will become darker and more disease-ridden.

In the Greek of Matthew 5:13–14, the word translated "you" is emphatic. Jesus is saying, "You are the *only* salt of the earth," and "You are the *only* light of the world." If we don't serve as salt and light, no one will. The world's corruption will not be reduced, and its darkness will not be illumined unless God's people are salt and light.[3] In Greek, the word for "you" is plural, stressing that the whole body of Christ, not just the ministers, is responsible for impacting the world as salt and light. Every believer—in the pulpit, the garage, the school, the hospital, the military, or wherever—must be the salt and light this dark world needs.

This Responsibility Describes the Core of Our Existence

When Jesus said, "You are the salt. . . . You are the light," he was stressing *being* rather than *doing*. Jesus was stating a fact, not giving a command or request. Salt and light represent what Christians are. The only question, as Jesus went on to say, is whether we are tasteful salt and seen light.[4]

Robinson says, "Jesus didn't call us to be magnificent chandeliers for people to admire. He called us to be a single bulb in a back hall to keep people from breaking their necks when they go to the bathroom in the middle of the night. He called us to make a difference in the darkness, for doing so makes us significant and gives us impact."[5]

Now let's learn why the workplace is one of the most effective places for being a "lightbulb."

2

Our Arena

In today's global community, the greatest channel of distribution for "salt and light" is the business community . . . the marketplace.

Bill Pollard, chairman, ServiceMaster

"You can't expect me to witness at work," John retorted. John, a salesman for a large pharmaceutical firm, was quite agitated as he spoke to me after a seminar I (Randy) had taught in South Carolina. "Think about it from my perspective. If someone asked me some tough questions or challenged me in my beliefs, I wouldn't know how to answer. That would be terrible for me professionally. At best, I would be seen as someone who believes in fairy tales—not very promotable, you know? At worst, I could be fired because I didn't fit in. No, witnessing and the workplace do not go together!"

Is Work a Curse?

Do you think God is punishing you because you have to work? Wouldn't it be wonderful to stay home and never have to work again?

If you think so, you might be surprised by what God has to say about work.

Work Is Not a Result of the Fall

We know from Scripture that work is not a result of the fall (Genesis 3) for two reasons.

1. *Man was given work before the fall, not after it.* "God blessed them and said to them, 'Be fruitful and increase in number; fill the earth and subdue it. Rule over the fish of the sea and the birds of the air and over every living creature that moves on the ground'" (Gen. 1:28). "The LORD God took the man and put him in the Garden of Eden to work it and take care of it" (Gen. 2:15).

2. *After the fall, only the* ground *was cursed, not work itself.* This has made work more difficult, but work in and of itself has dignity and is from God. "So the LORD God banished [the man] from the Garden of Eden to work the ground from which he had been taken" (Gen. 3:23). "[Lamech] named him Noah and said, 'He will comfort us in the labor and painful toil of our hands caused by the ground the LORD has cursed'" (Gen. 5:29).

God Is a Worker

We also know from Scripture that God himself is a worker. "In the beginning God created the heavens and the earth" (Gen. 1:1—the work of creation). "By the seventh day God had finished the work he had been doing; so on the seventh day he rested from all his work" (Gen. 2:2—"rested" here means he stopped working on creation, not that he stopped working altogether). "Jesus said to them, 'My Father is always at his work to this very day, and I, too, am working'" (John 5:17—proof that God is still working to this day).

So God is a worker, but *why* does he work? Here are two reasons.

1. *To meet the needs of his creatures.* He upholds creation (Col. 1:16–17), meets the physical needs of his creatures (Ps. 104:10–30), is working out his purposes in history (Deut. 11:1–7), and fulfilled the work of the atonement (John 4:34).

2. *God's work brings him satisfaction.* "God saw all that he had made, and it was very good. And there was evening, and there was morning—the sixth day" (Gen. 1:31). In the Genesis account of cre-

ation, God makes the heavens and the earth in six days. When all was said and done God essentially stepped back to comment on it all and said, "It is very good." So we see that God's work both expresses his care for others and brings him satisfaction.

Work Is Good

God sees work as something that is useful. "He who has been stealing must steal no longer, but must work, doing something *useful* with his own hands, that he may have something to share with those in need" (Eph. 4:28).

God also sees work as a part of his will and something that is good. "Slaves, obey your earthly masters with respect and fear, and with sincerity of heart, just as you would obey Christ. Obey them not only to win their favor when their eye is on you, but like slaves of Christ, *doing the will of God* from your heart. Serve wholeheartedly, as if you were serving the Lord, not men, because you know that the Lord will reward everyone for whatever *good* he does, whether he is slave or free" (Eph. 6:5–8).

The reasons God works are because it meets his creatures' needs and brings him satisfaction. We who are created in his image have the same reasons to work—work meets the needs of those around us and it can bring us satisfaction as well.

Work Is a Gift

To the concept of work as a gift, you might retort, "Work a gift? Now I know you're pushing this too far!" But consider the following verses from the book of Ecclesiastes: "A man can do nothing better than to eat and drink and find satisfaction in his work. This too, I see, is from the hand of God" (Eccles. 2:24). "That everyone may eat and drink, and find satisfaction in all his toil—this is the gift of God" (Eccles. 3:13). "Then I realized that it is good and proper for a man to eat and drink, and to find satisfaction in his *toilsome labor* under the sun during the few days of life God has given him—for this is his lot. Moreover, when God gives any man wealth and possessions, and enables him to enjoy them, to accept his lot and be *happy* in his work—this is a *gift of God*. He seldom reflects on the days of his life, because God keeps him occupied with gladness of heart" (Eccles. 5:18–20).

So work is a gift from God. When we work, it brings purpose to our lives. When we do a good job at work, it brings us satisfaction—a job well done. But what about the tough jobs or the tough times at work? Look again at verse 18. Notice something here: he mentions *"toilsome* labor." Solomon understands that work can at times be drudgery, but he still says that it is good for a man to find satisfaction in his work, even in the bad times. And there's no denying the fact that if you hate your job it affects your whole life: your home, health, attitude, everything. But if you're enjoying your job, no matter what it is, that's good. Be glad.

We Are Co-workers with God

Two very important concepts we need to understand concerning our identity and purpose as co-workers with God are as follows.

1. *God created people as workers.* "Then God said, 'Let us make man in our image, in our likeness, and let them rule over the fish of the sea and the birds of the air, over the livestock, over all the earth, and over all the creatures that move along the ground.' So God created man in his own image, in the image of God he created him; male and female he created them. God blessed them and said to them, 'Be fruitful and increase in number; fill the earth and subdue it. Rule over the fish of the sea and the birds of the air and over every living creature that moves on the ground'" (Gen. 1:26–28).

The word translated "subdue" (Hebrew: *kabash*) implies that Adam and Eve should get to work at making the resources of the earth useful for their own good. Notice that God didn't do this for them; they had to work at it. God meant for them to work and develop the earth so they could produce crops and raise animals, and create places to live in and furniture to sit on and so forth.

When you work you are doing something very godlike, significant and ordained by God.

2. *God created people to be his co-workers.* "Now the Lord God had planted a garden in the east, in Eden; and there he put the man he had formed" (Gen. 2:8). "The Lord God took the man and put him in the Garden of Eden to work it and take care of it" (Gen. 2:15).

God planted the garden; the man was to cultivate it—the first partnership. We are to manage his creation and care for and meet the needs of his creatures. As we work, we are the extension of God caring for his creatures and environment. We are his hand of blessing to those in need. A nurse is the caring hand of God, a police officer is the just hand of God, a sanitation worker is the cleansing hand of God preventing disease, and a carpenter is the creative hand of God building things that are both useful and beautiful.

So when you go to work tomorrow, you are doing something god-like; you go with a new Partner and you go with a good gift from God to enjoy life!

Our Work Is a Key Place to Impact Our Co-workers for Christ

Scripture shows us that our work is an instrumental part of our witness for Christ in the workplace. We need only consider how natural it was for God to work through the lives of believers and utilize their vocations in spreading the gospel. The following two points suggest that we should think about our work as a key to our evangelistic witness on the job.

1. *New Testament evangelism is* relational *evangelism.* While there are a few examples of witnessing to strangers in the New Testament (Acts 8:26–38), the majority of examples are of believers sharing Christ with someone whom they knew.

"The man from whom the demons had gone out begged to go with him, but Jesus sent him away, saying, 'Return home and tell how much God has done for you.' So the man went away and told all over town how much Jesus had done for him" (Luke 8:38–39). Instead of taking this formerly demon-possessed man with him as a trophy, Jesus sent the man back home. Why? Because the people back home would be able to see the before and after difference Jesus had made in his life!

Take a look at the evangelism approaches in the book of Acts. The first half of Acts (1–12) portrays Peter as the primary evangelistic leader. The primary approach is *proclamational* evangelism: standing on a street corner and publicly proclaiming Jesus as Savior. This approach is underscored by key Greek words used to describe these evangelistic engagements. The first key Greek word is *euanggelizō* and is found fifteen times, all the way through Acts. We get our word *evangelism* from *euanggelizō* and it means "to tell the good news." The second key Greek word used is *kerussō* and is found eight times, four in the first half and four in the second half of Acts. *Kerussō* means to preach or to proclaim as a herald the news of a king or special envoy.

The second half of Acts (13–28) has Paul as the primary evangelistic leader and the approach is more that of *relational* evangelism, which develops relationships with someone and then shares Jesus as Savior. This can be seen by the key Greek words used to describe these evangelistic engagements. The first key Greek word is *peithō* and is found eight times (13:43; 17:4; 18:4; 19:8, 26; 26:28; 28:23, 24). *Peithō* means "to convince or to persuade" and is done in a relational setting that requires time and many discussions. The second key Greek word is *dialegomai* and is found seven times (17:2; 17:17; 18:4; 18:19; 19:8, 9; 24:25). Our word *dialogue* is related to *dialegomai*, which means to discuss, reason with, and dialogue with someone.

Why the difference in approaches from the first half of Acts to the last half? In the first half of Acts, the church was primarily dealing with a Jewish culture that had a healthy view of God and a healthy view of the Scriptures. So when Peter mentioned the prophet Joel (Acts 2:16) everyone knew that Joel was a prophet of God and his words were from God. But in the second half of Acts, the church was dealing primarily with a Greek-Roman culture that had no particular view of God and no respect for the Scriptures. So time and relationships were required before the salt and light of the church would convince someone to forsake a polytheistic worldview and turn to Christ.

2. *Evangelism is most effective when we have time to develop relationships with the unchurched.* The question to ask is, do we live in a *Jewish* culture where everyone has a healthy view of God and a healthy view of Scripture, or do we live in a *Greek-Roman* culture where people do not have a healthy view of God or of his Scriptures? The answer is more the latter than the former. But regardless, if America ever really was a "Christian" nation, it certainly is not today. Many people believe in no God or many gods, plus they believe that the Bible is full of errors and fairy tales. Standing on a street corner and preaching the words of the prophet Joel will only result in mocking and rejection. To reach this culture will require a *peithō* and *dialegomai* approach, and that demands time and relationships. The question is, where do we have the time to develop such relationships?

Reasons to Be a Witness at Work

Why should we witness at work? We have just seen that we work because God is a worker, he has created us to find satisfaction in our work, and as we work, we are co-workers with him accomplishing his will on this earth. But there is another reason God sends us off to work. It is because the workplace is one of the most vital arenas in which Christians can engage unsaved people! Consider the following reasons.

Time

Where do the majority of Christians spend a majority of their time with a majority of the unchurched? The marketplace! We spend most of our waking hours at work. On average we spend 60–70 percent of our waking hours at work. The average time we spend at church is 2–3 percent. Yet many churches act as if the only thing that is important is the time people spend at church.

Where we spend the most time is where we will have the greatest impact. The apostle Paul tells us, "Mak[e] the most of your time, because the days are evil" (Eph. 5:16 NASB). Rather than thinking that God is *punishing* us by making us spend so much time at work, begin to see that God is *positioning* us to impact our marketplace for Jesus Christ!

Awareness

Someone has said, "On Sundays when we go to church we look good, smell good, and do good." We don't cuss, steal, or get angry. We all look the same. But at work when we live a Christlike life, we get noticed right away! The workplace is one of the most effective places for our changed lives to stand out and be noticed.

First Peter 3:15 is a key verse on the importance of apologetics. "In your hearts set apart Christ as Lord. Always be prepared to give an answer to everyone who asks you to give the reason for the hope that you have. But do this with gentleness and respect." Notice the reason people ask questions: when our friends and co-workers see that we handle the difficulties of life with an inner hope, they will become aware that we have something they do not possess. Then they will come and ask us questions about our hope.

In chapter 2, Peter writes about how believers are to respond in different areas of life. In verses 18–25, he tells slaves to submit with respect to their masters, even to harsh bosses! As Christian slaves responded with respect and submission, their co-workers would be so impressed that they would ask the believing slaves to give the reason for their hope.

Bridge

Have you ever tried door-to-door witnessing? It's not a lot of fun, and it's not very effective. People *shut* their doors in your face all the time. Think about this: every Monday to Friday, the world *opens* its doors to Christians and says, "Come on in; we need your help!" We don't invade their territory as intruders. We enter their world as companions. The workplace is the most likely place to have relationships with unchurched people, and we can utilize these opportunities as a bridge to share Jesus Christ.

We know what the Great Commission tells the church to do: "Go and make disciples of all nations, baptizing them in the name of the Father and of the Son and of the Holy Spirit, and teaching them to obey everything I have commanded you. And surely I am with you always, to the very end of the age" (Matt. 28:19–20).

Don't miss this: the Great Commission doesn't tell the church to go into the world and *invite* people to church; the Great Commission tells the church to go into the world and *be* the church! The most effective place to be the church is in the workplace.

In *Inside the Mind of Unchurched Harry and Mary*, Lee Strobel stresses that Christians must meet the unsaved (whom he characterizes as unchurched Harry and Mary) where they live—in their environment. Taking his cue from the example of Jesus and the woman at the well (John 4:1–6), Strobel says, "Rescuing people in spiritual peril frequently requires us to strategically venture into their environment."[1] The typical environment of unchurched Harry and Mary, their "Samaritan well," if you will, is the workplace. We get to enter this environment five days a week, and we are invited to do so!

Neglect

I asked the 130 men at a Christian men's conference (which included some pastors) where I was speaking, "When is the last time you heard a message on the workplace?" Not one person raised his hand. "Have you ever heard a message on the workplace by a credible speaker, one who was in the workplace and understood its difficulties?" Again, not one man had ever heard such a message. These were men who had been in church for most, if not all, of their lives.

At the end of this seminar, I opened the floor to questions. One man stood up and said, "Randy, this makes me mad!" (Immediately, I started thinking of what I had said that so angered this man!) He continued, "I have been in the church all of my life. Why have I never heard any of this? For the last fifteen years, I have gone to work only for my family and me. Now you're telling me that my job matters to God and that my job can be a key vehicle for evangelism. Why has this been kept a secret?"

As one who has pastored five churches and been a consultant to many churches, I admit that we as church leaders have, for the most part, neglected the workplace. Churches spend so much time trying either to evangelize strangers or get visitors to come to our building that we neglect the most potent harvest field of all—the workplace. And get this: the harvesters sit in our churches every Sunday, just waiting to be equipped, energized, and released for active service! Paul told us, "Conduct yourselves with wisdom toward outsiders, making the most of the opportunity" (Col. 4:5 NASB).

Success

Did you know that the Bible can teach you how to be a *business* success as well as a *spiritual* success? The Bible is a businessperson's success manual. The book of Proverbs, for example, has business principles on subjects like not being lazy, working hard, controlling greed, being profitable, having integrity, excelling in our jobs, and much more.

We are not proclaiming the "health, wealth, and prosperity gospel" that some TV evangelists espouse. God may not want you wealthy, but we believe that God does want you to be the best employee or employer you can be. What Paul had to say to slaves is also appropriate for employees: "Slaves, obey your earthly masters with respect and fear, and with sincerity of heart, just as you would obey Christ. Obey them not only to win their favor when their eye is on you, but like slaves of Christ, doing the will of God from your heart. Serve wholeheartedly, as if you were serving the Lord, not men" (Eph. 6:5–7). When a Christian employee works with his or her "whole heart," the earthly boss will take notice, as will the heavenly Boss!

We all remember the story of Daniel and the lions' den in Daniel 6. But do you know that the lions' den came about because Daniel was a success with God as well as a success in business? We know that Daniel was a success with God, for God rescued him in the lions' den by shutting the lions' mouths. But look carefully at the last verse of chapter 6: "So this Daniel enjoyed success in the reign of Darius and in the reign of Cyrus the Persian" (v. 28 NASB). Daniel was a successful businessman—so successful that his boss, Darius the king, wanted to promote him to being number two over all the land. This promotion sparked jealousy in the hearts of some of Daniel's co-workers, and that is why they concocted the plan of the lions' den. But the point is that Daniel was a success with God and in business. As a businessman, I wanted the same balance, so I studied Daniel 6 and found six key principles from Daniel's life that made him a success with God as well as a success in business.[2] The good news is that these same principles are applicable today!

When we are good businesspersons, we will have a profound impact in our workplaces just as Daniel had a profound impact on his boss, his co-workers, and his world (Dan. 6:24–28).

Evangelism

Is this interest in the workplace by Christians a momentary fad or denominational program, or is it a movement of God? Consider the following opinions:

- Dr. Billy Graham: "I believe one of the next great moves of God is going to be through the believers in the workplace."
- Dr. Henry Blackaby, author of *Experiencing God*: "I think [the workplace] is the choice of God."
- Franklin Graham: "God has begun an evangelism movement in the workplace that has the potential to transform our society as we know it."[3]

These are powerful statements by godly men and visionaries. These key visionaries believe that the workplace is one of the greatest harvest fields available to the church today.

Revival

What happens when Christians in the pew decide to impact the workplace for Christ? Revival breaks forth in their hearts! They get on fire for God, hunger for the Word, begin to pray for co-workers, look for witnessing opportunities, and really love their church. When Christians are revived, they are a powerful force for God in their world of influence. May this spirit of revival break forth in all of our hearts.

Excuses Given for Not Being a Witness at Work

We have heard many excuses why people don't witness at work. We call them the five Ds for not witnessing at work.

Deny—"It is not allowed." Some Christians believe they could be fired if found discussing religion at work. Yet I have never been on a job or in a business where co-workers did not discuss a variety of topics, including religion. It is possible that the company has reacted to an overzealous Christian employee who has actually repelled people from Christianity rather than attracted them. Christians in the workplace do have rights and cannot be persecuted for their beliefs.[4] Practicing discrimination against Christians in the workplace is illegal, and victims can even file a grievance with the Equal Employment Opportunity Commission. A must-have for every Christian in the workplace is the American Center for Law and Justice's (ACLJ) booklet *Christian Rights in the Workplace.*[5]

Dilemma—"It will not be helpful to my career." As we saw earlier, John feared that being seen as a "holy Joe" would prevent him from being promotable. Yet he saw that when a Christian lives for God at work, it actually makes him or her stand head and shoulders above everyone else. As a boss, I do the hiring and firing of people all the time for my retail stores. I know that most employers are faced with employees who have little if any integrity, don't care about their job, have a rotten attitude, and want the customers to serve them, not vice-versa! But Christians who impact their workplaces for Christ will work with integrity, fulfill their divine design, see their jobs as a way to fulfill their purpose for existence, have outstanding attitudes, and be a blessing to co-workers and customers. Now what boss would not notice that? I would love to hire employees with these characteristics, and they would be on the fast track for promotion in our company!

Defeated—"I can't witness at work." This occurs when a Christian has been conformed to the "pattern of this world" (Rom. 12:2) while at work. In short, his or her life has been compromised and is a poor representation of Jesus Christ. The answer to this is to remember the height from which you have fallen, repent, and return to the pure living you practiced before (Rev. 2:5).

Divisive—"I don't know how to witness." Many Christians think to witness and discuss religion is to be divisive in our "politically correct" world. While it is easier to say, "What you believe is okay, and what I believe is okay," it is also wrong. What one believes affects a person's eternal destiny, and it is our job to be a light to them. In chapter 4, we'll show you how to witness with a dialogue approach rather than a dagger approach. You need to know two things to be an effective witness at work: truth and timing. By *truth* we mean the plan of salvation shared in a way that is easily remembered and clearly presentable (two excellent examples are the Bad News/Good News[6] approach by Larry Moyer of EvanTell and the Conversational Evangelism model by Dave Geisler; see appendix B). *Timing* refers to sharing the truth at an appropriate time. Taking up company time or not doing your job because you are witnessing will not win you any brownie points with your boss or with God!

Daunting—"I don't know how to answer questions or objections to Christianity." A lot of Christians have this problem. Recently I surveyed 130 men at a Christian men's conference at which I was speaking. I asked them what area of witnessing they struggled with the most—credible life, timing, clear presentation, or answering questions or objections? Fifty-five percent marked that they struggled with answering questions or objections to Christianity. Next I asked them to list the difficult questions or objections to Christianity they have faced while at work. After this I asked the most probing question: "Do you feel that you handled the objection well?" Seventy-seven percent responded, "No." That is why we have written this book. We want to provide you with the answers and help you to be a confident witness for Christ while at work. We'll discuss this in greater detail in the next chapter.

Remember John who was concerned about being promotable? I replied to him, "Yes, John, if you don't know how to answer questions or objections, you will look foolish. But worse than that, Christianity will not be deemed credible. So the solution is not to be passive about workplace witnessing but rather to become aggressive about learning how to answer questions and objections to Christianity! Knowing how to answer a co-worker's questions (1 Peter 3:15) will yield two results. First, you will be seen as an intelligent person, as one who has examined the issues and come to a plausible conclusion for Christianity. Second, Christianity will be seen as credible in the eyes of your co-workers." John admitted that made sense but then asked how he could learn such answers. I told him that this book was coming to help him and other Christians become the "light."

How to Be Salt and Light at Work

In the same way, let your light shine before men, that they may see your good deeds and praise your Father in heaven.

Matthew 5:16

As Salt We Are to Be a Preservative in Our World

For a Christian to be salt means that we keep the world from decaying, or becoming more morally corrupt. To do this we have to live a life of integrity before others. To be salt in the workplace we will have to shake this salt on the moral wounds that we encounter on the job.

This means that we will have to refuse to go along with those who want to lie, cheat, or steal. This means that we may have to stand up and confront those who are leading others astray. This means that we will have to resolve ethical dilemmas and difficulties in a biblical manner. Yes, the Bible does give us guidance in how to make ethical decisions, especially in the workplace! The bottom line is that salt is integrity—doing the right thing at all times no matter what! Making the right choices no matter who comes with us. Taking a stand against evil even when we may stand alone. If our saltiness remains unleashed or is washed away because of a poor testimony due to a lack of integrity or poor work effort, we become useless.

Salt Is Ethics in Action

To live as salt at work does not mean we become Pharisees or condemning, finger-pointing preachers. Rather, it means that we live a life of integrity among others. Salt is ethics in action, which seems to be sadly missing in our corporate boardrooms today. Salt is taking a stand against doing what is illegal and immoral at our jobs. Salt is guiding our co-workers to a better alternative to accomplish the same results. When a person lives like that at work, people will take notice, and he or she will stand head and shoulders above the rest.

We Are to Be a Light to Our World

For a Christian to be light means that we are to reveal the perilous dark path our friends are taking. It means that we guide them to the path of Jesus Christ. And our light is never to be hidden but seen by all—even in the workplace. In fact, we are the "bought ones" of Jesus Christ (see 1 Cor. 6:20; 7:23) and are expected to shine at all times.

So to be light means that we show nonbelievers that their lifestyle, their worldview, or even their religion is a path filled with rocks and holes and eventually will lead them off a cliff. It means that we must listen to others and answer their questions about and even their objections to Christianity. This is *apologetics*—being light in action.

To be light means that we then guide our friends to the path of Jesus Christ and all he offers. It means that we share the gospel of Christ in an attractive and effective manner. We must never hide our light, for if we do, we bring peril to all.

Haddon Robinson asks, "Is your office a black place, full of moral corruption, greed, and cold cruelty? Remember this: The blacker the night the greater the need for light. Darkness cannot put out a light. Darkness only gets darker when the light fails. When we fail to reflect Christ's light, we let the darkness win."[7]

Light Is the Gospel Discussed and Defended

Always be prepared to give an answer to everyone who asks you. . . .

1 Peter 3:15

Remember that light is guiding people to the right path and revealing the obstacles in their way. For our light to be *guiding*, we must share the gospel of the Light of the World (John 8:12). For our light to be *revealing*, we must answer people's questions and objections to Christianity as well as reveal the flaws in their own world and life view.

As we live a Christlike life (salt) at work, our co-workers will notice that we are different. They will come to us and begin to question why we think differently, respond to the boss differently, and have an attitude that is hopeful and positive. This is when we share our faith with them. Being light at work is sharing the gospel and answering questions that arise.

Most people will have some basic questions about God, Jesus Christ, the Bible, and Christianity. This doesn't mean they are evil; they are just confused. If we cannot answer their questions, they will assume that Christianity is either not true or just a psychological crutch we are using, or both.

We must know how to answer their questions! Apologetics is answering the questions people have about Christianity. Christianity is a credible religion, and answers to people's questions and objections are available.

But docs Christianity need to be "defended"? Is this something we should be doing, and if so, how? The next two chapters will answer these critical questions.

3

Why Apologetics?

"What do you think of that new Mel Gibson film about Jesus, *The Passion of the Christ*?"

This was a day at work that Mike would never forget. Every Monday the management team of his computer engineering company got together for a staff meeting and an informal lunch. During lunch the issues of the world were discussed, debated, and rarely solved. Nita was the one who brought up the new controversial film about Jesus Christ that was taking the country by storm.

Various responses were given to Nita's question. "Interesting." "Courageous." "Disturbing." Then Doug, the opinionated self-proclaimed expert in any field, chimed in. "I think the story of Jesus is a farce. Nothing in the movie really happened. The story of Jesus is just a fantasy tale like Star Wars or Lord of the Rings."

"How could you think the story of Jesus is just a fantasy?" asked Shakeima. "Everyone believes that Jesus once lived."

"No they don't," Doug said sharply. "No intelligent person believes that a man named Jesus ever lived and then died on a cross like the movie portrayed. Certainly no rational person could believe that a man so tortured and killed could rise from the dead like a ghost. Not if you check the facts."

"What facts?" Nita asked.

"That's just it," Doug smirked. "There are none. All the 'facts' about Jesus we have are from the Bible, which is only spewing forth the company line and selling the merchandise. If Jesus were really the 'Son of God,' then one would think there would be some evidence for him outside the Bible apart from the ones who were making up the stories about him. Can anyone here at this table give me one piece of evidence for the existence of Jesus outside the Bible? Anyone?" The table was silent.

Doug targeted his eyes on Mike, who was looking down at his salad. "Hey Mike, what about you? You go to church every Sunday and you believe in this Jesus. How about it? If you can give me one piece of evidence for Jesus *outside* the Bible, I'll listen to one piece of evidence about Jesus from the Bible."

Mike silently prayed for help as his mind tried to remember any sermon, any scrap of information he could retrieve that would satisfy his inquisitor. But nothing came to his mind, and Mike bravely said, "Doug, it's a matter of faith. You just have to believe, and when you do, everything falls into place."

"Faith!" laughed Doug. "How about foolishness, folly, or just plain bedtime stories and fables to comfort you in the night? No offense, man. You believe what you want to believe. But before I place my 'faith' in someone who claimed to be God and died for my sins, then rose from the dead, I'd have to see some proof. I don't think that is asking too much, do you?"

Once again the lunchroom was quiet.

Why Should We Do Apologetics?

While the names and some statements in this story were changed for the sake of privacy, this incident really happened. As a result of Mel Gibson's film *The Passion of the Christ*, a lot of similar discussions were happening all over America, from lunchrooms to office watercoolers to high school classrooms to dinner tables. What does this story tell us about the need for apologetics? What can we learn from Mike's bad day?

1. Unbelievers have good questions.
2. We have good answers to good questions.
3. Our responsibility is to be prepared apologetically.

4. There are opportune moments for evangelism.
5. The workplace is a key place for apologetics.

Let's examine each of these points.

1. Unbelievers Have Good Questions

While we may not like Doug's smugness or unrelenting attack, we must admit that he does raise a legitimate question. Is the story of Jesus just a fantasy like the story of Luke Skywalker of Star Wars or Frodo of Lord of the Rings? Or is the story of Jesus the truth on which our eternal destiny depends? These are good and important questions.

God created people with the ability to reason. In fact, this is one of the things that distinguishes us from "unreasoning animals" (Jude 10). God calls upon us to use our reason (Isa. 1:18) to discern truth from error (1 John 4:6) and right from wrong (Heb. 5:14). A fundamental principle of reason is that we should have sufficient grounds for what we believe. An unjustified belief is just that—unjustified. Socrates said, "The unexamined life is not worth living." Likewise, the unexamined belief is not worth believing.

Like Doug, many people refuse to believe without some evidence, and they are right in doing so. Since God created us as rational beings, he does not expect us to live irrationally. He wants us to look before we leap. This does not mean there is no room for faith, as Mike tried to suggest. But God does not want us to leap in the dark. Rather, he wants us to take a step of faith in the light of evidence.

We should have evidence that something is true before we place our faith in it. For example, no rational person steps in an elevator unless he has some reason to believe it will hold him up. Likewise, no reasonable person gets on an airplane that has a broken wing and smoke coming out the tail end. And a rational person like Doug will want some evidence that God exists before he places his faith in God. Rational unbelievers will want evidence for the claim that Jesus is the Son of God before they place their trust in him. Their questions must be answered.

The objections that unbelievers raise are not trivial. They often cut deep into the heart of the Christian faith and challenge its very foundations. If miracles are not possible, then why should we believe Christ was God? If God can't control evil, is he really worthy of worship? Face it: if these objections can't be answered, then we may as well believe in fairy tales. These are reasonable questions which deserve reasonable answers.[1]

2. We Have Good Answers to Good Questions

Most skeptics have only heard the questions and believed that there were no answers. But we have some great answers to their questions. Christianity is true. That means that reality will always be on our side, and we just need to find the appropriate evidence to answer whatever question is asked.[2]

Had Mike been able to answer Doug's jabbing attacks about Jesus Christ, the whole situation would have turned out differently—for Doug, Mike's co-workers, and even Mike. Had Mike known about the evidence that shows that a man named Jesus really lived, died on a cross, and rose from the dead, leaving his tomb empty, he would have been able to take advantage of a powerful opportunity to share Jesus Christ. And get this: the evidence we just mentioned comes from outside the Bible, not from the Bible itself. As we will see in chapter 12, our evidence for Jesus is overwhelming and comes from both the Bible and outside sources.

3. Our Responsibility Is to Be Prepared Apologetically

Mike was never interested in studying up on his faith and digging into apologetics. He admitted that he, like many Christians, had a lot of misconceptions about apologetics. Judy Salisbury, founder of Logos Presentations, and author of *A Time to Speak* and *A Christian Woman's Guide to Reasons for Faith*, gives five misconceptions in the way people perceive apologetics.[3]

Apologetics is about arguing, and arguing is divisive. The last way Mike wanted to be viewed at work was as a divisive person. At work divisive people were tolerated at best and fired at worst. The two things employees shouldn't talk about at work were religion and politics. Both subjects could get people into trouble and force them to take sides. So the best course of action was to keep one's mouth shut and let people say (and think) what they wanted. Now Mike realized that his desire to be nondivisive was all about protecting himself and not about protecting others (and their souls). It was as if he were in a hotel on fire, and he escaped without ringing the fire alarm so there would not be a crush of people escaping at the door.

Apologetics is too hard to get your arms around. Even the word *apologetics* was confusing to Mike. Did he need to learn to apologize for his faith? And then there was the time issue. There were too many apologetic subjects to brush up on and too many books to read for a busy working man. Now, however, he wished he had invested his time more wisely.

Apologetics is only accessible to the well educated. Who can understand all the issues apologetics deals with? How could Mike debate subjects such as evolution versus creation or Jesus versus Muhammad? Mike had thought that only geniuses with Ph.D.s were equipped to handle such deep debates. Yet he now realized that he had become an expert in his job and had learned to evaluate a software glitch, eliminate the potential causes for the error, and then fix the faulty program. Could he not invest some time to approach his faith with such an intellectual pursuit?

We believe that training Christian businesspeople like Mike in apologetics will reap a harvest such as we have rarely seen. We have been negligent in training Christian businesspeople in apologetics. Most apologetics training has been for scholars with a technical language and mind-set far above the average Christian. It is time that we focus our apologetics training on Christians on the front lines, that is, Christian workers. It is time that we adapt our language and concepts in ways that can be grasped and used by the "person in the street."

Apologetics is irrelevant to daily life. Mike could not remember one sermon his pastor had preached on apologetics or even one Sunday school lesson ever taught on the subject! No one at church ever asked apologetic questions, but now he understood that no one at church *would* ask such questions. The ones asking the questions were not coming to his church, but they were coming to his workplace. The subject he once thought was above his head and the discourse of intellectuals or those who simply liked to argue had now come kicking in the door to his office, and the intruder was there to stay!

Apologetics is only about reaching the head. Mike had known some Christians who had "all of the answers" but were as arrogant as Doug! He never wanted to be like them, for they always seemed to be looking for someone with whom to argue. While they had the right answers, they did not have the right heart, for Peter tells us to respond to people who ask questions with "gentleness and respect" (1 Peter 3:15).

What is apologetics all about? First Peter 3:15 is the classic text for apologetics: "In your hearts set apart Christ as Lord. Always be prepared to give an answer to everyone who asks you to give the reason for the hope that you have. But do this with gentleness and respect." The Greek word translated "reason" is *apologia*, from which comes our English word *apologetics*. Beside our current text, it is found in many other New Testament passages (see, e.g., Acts 22:1; 24:10; 25:8, 16; 26:1, 2, 24; 1 Cor. 9:3; 2 Cor. 7:11; Phil. 1:7, 16; 2 Tim. 4:16).

Apologia was a Greek legal term meaning among other things an answer, a defense, a verbal defense, a speech in defense, a speech of defense, and a reply. An apologetic is a defense, or a statement of a position one holds or wants to defend or prove. In this case, the cause is Christ and Christianity.

In the Bible, an apologetic does not mean an excuse or "apology" for what one believes. Rather, apologetics is the presenting of evidence and logical arguments or reasons why a person ought to believe in Christ.

In the preceding chapter, we saw that to be "light" is to guide people to the right path and reveal the obstacles in their way. For our light to be *guiding* means that we share the gospel of the Light of the World (John 8:12). For our light to be *revealing* means that we answer people's questions and objections to Christianity as well as reveal the flaws in their own world and life view. This is apologetics.

Why should someone like Mike be involved in apologetics?

We are commanded to do apologetics. First Peter 3:15 tells us three things: first, we must be ready to answer tough questions about our faith; second, we are to give a reason to those who ask the questions; and third, giving these answers helps to prepare a person's heart for salvation.[4] Paul tells us in Colossians 4:6 that we should know how to respond to unbelievers.

To reveal the flaws in non-Christian worldviews. A light shows the pitfalls along a dark path. We live in a world with non-Christian worldviews (such as postmodernism and relativism) and pagan philosophies and ideologies (such as pantheism). We must show people that the views they have been trusting or believing in are not true and cannot help or save them.

To guide non-Christians to the faith. The guiding function of light is to show those living in darkness the only path that will lead them to salvation. Apologetics offers sound evidence and reasons why one ought to consider the claims of Christ. Apologetics also helps to clarify to non-Christians what Christianity does and does not believe or teach. Christianity has been misrepresented (both by friend and foe), and many times a believer must deal with the errors presented about Christianity before moving on to its truths.

What happens if someone like Mike rejects getting involved in apologetics?

I (Randy) recently heard about a woman who went on vacation and came back to a disaster in her house. Right before she left, she used the toilet. Unknown to her, the toilet malfunctioned after she flushed it and began to leak slowly. When the woman returned ten days later, she came back to more than sixteen thousand dollars of damage to her house, and her walls and clothes were covered with mold. A slow leak can cause great damage. If we do not get involved in apologetics, a LEAK occurs.

L—*Loss of opportunity.* As we will see under point number 4, below, there are opportune moments for evangelism. If we are unprepared or unwilling to engage in apologetics, we will lose valuable opportunities to witness for Christ.

E—*Erosion of our faith.* Not answering attacks on our faith will have a negative effect on us, much like being punched and not defending ourselves. After a while we will be bruised, sore, and damaged. We will begin to wonder whether Christianity is credible or not. If we don't know the answer or don't care to find out, Satan will use our lack of offense as an opportunity to cast doubt in our mind, much as he did with Eve in the garden (Gen. 3:1).

A—*Affirmation of our opponent's position.* If we cannot give an answer, two negative things will happen. First, our opponent will think his or her false views are correct and continue in error. Second, our audience (either those listening or those our opponent will tell later) will also think the opponent was correct.

K—*Kids fall away from the faith.* Why do so many Christian kids lose their faith when they go to a secular college? We will discuss this under point number 5, below, but I believe that as our children become adolescents, they naturally begin to question everything, even their faith. If the only answers teenagers hear are "I don't know," "Because I said so," and "That's just the way we believe," it will not be enough to satisfy their God-given curiosity. Remember point 1, that unbelievers (and teenagers) have good questions, but don't forget point 2, that we have good answers to good questions. If parents don't know why they believe the things they do, their kids, when they go to college, will naturally look for someone who can defend his or her beliefs and will follow that person's example.

4. There Are Opportune Moments for Evangelism

Peter had a reason for telling us to "always be prepared." Mike had a great witnessing opportunity dropped in his lap, but he wasn't ready for it. Opportune moments for evangelism come our way almost every day if we will just look for them. The movie *The Passion of the Christ* provided opportune moments for the subject of Jesus's passion to be discussed and decided on all over the United States and the world. After September 11, 2001, one question on everyone's mind, from the boardroom to the washroom, was, "Where was God on 9/11? How could a good God allow such evil?"

We must be alert to the opportune moments that come our way. Sometimes they will be public happenings, such as a movie or tragedy. At other times they will be more personal, as when a co-worker experiences some private pain and is open to the hope of the gospel.

There are three keys to seeing the opportune moments.

Pray for opportunities. Paul asked for prayer in Colossians 4 when he said, "And pray for us, too, that God may open a door for our message, so that we may proclaim the mystery of Christ, for which I am in chains. Pray that I may proclaim it clearly, as I should" (vv. 3–4). Paul asked for an open door to share the gospel with others and the wisdom to do it well. When we pray for opportunities to witness, God loves to answer our prayer!

Open your eyes. Paul tells us, "Conduct yourselves with wisdom toward outsiders, making the most of the opportunity. Let your speech always be with grace, as though seasoned with salt, so that you will know how you should respond to each person" (Col. 4:5–6 NASB). Paul tells us to use great wisdom in seeing the opportune moments to witness to nonbelievers and to seize those moments for Jesus's sake. Look at public happenings, such as news events, current movies, even things such as problems within your own company (such as downsizing or financial difficulties). Look at what is happening in the lives of your co-workers. Are they going through marital difficulties, financial problems, or an illness of someone in their family?

Listen to what your co-workers are saying about these public events and be prepared to answer their questions. Hear the pain behind the pleasant facade of your co-workers, and be sensitive to what issues are really involved.

Follow the Holy Spirit's leading. In Acts 8:30 we read that when the Spirit prompted Philip to join himself to the chariot of the Ethiopian eunuch (who was reading Isaiah 53), Philip asked the man, "Do you understand what you are reading?" The eunuch replied, "How can I unless someone explains it to me?" The Holy Spirit will lead the praying Christian to people who need help in understanding spiritual truth. While the Holy Spirit will provide a "door for our message" (Col. 4:3), we must walk through it and "proclaim it clearly" (Col. 4:4).

5. The Workplace Is a Key Place for Apologetics

There are four key places for apologetics.

Secular college campuses. J. Budziszewski shares that a secular college is a war zone and then lists twelve reasons why collegians lose their faith.[5] Some of these reasons are as follows:

- Young believers don't know the reasons for God's rules.
- They think that faith and knowledge are opposites.
- They believe that Jesus forbids moral judgment.
- They don't realize that their adversaries have faith commitments.
- They don't know how to call a bluff.

College is a gathering of seeking students and knowledgeable professors thrown together in one setting. Therefore, having one's beliefs challenged is as much a part of college as dorm life and all-nighters. Knowing that such attacks are coming and preparing students for them is vital.

Relationships with unsaved relatives. If you have unsaved relatives, you eventually will be drawn into a discussion (if not an argument) about your differing beliefs. Many Christians say, "Humbug!" to the Christmas holiday season because they will have to visit relatives, some of whom are unsaved, and the visits with these scrooges is never a "wonderful life"! As 1 Peter 3:15 guides us, knowing how to defend your faith with gentleness and respect is key here.

The church. In their book *Is Your Church Ready? Motivating Leaders to Live an Apologetic Life*, Ravi Zacharias and Norman Geisler make the point that it is essential for churches to train their people in apologetics. As mentioned above, many young people who were raised in the church leave the church when they enter college or the workplace because they were never taught that the Christian faith is credible and holds the answers to unbelievers' questions. Where but in the church will they find trained leaders and the time for training (as in Sunday school, youth group, or sermons)? Zacharias and Geisler then provide a guide for church leaders to use for apologetics training in the church, touching on how preaching, teaching, and even worship can be used to help Christians develop an apologetic lifestyle.

The workplace. This environment has the following elements.

- *Diversity.* It is not unusual to find in the workplace today a gathering of males and females who are Catholics, Protestants, Muslims, New Agers, atheists, agnostics, and who knows what else!
- *Time.* As mentioned in the preceding chapter, we spend an average of 60–70 percent of our waking hours at work and thus with our co-workers. We may be able to avoid troublesome relatives, but pagan, ungodly co-workers are around us at work all of the time.
- *Opportunity.* Rather than see the time spent with co-workers as a negative, it is time we see it as a positive. Instead of having the perspective that all day long we are surrounded by minions of the devil, it is time we grasp the perspective that all day long the minions of the devil are in the presence of an overcomer who is empowered by the Holy One! Instead of allowing their evil to influence us, it is time we use our righteousness to influence them. Dark is only dark until light appears. When we shine our light boldly and proudly, the darkness flees away.

Diversity, time, and opportunity are why we believe the workplace is a key place for apologetics and why this book is so important. In Antioch, Paul adapted his witnessing strategy to include not just the synagogues but also the marketplace (Acts 17:17–18). The result was that people began to listen and Paul had an opportunity to witness on Mars Hill (v. 22). We believe that there are many "Mars Hill" opportunities just waiting to be seized when Christian businesspeople take Jesus to the workplace. But how we engage others in apologetics will make the difference between winning a hearing and offending an audience, as our next chapter will show.

4

How Should We Do Apologetics?

"God says you're a fool, Tim. A fool!"

Bruce heard the yelling all the way down to his office. It sounded like two of his administrators were having a knock-down fight, and since he was the boss, he would have to investigate. He gingerly walked down to Sarah's office, where the yelling had been coming from, and saw her at her desk with her head in her hands. Bruce knocked on her half-opened door and asked, "Sarah, is everything all right?"

"No, everything is not all right!" snapped Sarah.

"Well, what happened?" Bruce questioned.

Sarah replied, "I was having a religious discussion with Tim, and things got a little out of control."

"Sarah, it sounded like things got a *lot* out of control. And this was over a *religious* discussion?"

"Yes, I was sharing with Tim how I believe God guides me in my daily life, especially while at work," Sarah explained. "Tim just smiled, shook his head, and said, 'That's good for you, Sarah. But I don't believe any intelligent person can believe in the existence of some God out there.' 'So I'm not an intelligent person because I believe in God?' I asked. Tim smirked and said, 'You said it, not me.' Bruce, that is when I snapped. I said, 'You know what, Tim? The Bible says that only a fool would not believe in God. That's right.

"The fool hath said in his heart, There is no God."[1] God says you're a fool, Tim. A fool! What do you think of that?' Tim then got up, and as he walked out of my office, he said, 'What difference does it make what a made-up being thinks about me? That would be like being upset that one of my daughter's dolls is mad at me. Who cares?'" Sarah looked at Bruce and said, "Bruce, you're a Christian. What I said about Tim was true. It's in the Bible."

Bruce shook his head and said, "Yes, but how you said it was not loving. That approach is not going to win him to Christ."

Sarah sighed, "It is so hard to discuss religious differences without having it turn into a battle. How should I have handled that situation better?"

Now it was Bruce's turn to sigh as he said, "I honestly don't know, Sarah. I don't."

Silence now filled the office.

Knowing the Bible and other important information for defending your faith is crucial to effective apologetics. But as Sarah found out, how she uses this knowledge is the key to how effective she is for the cause of Christ. She can attract people to Christ or repel them from Christ just by the way she shares her insights. No one likes to be called a fool, even if the Bible says it's true. Remember that Peter told us to share the reason for our hope with "gentleness and respect" (1 Peter 3:15). Someone has said, "The same sun can melt ice and burn skin." How do we "melt the ice" of our co-workers' hearts and not end up "burning their skin"?

Christians have different approaches to questions about their faith and the use of apologetics.

- *Defensive approach.* This Christian works hard to build up high walls, not wanting or willing to discuss Christianity or religious topics with unsaved people.
- *Defeatist approach.* This Christian simply gives up because he or she thinks that the subject of apologetics is too deep for comprehension. Or even worse, he or she fears there may not be an answer to the question being asked.
- *Devotional approach.* This Christian studies these truths only for personal use. Mental stimulation and the pursuit of knowledge is very fulfilling, but study only for the sake of oneself will lead to arrogance (1 Cor. 8:1).

- *Dagger approach.* This Christian enjoys using apologetic information to attack non-Christians and their beliefs. This Christian "Rambo" loves a good fight and is always looking for one. The smug smile and satirical tongue of this person are so repelling that even mosquitoes look for their meal elsewhere!

- *Dialogue approach.* This Christian uses apologetic information to talk with seekers and develop relationships with them. The apostle Paul was a master at this. Acts 18:4 shows Paul's approach. Paul at Corinth "was reasoning in the synagogue every Sabbath and trying to persuade Jews and Greeks" (NASB). "Reasoning" is from the Greek word *dialegomia*, which means to discuss and debate. Our English word *dialogue* comes from this word. "Trying to persuade" comes from the Greek word *peitho*, which means to convince by argument. These same words are also found in Acts 19:8. Paul's approach was to get to know someone, open a dialogue about Jesus, and using apologetic proofs, try to convince this person that Jesus was the Messiah.

There are two ways to keep your dialogue approach from turning into a dagger approach. First, you must prepare for apologetic encounters at work before they occur, and second, you must learn to develop a dialogue style that you will never forget.

Being Ready for an Apologetic Encounter at Work

1. Know Your Stuff

If a soldier goes into battle with an empty rifle, he or she won't last long. As we saw in chapter 3, Mike went to work and entered a war zone. He was attacked by Doug and had only an empty rifle to defend himself and Christianity.

Some basic questions concerning Christianity come up from time to time, and you must know how to respond to them. Below we will give you these answers in a user-friendly format.

2. Pray

As mentioned earlier, Paul asked for prayer in Colossians 4 when he said, "And pray for us, too, that God may open a door for our message, so that we may proclaim the mystery of Christ, for which I am in chains. Pray that I may proclaim it clearly, as I should" (vv. 3–4).

- *Pray for yourself.* Pray for God to give you the strength and wisdom to be a good witness. Paul asked for personal prayer, and you can ask others to pray for you too.
- *Pray for the opportunity.* Paul asked for an open door to share the gospel with others. Pray for opportunities as you approach work and spend the day there.
- *Pray for your co-workers.* Pray for your boss, co-workers, clients, and customers. In the churches we pastored, many Saturdays we would spend time in the church auditorium touching and praying over each pew. We prayed for the people who would be there on Sunday, asking God to move in their lives. You can do the same thing at work. When possible, pray over your co-workers' offices, cubicles, and workstations. Walk around your company or business and claim it for God and his kingdom. Remember that you are the only pastor, the only shepherd some of your co-workers will ever know.

3. Make People Thirsty

I (Randy) teach conflict resolution skills in a seminar I have entitled "Office Zoo."[2] In this seminar, I identify the different animals we face at work and then share four "taming tools" that help to tame our "animals" as they are being difficult and then train them from attacking in the future. I have taught these concepts for years and found them to be effective in resolving conflict whether it is in the secular workplace, a church, or even marriage. One of these taming tools I teach is the "salt principle." Psychologist Gary Smalley developed this principle. It makes sure that you have the full attention of the person to whom you are speaking by motivating that person to listen to you and see things from your perspective.[3] To get that attention, you have to pique that person's interest until he or she is "thirsty."

Smalley says, "You know the old saying that you can lead a horse to water, but you can't make it drink? Well, you CAN make it drink by dumping a lot of salt into its oats before you take it to water."[4] The more curious you make someone, the more that person will want to listen. The principle is this: never communicate your feelings or information you consider to be important without first creating a burning curiosity within the listener.

In doing apologetics, you can learn how to build a burning curiosity in your co-workers to hear the truths of Christianity. Paul said, "Let your conversation be always full of grace, seasoned with salt, so that you may know how to answer everyone" (Col. 4:6). Salt in this verse refers more to seasoning than to the purifying aspect of Matthew 5:13.

When various topics come up at work that can be witnessing opportunities, listen to what is said and sprinkle some salt! For example, the following scenario could take place when a tragedy occurs.

> Comment: "I don't know what this world is coming to."
> Salt: "I know how you feel. I used to be very afraid when I saw these tragedies. But I'm not anymore."
> Response: "Really? Why aren't you afraid anymore?"
> More salt: "Do you really want to know my secret?"
> Response: "Yes, I'm listening!"

As you can see, the salt principle can actually get people to beg you to tell them your secret, which of course is the gospel. I have tried this principle many times and found it to be very effective in winning a hearing.

Developing a Dialogue Apologetic Style

Being involved in an apologetic encounter at work can seem daunting if not terrifying. Christians tell us that the two major reasons they avoid apologetic encounters at work are the *knowledge* factor (knowing evidences of God, evolution, reasons for evil, etc.) and the *divisive* factor (fearing that discussing the things of God will lead to division). This book is written with these two reasons in mind. It is designed to be a handy reference tool that you can keep at your workstation. When a subject comes up, you can turn to the relevant chapter and especially the reference guide at the end of the chapter. We use acrostics with each subject to emphasize the core elements and make them easy to remember.

In reference to being divisive, there are two points to keep in view. First, anytime one takes a stand for Christ, there will be division

(John 15:18–21). Second, although the cross is offensive, we are not to be offensive (Gal. 5:11). We have developed a tactful approach to engaging in apologetics that is both loving and effective. We use the acrostic PROVE to guide us in the important steps of talking with a person. It helps to keep us from being sidetracked and to be gentle and respectful when dealing with someone with whom we disagree (1 Peter 3:15). The PROVE approach may not work with every person or in every situation, but we have found it to be effective most of the time. (For another approach to sharing the gospel, the THINK approach by Dave Geisler, Norm's son, see appendix C.)[5]

P — *Partner*

Begin your dialogue by getting the person to agree to be partners in discovering the facts about the issue the two of you are discussing. There are two reasons for beginning with the partner approach. First, treating someone as a partner is a positive way to begin a disagreement. In his classic book, *How to Win Friends and Influence People*, Dale Carnegie says: "In talking with people, don't begin by discussing the things on which you differ. Begin by emphasizing—if possible—that you are both striving for the same end and your only difference is one of method and not of purpose. Get the other person saying, 'yes, yes,' at the outset."[6]

Let's think about how Mike from chapter 3 could use this approach. Mike could begin his dialogue with Doug by saying, "Doug, you sure have given the subject of Jesus a lot of thought, haven't you? ("Yes, I have.") And you only want to believe in something that is true, right? ("I sure do!") Well, so do I. Let's agree to deal only with the facts together. Let's find out what we believe about Jesus and how we came to our conclusions. Now, I may be wrong or you may be wrong. But let's wrestle with the facts together. What do you say about that?"

I am sure that Doug would readily agree. Why? First, he would be shamed before the others for rejecting such a gracious offer. Second, people like Doug are creatures of logic and only want to deal with factual evidence. Third, getting Doug to say yes a few times helps to set his psychological processes moving forward in the affirmative direction.[7] Fourth, entering into a partnership assumes some time involved and a series of dialogues rather than lectures. Finally, being asked to be a partner shows Doug that he is respected and not viewed as an opponent by Mike.

The second reason to start as a partner is that you now have the liberty to ask probing questions of your partner. You have to know who your partner is and where he or she is spiritually. Your "partner" should not resist such questions, for this is now allowed. How do you do this? By being like Sherlock Holmes or a good doctor. The great fictional detective Sherlock Holmes used his powers of observation in conjunction with asking probing questions to solve a mystery. A good doctor doesn't give medications without first asking questions to obtain the patient's diagnosis. Your task is to do the same. We like to use a set of questions we call the "CT SCAN." In medicine a CT (or CAT) scan is a three-dimensional image of the body made by computerized tomography. The machine sees inside the body in a noninvasive way. Likewise, the following six questions are designed to help you discover information about your partner without being overly invasive.

> **C**—*Curiosity. "I'm curious—why do you believe (or not believe) this?"*
>
> **T**—*Time. "How long have you believed (or not believed) this?" "When did you change your mind on this?"* Years ago when I was a new police officer, I was assigned a partner named Jim. As we began to spend time together, eventually the subject of religion came up. Jim bluntly told me, "I don't believe in God, and no one can convince me otherwise!" I tried sharing some evidences for God, but he would not budge. Finally, I asked him the key question of time: "When did you begin to believe there was no God?" Jim spoke in almost a whisper: "My daddy was a drunk who beat me and my mom every night. I prayed every day for God to make it stop, but it never did until I moved out. If there really were a God, he would have answered my prayers." The obstacle for Jim was not the existence of God, but the problem of evil! If there is a God, then why is there evil? (We cover this difficult issue in chapter 8.) Once I knew the obstacles, I was able to change my approach, answer his questions, and see God soften Jim's heart to the gospel.
>
> **S**—*Smug factor. "What do you like about your position?"* This tells you what obstacles you must overcome in your partner's mind concerning his or her position.
>
> **C**—*Catalogue. "What are your facts?" "Is this your opinion or is this a fact? How do you know it is a fact?"* Sergeant Joe Friday on

the old *Dragnet* show used to say, "Just the facts, ma'am. Just the facts." Getting a person to agree to dealing only with facts is critical. As the "facts" are mentioned, be sure to write them down. This will show that you are listening and ensure that you won't forget his or her points.

A—*Analyze. "What would or should you accept as evidence for this position?"* Analyze the basis for the "facts" that have been given. Dealing with "evidence" is objective and fact-oriented. Dealing with "proof" is subjective. What is proof to you may not be proof to me. For example, no one can "prove" or disprove the existence of God. But you can look at the evidences. Try to determine what constitutes evidence for this person.

N—*Negotiate. "Would anything convince you, or is your mind already made up?" "Are you open to looking at your position and my position with an open mind, or will we just be wasting our time?"* These are important questions, for as you dialogue with your partner, he or she may become close-minded and refuse to consider your viewpoint. If at the partner stage your partner says that his or her mind is made up, then not only will your dialogue fall on deaf ears, but it will be evident to all that you are the one willing to dialogue and he or she is not. This will position you positively for the next person in your workplace who truly is seeking to know the answers.

Ravi Zacharias, in speaking to pastors, says something that I think applies to all involved in answering questions: "We must listen to our congregations—and often the question behind their question. When met with gentleness and respect, many people admit their vulnerability."[8] We must listen to our co-workers—and the question behind their question. When met with love and respect, their hard hearts may melt.

R—*Rephrase*

Rephrasing, a key tool for listening to others, is another taming tool I teach in my Office Zoo seminar. Listening to people is a difficult skill to develop, especially when we are under attack. Often when we are involved in a disagreement, we either respond to what we thought we heard the person say or justify and defend ourselves. The natural human reaction is to become defensive and offer a list of reasons why the comment is untrue. Either way the person feels that we have not listened. And they're right! If we are not listening in an apologetic encounter, we will anger and insult the person we are trying to reach for Christ.

The Bible tells us the following:

Proverbs 1:5: "Let the wise listen and add to their learning, and let the discerning get guidance."

Proverbs 18:13: "He who answers before listening—that is his folly and his shame."

Proverbs 21:23: "He who guards his mouth and his tongue keeps himself from calamity."

James 1:19: "My dear brothers, take note of this: Everyone should be quick to listen, slow to speak and slow to become angry."

Again I am indebted to Smalley, who calls the rephrasing concept "drive-through talking."[9] When you visit the drive-through at a fast-food restaurant, you place your order by talking into the speaker, and the clerk repeats it. If you agree, you say yes and then proceed. If the clerk is wrong, you repeat your order until it is right.

Rephrasing during an apologetic dialogue is done in three simple steps:

1. *Share.* Let the person share his or her complaint. Doug shared why he could not believe in Jesus.
2. *Repeat.* Repeat in your own words what you think the other position is. Mike could say, "Doug, let me make sure I heard you correctly. You said that you could not believe in Jesus because you know of no evidence for him outside the Bible. Is that what you said?"
3. *Agree.* Wait until the person says yes. If he or she says no, continue to rephrase until there is agreement.

Now you have listened and the other person knows you have listened. This is a major step not only to defusing anger but also to making sure that both of you are talking about the same thing. Rephrasing every answer you receive from your CT SCAN questions is important, for in doing so, you will truly know your new partner.

O — Oreo Cookie

The Oreo cookie method is another Office Zoo taming tool that is effective for confronting a person or, in this case, sharing a differing position. To openly share that you disagree with another person, especially about religion, is very difficult to do well. That is why many Christians would rather hide like an ostrich than get involved in apologetics.

I learned the Oreo cookie method years ago when being trained as a police officer. I used this approach with people I had to arrest and found that it worked with every person sober or sane enough to understand my words. This approach was so effective that when I had finished using it, even most of the drunks I arrested actually told me that I had to arrest them! With the Oreo cookie method, you will be able to share a differing position with someone that will not anger them and will even motivate them to consider your position.

Just use the parts of an Oreo cookie—cookie, cream, and cookie—as your model.

Cookie. Begin by mentioning something you respect or appreciate about the person or an area on which the two of you can agree. It is important to begin with appreciation, not flattery, for most people can see through that. I guarantee that you will strike a responsive chord within a person, which will break open the hard ground of their heart for the cream.

Cream. Share your position on the issue. The "cream" of the cookie is the negative that must be shared, whether it is a point of confrontation or a differing position.

Cookie. Finish by sharing positive intent by assuming the best about the person and giving the benefit of the doubt. This gives the person a good reputation to live up to and encourages the person to consider your position.

In 1 Corinthians the apostle Paul used this approach. He started off positive by first using the cookie in telling the Corinthians that they were the sanctified church of God and that he was always thankful for them (1:2, 4). Then he gave them the negative cream, whereby he dealt with their behavior, such as challenging Paul's authority (chap. 4); condoning immorality (chap. 5); suing one another (chap. 6); and abusing their marriages (chap. 7), their

Christian liberty (chap. 8), the Lord's Supper (chap. 11), and their spiritual gifts (chaps. 12–14). But Paul ended his letter with the positive cookie by saying that he couldn't wait to see them (16:6), he wanted to spend quality time with them (16:7), all the churches thought highly of them (16:19–20), he cared so much for them that he wrote the letter himself (16:21), and he loved them (16:24). While the Corinthian church received an apostolic spanking, they knew it was done by someone who loved them. The positive results of Paul's approach can be seen in 2 Corinthians, where the church addressed the issues Paul had raised.

Let's see how Mike could use the Oreo cookie method to deal with Doug.

Cookie. Starting positively, Mike could say, "Doug, you are a wise man. I know that you are the kind of person who likes to consider all of the facts when studying something, whether it is here at work or with politics or religion. You examine both sides of an issue and then you come to a decision. I really respect that about you."

Cream. Sharing his differing position on the issue, Mike could say, "Perhaps you are not aware of the evidence outside the Bible that shows that a man named Jesus actually lived, was put to death on a cross, and was reported to have risen from the dead. Some of this evidence was actually reported by the foes of Jesus."

Cookie. Finishing by giving Doug a good reputation to live up to, which would encourage him to consider Mike's position, Mike could say, "Doug, since you are a wise and thorough man, I know that you will want to look at all of the evidence and see what it has to say." A person who is truly open will not resist this approach.

V — Verdict

After you have dialogued and considered both sides of an issue, it is time to make a decision, time to cast a verdict. Which position is most credible? Jurors listen to both sides of a court case, but their job is not done until they cast a verdict for one side or the other. Calling for a verdict is "funneling" the person to making a decision for the gospel.

Mike could say to Doug, "Now let's conclude what we have learned. We looked at some of the evidence about Jesus. We saw that legitimate sources outside the Bible say that a man named Jesus actually lived, died on a cross, and was reported to have risen from the grave. And we saw that these reports came from people who were unbiased and unforced, right Doug?[10] What do you say to the evidence? What is your verdict?"

Hopefully, Doug's verdict will be to agree with your side. My advice would then be to remind him of his earlier challenge. Remember that Doug said if he saw one piece of evidence for Jesus outside the Bible, he would consider one piece of evidence for Jesus from the Bible. Start over with the PROVE approach and consider the facts as partners concerning the empty tomb.

E — *Educate to the Gospel*

As you come to the verdict about Jesus, share the gospel. In sales this is what we call the "close." As a former salesman and director of salespeople, I had to learn that it was not enough to know your product and the person to whom you were selling; you had to know how to get that person to "sign on the dotted line."

After Doug looks at the evidence of the empty tomb, Mike can then share the meaning of the resurrection. He can share why Jesus came to this earth and died on the cross. He can tell Doug that three days later Christ arose to bring new life to all who would place their faith in him. Never fail to share the gospel with a partner, even if only in a nutshell. The Holy Spirit will take these "seeds" that you have sown and work in the person's heart to convict of sin and reveal the righteousness he offers and the judgment that will result if Christ is rejected (John 16:8).

It is fitting that we close our chapter on defining and defending the gospel by considering both the problem and the power. The problem facing our co-workers is not that they are dumb and cannot comprehend the obvious truths about God and Jesus; it is that they have been blinded. In 2 Corinthians 4, the apostle Paul wrote, "And even if our gospel is veiled, it is veiled to those who are perishing. The god of this age has blinded the minds of unbelievers, so that they cannot see the light of the gospel of the glory of Christ, who is the image of God" (vv. 3–4).

If Paul had stopped there, our task would be daunting and discouraging, if not impossible. But in verse 6, Paul shared the solution to the blindness: "For God, who said, 'Let light shine out of darkness,' made his light shine in our hearts to give us the light of the knowledge of the glory of God in the face of Christ." The solution to our friends' and co-workers' spiritual blindness is not up to us; it is up to God. God will overcome the enemy's darkness in victory every time!

Part 2 will deal with some "hot topics around the watercooler." Each chapter will discuss difficult apologetic topics Christians face with unbelievers while at work.

PROVE Dialogue Approach

P—*Partner*
- C—*Curiosity.* "I'm curious— why do you believe (or not believe) this?"
- T—*Time.* "How long have you believed (or not believed) this?" "When did you change your mind on this?"
- S—*Smug factor.* "What do you like about your position?"
- C—*Catalogue.* "What are your facts?" "Is this your opinion or is this a fact? How do you know it is a fact?"
- A—*Analyze.* "What would or should you accept as evidence for this position?"
- N—*Negotiate.* "Would anything convince you, or is your mind already made up?" "Are you open to looking at your position and my position with an open mind, or will we just be wasting our time?"

R—*Rephrase*
- *Share.* Let the person share his or her viewpoint.
- *Repeat.* Repeat in your own words what you think the other position is.
- *Agree.* Wait until the person says yes. If he or she says no, continue to rephrase until there is agreement.

O—*Oreo* Cookie
- *Cookie.* Mention something you respect or appreciate about the person or an area on which the two of you can agree.

• *Cream.* Share your position on the issue. The "cream" of the cookie is the negative that must be shared, whether a point of confrontation or a differing position.
• *Cookie.* Finish by sharing positive intent by assuming the best about the person and giving the benefit of the doubt.

V—*Verdict*

• This is the time to ask the person to decide on the facts you have shared.

E—*Educate* to the Gospel

• Always share the gospel, even if only in a nutshell.
• Remember that it is God who will work in the other person's heart!

Hot Topics around the Watercooler

5

Are All Religions True?

"Because of the diversity of our employees and our desire to respect each person's religious preferences, we have decided not to celebrate Christmas at work this year," the boss told the staff of the marketing firm. "Celebrating Christmas would elevate Christianity over other religions, and we want to be tolerant of everyone. Therefore there will be no Christmas party this year. That also means no gift giving, no Christmas songs on the radio, no decorations, and no Christmas cards. I know this will not be popular with you, but believe me, it is necessary." With that, he turned and walked out of the conference room.

As soon as he left, everyone exclaimed their disbelief. Someone even called the boss a scrooge. After the employees went back to their cubicles, Gene cornered Tony, the operations manager, and asked why this decision was made. Gene was a Christian and had developed a good friendship with Tony. Tony told Gene that the company had no choice. "An Asian employee in the IT department had complained about Christmas being observed at work and not his religious holidays. The human resources department recommended that it is all or none—either we observe all religious holidays or none at all. Here, look at all the holidays just for November and December."

With that he pulled out a sheet from his folder and showed it to Gene. Some of the dates for November were: 11/1—All Saint's Day

(Christian); 11/12—Birth of Baha'u'llah (Baha'i); 11/14—end of Ramadan (Islam); 11/24—Martyrdom of Guru Tegh Bahadur (Sikh), Thanksgiving (Interfaith); 11/26—Day of Covenant (Baha'i); 11/27—Advent (Christian); 11/28—Ascension of Abdul-Baha (Baha'i). December dates included: 12/8—Bodhi Day (Buddhist); 12/21—Yule/Winter Solstice (Wicca); 12/25—Christmas (Christian); 12/26–1/1—Kwanzaa (Interfaith); 12/26–1/2—Hanukkah (Jewish).

"So since we couldn't observe all of the religious holidays, we had to decide to observe none of them. I know you don't like it, but I think it was the right call."

Gene pouted. "But Tony, no Christmas? This still is a Christian nation, you know."

"Not anymore, my friend," Tony replied. "Besides, they've got a point. Why should we elevate one religion like Christianity over another?"

"But," Gene stammered, "the other religions are wrong. They're not telling the truth."

Tony just shook his head. "Gene, religions are like McDonald's and Burger King. They're all selling the same product, just with different window dressings. All religions say basically the same thing and have the same core truths. They all have a common theme—live a good life. They all have a central character, whether it be Jesus or Buddha or Muhammad. And they all have sacred writings and a common destination—heaven or their version of it. My friend, all roads lead to heaven. It doesn't matter which one you take. We just need to respect each person's perspective of the truth as they know it."

Gene had no reply.

Tolerance is the new mantra in America today. Tolerance today no longer means you put up with something you do not believe, but rather, like Tony, you are now supposed to accept every belief as true. You are supposed to be especially tolerant of religions and are not allowed to question anyone else's beliefs. This is called "religious pluralism"—the belief that all religions are equal and true. Judaism, Hinduism, Islam, Taoism, Buddhism, and Christianity are seen as different restaurant chains peddling the same product.

The Truth about Truth

Critics of truth today are found in two different camps. One says, "There is no truth," while the other says, "What's true for you is not what's true for me." Actually, the latter camp is just the logical outflow of the former camp, as we will see. The truth is (no pun intended), most people today believe there is some truth, but you'd better allow them to have their own or else!

Six Blind Hindus and an Elephant

I'm sure you have heard the parable of the six blind men and the elephant—a favorite of many university professors. In this parable, each blind man feels a different part of an elephant and comes to a different conclusion about the object in front of him. One grabs the tusk and says, "This is a spear!" Another holds the trunk and says, "This is a snake!" The one holding the leg exclaims, "This is a tree!" The one holding the tail feels sure that he holds a rope. The one feeling the ear concludes, "This is a fan!" Finally, the one leaning on the elephant's side says, "No, this is a wall!" These six blind men are supposed to represent world religions that have come to a different conclusion about what they are sensing. We are told that, like each blind man, no one religion has the truth, but each has a portion of it. Truth is relative to the individual; it is subjective.

Three observations thunder forth from this elephant parable. First, all the men are wrong! They are not holding a tree or a fan or a snake. No, they are feeling an elephant. Second, they are all blind. They are wrong because they are blind. They do not know what is in front of them. Third, they are in danger. Elephants have been known to trample people and things, especially when strangers are pawing at them! These same three observations thunder forth from the conclusion that all religions hold the truth. As we will soon discover, all religions do not contain the truth, and so some of them are wrong. Those who adhere to these religions are wrong because they are blind like the blind men examining the elephant. They are sincere in their beliefs, but they are sincerely wrong. Finally, they are dangerous. If their religion does not contain truth, then it is error. Believing error in religion is no less dangerous than swallowing poison—both will change your future!

But how do we know that not all religions contain truth? How do we know which religion, if any, contains the truth? Who possesses the truth? The process of discovering truth begins with the self-evident laws of logic called "first principles." They are called first principles because there is nothing behind them. They are not proved by other principles; they are simply inherent in the nature of reality and are thus self-evident. So you don't learn these first principles; you just know them. These principles are so logical that when you hear them, you respond, "Of course, that makes sense."

Who is the "possessor" of truth? Everyone? No one? Or someone? To discover this, we have developed the acrostic **POSSESSOR** to guide us through the principles to discover truth.

Truth . . .

P—*Parallels the Facts*

Truth can be defined as that which accords with the facts. In short, truth "tells it like it is." Truth matches its object. For example, when someone looks at a table and says the object is a table, that person is telling the truth.

Well, if that is truth, then what is falsehood? When something is false, it does not accord with the facts, does not tell it like it is, and does not match its object. For example, when someone points to a tree and says it is a table, that person is telling a falsehood.

O—*Opposite of True Is False*

The opposite of true is false. This is the *law of noncontradiction*. The law of noncontradiction is another self-evident first principle of thought that says that contrary claims cannot both be true at the same time in the same sense. In short, it says the opposite of true is false. We all know this law intuitively and use it every day.

Opposite ideas cannot both be true at the same time and in the same sense. Consider the following examples:

- The earth is round. The earth is flat.
- Christianity says there is a God. Atheism says there is no God.
- The Bible says Jesus rose from the dead. The Qur'an says Jesus did not rise from the dead.

All truths exclude their opposite. A medieval Muslim philosopher by the name of Avicenna suggested a surefire way to correct someone who denies the law of noncontradiction. He said that "anyone who denies the law of noncontradiction should be beaten and burned until he admits that to be beaten is not the same as not to be beaten, and to be burned is not the same as not to be burned."[1]

S — Is Selective

Truth is absolute, not relative. If something is true, it is true for all people at all times in all places. For example, 3 + 3 = 6 in London, Moscow, Peking, and Washington. Even seemingly relativistic statements like "I feel warm" are true everywhere, for the fact that *I* feel warm is true for everyone, even for people who feel cold. So, whatever is true anywhere is true for everyone everywhere.

Now let's go back to the parable of the blind men and the elephant. Were the six blind men right? No, they *all* were wrong. The only one who was right was the one with his eyes open to the truth and could see that it was an elephant. That was the absolute truth!

Not only is truth absolute, but all truth claims are narrow and exclusive. Stop and think about it for a moment. Even the claim that "every religion is true" (which is an absolute statement) excludes all opposing views, such as "only one religion is true." But isn't this intolerant? No, it isn't intolerant to say that "7 x 3 = 21." It is simply true. Likewise, it is not intolerant to say, "Washington, D.C., is the only capital of the United States," because it is. To say that it is intolerant and narrow to question another person's beliefs is in itself an intolerant and narrow position!

Your greatest tool in answering these objections is to use the Road Runner approach and apply the claim to itself. I'm sure you remember the cartoon characters Road Runner and Wile E. Coyote. Coyote's only goal in life was to catch Road Runner, who was too fast and too smart for him. Over and over Wile E. Coyote would miss Road Runner and find himself suspended in midair, supported by nothing, and soon would go crashing down to the valley floor. That is what the Road Runner tactic does to the relativists of our day. It helps them realize that their arguments have no support, and those arguments go crashing down to the ground.[2]

The Road Runner approach helps to identify a self-defeating statement as one that fails to meet its own standard. Here are some examples:

- "I can't speak a word in English." Didn't he say *that* in English?
- "Truth is not telling it like it is." Isn't *that* telling it like it is?
- "Opposites can both be true." Is the opposite of *that* true?
- "There is no truth." Is *that* true?
- "You can't know truth." How do you know *that* is true? This is a self-defeating statement because it claims to be a known, absolute truth.
- "There is no absolute truth." Is *that* absolutely true?
- "It's true for you but not for me." Is *that* just true for you but not for me? Try saying that to your bank teller, the police, or the IRS and see how far you get!
- "No one knows the truth." Then how do you know *that* is true?

By turning a self-defeating statement on itself, you can expose it for the nonsense it is. It shows people that their arguments cannot sustain their own weight, and they plummet to the valley floor just like Coyote chasing Road Runner.

S—*Is to Be Sought, Not Invented*

Truth is discovered, not invented. The "invention" of a truth is a clear indication that it is not really a truth. Truth exists independently of anyone's knowledge of it. For example, gravity existed prior to Newton discovering it in the 1600s. Likewise, we did not invent the mathematical tables. We simply discovered them. We must discover the truth that is already out there, and to do so, we must seek it.

E — *Is Elevated above Culture and Attitude*

Truth is transcultural. If something is true, it is true for all people in all places at all times. The equation $4 + 4 = 8$ is true for everyone everywhere and at every time. Being raised in a given culture doesn't make a person's beliefs true. For example, being raised a Nazi doesn't make Nazism true. Being raised a racist does not make racism true. Being raised a bigot does not make bigotry true.

Furthermore, our attitude doesn't change the truth either. A person with a bad attitude about truth does not make truth an error. Just because a person is arrogant does not make the truth he or she professes false. On the other hand, a person with a good attitude about error does not make error true. A humble person does not make the error he or she professes true.

S — Is Not Grounded in Sincerity

Truth is unchanging even though our beliefs about truth change. When humans began to believe the earth was round instead of flat, the truth about the earth didn't change; only their belief about the earth changed. Beliefs cannot change a fact no matter how sincerely they are held. People sincerely used to believe the world was flat, but that only made them sincerely wrong.

So contrary beliefs are possible, but contrary truths are not possible. We can believe everything is true, but we cannot make everything true by believing it.

What have we learned so far? Truth *can* be known when it . . .

P—parallels the truth
O—is opposite of that which is false
S—is selective in that it is exclusive
S—is sought, not invented
E—is elevated above culture and attitude
S—is not grounded in sincerity

Now let's take these points and apply them to religions and the truth. Have you ever noticed that people demand absolute truth when it comes to safety, money, medicine, advertising, relationships, transportation, and court proceedings? So why not demand absolute truth with religion? We will continue with the last three letters of POSSESSOR to help us evaluate whether all religions are true.

Religions and the Truth

S — Have Some Truth

Do other religions have *some* truth? I (Randy) once heard a preacher say that no other religion had even a kernel of truth but that Christianity had the whole bushel of it. Well, that is not true. Nearly all religions have some beliefs that are true. Every system of error must have enough truth in it to keep it "afloat." For example, Judaism, Islam, and Christianity all believe that there is one God and that he is the maker of all. Theism is the truth, so at least these three religions hold to the same truth. Confucianism believes that "we should not do to others what we do not want them to do to us." This is just the flip side of the Judeo-Christian "Golden Rule" (Matt. 7:12).

O — Teach Opposites

Most religions have some beliefs that are true, but not *all* religious beliefs can be true, because they are mutually exclusive—they teach opposites or contradictory beliefs (remember the law of non-contradiction).

While most religions have some kind of similar moral code because God has implanted the discernment of right and wrong in our consciences, they disagree on virtually every issue, including the nature of God, the nature of man, sin, salvation, heaven, hell, and creation.

Let's go further and contrast one religion with another, say Islam with Christianity.

ISLAM	CHRISTIANITY
God: only one person	God: three persons in one God
Humanity: good by nature	Humanity: sinful by nature
Jesus: merely a man, not God	Jesus: more than man, is also God
Death of Christ: not on cross and no resurrection	Death of Christ: died on cross, rose again in same body
Bible: corrupted	Bible: not corrupted
Salvation: by faith plus works when good deeds outweigh bad deeds	Salvation: not by works but is a free gift of God for all who believe

But wait a minute. Don't Islam and Christianity have things in common? Yes, but so do a counterfeit twenty-dollar bill and a real twenty-dollar bill. Both are paper, both are rectangular, and both have the number twenty on them. But one is a counterfeit! How can we tell a counterfeit from the real twenty-dollar bill? Not by comparing superficial similarities, but by comparing crucial differences. Since the opposite of true is false, if one religion is true, then all opposing beliefs in other religions are false.

R—*Must Correspond to Reality*

Any teaching—religious or otherwise—is worth trusting only if it points to the truth. Apathy about truth can be dangerous. In fact, believing error can have deadly consequences temporally and eternally as well.

Many beliefs that people hold today are not supported by evidence but only by their personal preferences. As Pascal said, many people invariably arrive at their beliefs not on the basis of proof but on the basis of what they find attractive.[3] But truth cannot be a subjective matter of taste—it is an objective matter of fact. To find truth with which to govern our lives, we must give up our subjective preferences in favor of objective facts.

So the only religion worth following must point to the truth, to the reality that is evident around us. What is the reality to which truth corresponds? We need to discover the reality about subjects such as:

- the existence of God
- the beginning of the universe
- the beginning of man
- the possibility of the supernatural
- whether God has communicated to us
- who Jesus is
- how one has a relationship with God

The religion that tells the truth about these subjects is the religion that is true and worth following.

Summary: Can All Religions Be True?

Can *all* religions be true? No, they teach opposites, and opposites cannot both be true.

Do other religions have *some* truth? Yes, but since the opposite of true is false, if one religion is true, then all opposing beliefs in other religions are false (even if some beliefs are true).

Can *one* religion be true? Yes, we must take off our blinders and see which religion corresponds to reality.

We purposely began "Hot Topics around the Watercooler" with the subject of truth and how to recognize it. Setting the ground rules for truth establishes the foundation for every other discussion. This is the approach that Gene can take with Tony. Using the PROVE acrostic of chapter 4, Gene could get Tony to agree to be partners at exploring the truth about truth. Then he could follow through the POSSESSOR acrostic, which sets the ground rules for truth. Once they have agreed on these ground rules, Gene and Tony are ready to explore the truths about the existence of God, which is the subject of our next chapter.

POSSESSOR of Truth Checklist

Truth . . .

P—*Parallels* the Facts
- Truth accords with the facts, tells it like it is, and matches its object.
- That which is false does not accord with the facts, tell it like it is, and match its object.

O—*Opposite* of True Is False
- The opposite of true is false.
- Opposite ideas cannot both be true at the same time and in the same sense.

S—Is *Selective*
- Truth is absolute, not relative.
- Truth claims are selective, narrow, and exclusive.
- We can use the Road Runner tactic to identify self-defeating statements.

S—Is to Be *Sought*, Not Invented
- Truth is to be discovered.
- Truth exists independently of anyone's knowledge of it.

E—Is *Elevated* above Culture and Attitude
- Truth is transcultural.
- Being raised in a given culture doesn't make one's beliefs true.
- One's attitude doesn't change the truth.

S—Is Not Grounded in *Sincerity*

- Truth is unchanging even though our beliefs about truth change.
- Contrary *beliefs* are possible, but contrary *truths* are not possible.

Religions . . .

S—Have *Some* Truth

- Nearly all religions have some beliefs that are true and correspond to a similar moral code.

O—Teach *Opposites*

- All religions can't be true, because they teach opposites.

R—Must Correspond to *Reality*

- Any teaching—religious or otherwise—is worth trusting only if it points to the truth.
- Many beliefs that people hold today are not supported by evidence, but only by their personal preferences.
- The only religion worth following must point to the truth, to the reality that is evident around us.

Digging Deeper on the Subject of Truth

Geisler, Norman. *Baker Encyclopedia of Christian Apologetics.* Grand Rapids: Baker Books, 1999, 741–45.

Geisler, Norman, and Ron Brooks. *When Skeptics Ask.* Grand Rapids: Baker Books, 1990, 255–72.

Geisler, Norman, and Abdul Saleeb. *Answering Islam.* Grand Rapids: Baker Books, 2002.

Geisler, Norman, and Frank Turek. *I Don't Have Enough Faith to Be an Atheist.* Wheaton: Crossway, 2004, 35–69.

6

Does God Exist?

"I don't believe there is a God," Lin's boss, Ted, told him as they were riding to a business meeting.

Lin hadn't been sure if Ted was a Christian, so he had continued to look for opportunities to discuss spiritual topics with him. Riding in a car together for a couple of hours would be an optimum time to really talk! As Lin maneuvered the conversation once again to God, Ted startled Lin with his declaration that he didn't believe there was a God.

Lin blinked and replied, "How can you say there is no God? How can you know that for sure?"

Ted replied, "Well, okay, let me clarify my view a bit. Maybe there is a God, maybe there isn't. I don't know. I can't be sure. But how can you be sure there is a God? You believe it on the basis of what you call 'faith,' and that's fine for you. But I'm a facts and cold logic man like old Joe Friday of *Dragnet*. Remember what he used to say—'Just the facts, ma'am. Just the facts'? Okay, what are your facts for believing that some being like God exists?"

Ted had experienced a harder life than most, for he was raised in an orphanage, so it was hard for him to believe in a caring God. In the military, he learned to be strong and self-sufficient, and he carried these traits over into business. Now at fifty-five, he was considered a business success and thus found it hard to feel he needed God. So, on the one hand, he mentally lived as if God did not exist. Yet on the other hand, he seemed to enjoy spiritual discussions and debates with Lin. Was it because he wanted to prove Lin wrong, or was it because he secretly hoped Lin would prove him wrong?

Lin needed to respond wisely to his boss, for this was an opportune time (Eph. 5:16). How could Lin respond to his friend? Before we can determine that, we need to discover two things: (1) What does Ted believe about God? and (2) Does he want evidence or proof?

Who Believes What?

Did you notice that Ted started out as an atheist but just as easily became an agnostic? What is the difference, and is it important? Let's consider the major views of God.

- *Theist.* Believes that God created the universe but is not the universe. Rather, he is actively involved in the world and the affairs of his creatures. He made the world, but he is not the world. God is as different from the world as a painter is from his painting. But God is still *in* the world the way a painter's mind is expressed in his painting.
- *Pantheist.* Thinks God *is* the world. He is everything and is literally the universe. God is not the creator of the world. He is the painting, not the painter.
- *Atheist.* Maintains there is no God in the first place and all that is has occurred as a result of pure accident. While the theist says, "I know there is a God," the atheist says, "I know there is no God." Atheists believe that the painting always existed and no painter ever painted it.
- *Agnostic.* Claims "I don't know if there is a God." This person says that he doesn't know if there is a painter or not.
- *Deist.* Maintains that God created the universe and set up natural, scientific laws by which it runs but then disassociated himself from it. The deist disdains a personal God who answers prayers, extends grace, or enters in any way into the affairs of humans. God, to the deist, is an "absentee landlord." He worked in the past but is absent in the present. God painted the painting but left it abandoned by the road somewhere.

There are two key ways to approach an agnostic like Ted. First, show him the fallacy of his skepticism by using the Road Runner approach. I (Norm) was witnessing to a man at his house and used the Road Runner approach to move him to Christ. Here's how it went.

Knock, knock.

"Who's there?" said the man who came to the door.

I stuck out my hand and said, "Hi! My name is Norm Geisler. This is my friend, Ron, and we're from the church at the end of the street."

"I'm Don," the man replied, his eyes quickly sizing us up.

Immediately I jumped into action with a question. "Don, do you mind if we ask you a spiritual question?"

"No, go ahead," Don said boldly, apparently eager to have a Bible thumper for dessert.

So I asked him, "Don, if you were to die tonight and stand before God, and God were to ask you, 'Why should I let you into my heaven?' what would you say?"

Don snapped back, "I'd say to God, 'Why *shouldn't* you let me into your heaven?'"

After a quick prayer, I replied, "Don, if we knocked on your door, seeking to come into your house, and you said to us, 'Why should I let you into my house?' and we responded, 'Why *shouldn't* you let us in?' what would you say?"

Don pointed his finger at my chest and sternly replied, "I would tell you where to go!"

I immediately shot back, "That's exactly what God is going to say to you!"

Don looked stunned for a second but then narrowed his eyes and said, "To tell you the truth: I don't believe in God. I'm an atheist."

"You're an atheist?"

"That's right!"

"Well, are you absolutely sure there is no God?" I asked him.

He paused and said, "Well, no, I'm not *absolutely* sure. I guess it's possible there might be a God."

"So you're not really an atheist, then—you're an agnostic," I informed him, "because an atheist says, 'I know there is no God,' and an agnostic says, 'I don't know whether there is a God.'"

"Yeah, all right; so I guess I'm an agnostic, then," he admitted.

Now this was real progress. With just one question, we had moved from atheism to agnosticism! But I still had to figure out what kind of agnostic Don was. So I asked him, "Don, what kind of agnostic are you?"

He laughed as he asked, "What do you mean?" (He was probably thinking, *A minute ago, I was an atheist—I have no idea what kind of agnostic I am now!*)

"Well, Don, there are two kinds of agnostics," I explained. "There's the *ordinary* agnostic who says he *doesn't* know anything for sure, and then there's the *ornery* agnostic who says he *can't* know anything for sure."

Don was sure about this. He said, "I'm the ornery kind. You can't know anything for sure."

Recognizing the self-defeating nature of his claim, I unleashed the Road Runner tactic by asking him, "Don, if you say you can't know anything for sure, then how do you know *that* for sure?" I could see the lightbulb coming on but decided to add one more point. "Besides, Don, you can't be a skeptic about everything, because that would mean you'd have to doubt skepticism; but the more you doubt skepticism, the surer you become."

He relented. "Okay, I guess I really *can* know something for sure. I must be an *ordinary* agnostic." Now we were really getting somewhere. With just a few questions, Don had moved from atheism through *ornery* agnosticism to *ordinary* agnosticism.

I continued, "Since you admit now that you *can* know, why *don't* you know that God exists?"

Shrugging his shoulders, he said, "Because nobody has shown me any evidence, I guess."

Now I launched the million-dollar question. "Would you be willing to look at some evidence?"

"Sure," he replied. This is the best type of person to talk to: someone who is willing to take an honest look at the evidence. The Road Runner approach helps to show a person his or her position is faulty and gently nudges the person to be willing to listen to your position. Being willing is essential. Evidence cannot convince the unwilling. Now we are ready to move to the second point.

The second way to approach an agnostic like Ted is to show him the evidences of the Painter by showing him the marvels of the painting.

Evidence or Proof?

Remember that Ted wanted "facts and cold logic." But the important question is whether he wants good *evidence* or absolute *proof*. The latter is not possible for most things, except mathematical statements (like 2 + 2 = 4) or basic statements like "I exist." So it would be self-defeating to say, "I don't exist," since I would have to exist in order to say I didn't exist. So proof in the sense of good evidence exists. But "absolute" proof does not exist for most things. For example, I don't have absolute proof that the words "Drink Coke" in the sky are an advertisement rather than an unusual wind formation, but I have good evidence they are.

Finally, there is a difference between proof (good evidences) and persuasion. Evidence is objective. It provides the facts any reasonable person *should* accept. However, as the saying goes, "You can lead a horse to water, but you can't make it drink." Likewise, providing proof (objective evidence) is no guarantee the person is going to be subjectively persuaded. Many people can accept the proof factually that mile for mile airplanes are safer than cars, yet they can't be persuaded to get in one. Proof for the *mind* is no guarantee of persuasion of the *will*.

Why is this important to know? If you say to someone, "I'm going to prove to you that God exists," that person may view your statement as an attack and respond defensively, "Oh yeah, bring it on!" If a person shouts, "You can't prove to me that God exists!" you will not be able to do so, for the person has already formed a conclusion that God does not exist.

The question arises of how we can establish the existence of a God who is invisible. The answer is to use observation and reason to investigate God the same way we use these tools to investigate other things we cannot see—by observing their effects and drawing reasonable conclusions from them.[1] Take gravity for example. We can't see gravity and believe in it. But we can see its effects and reasonably conclude that there must be some force that is causing these effects.

Greg Koukl described an attorney who would only believe physical proof for the existence of God. God would have to come and appear to the attorney for the man to believe. Koukl thought this was odd coming from an attorney and countered by asking, "Is that the kind of evidence you would require in a court of law for something to be demonstrated as true?" Think about it. Attorneys try to convict criminals by showing that they had a motive for committing a crime. A motive is not a physical thing. You can conclude a motive from physical circumstances or from physical evidence, but the motive itself is not physical.

There are many ways to prove something's existence. If a thing is physical, such as DNA or a weapon, then some physical test should generally be able to reveal it. But if a thing is not physical—like a motive, a soul, an idea, or God—then you have to confirm its existence by different means and evidence. Attorneys conclude the existence of a motive by other means of reasoning and evidence. Why can't God be demonstrated to exist, at least in principle, in the same way?[2]

So we prefer to talk about good evidences for the existence of God rather than absolute proofs or persuasion. If a person is open to consider the evidence for God, to look at his "painting," then you can have a profitable discussion. The PROVE acrostic we shared in chapter 4 is very effective to use with agnostics.

What determines evidence? For most people, it boils down to simple cause and effect. If there is a house (an effect), then we can "know" there was someone who built it (a cause). Furthermore, we know that wind, rain, dirt, trees, stones, and such are not a sufficiently complex cause to explain the house as an effect. With our analogy, if there is a painting (the universe), then there must have been a cause that brought the painting into existence. The *Mona Lisa* is a great painting, but no one thinks the *Mona Lisa* painted itself or had no painter. No, the existence of the *Mona Lisa* painting implies an artist who painted it.

Evidences to Consider—BIG

There are three key cause-and-effect evidences that show it is reasonable to say God exists. They are the cosmological, teleological, and moral arguments. Right now you may be saying, "I can't even spell some of those words, much less understand and defend them! That is why apologetics is beyond me and I am better off being quiet at work!"

Slow down and take a deep breath. Remember that we said this book is not written for people with Ph.D.s, but for "the person in the street"? We will use the acrostic BIG to help you remember the evidences for the existence of God.

- **B**—*Universe that began requires a **Beginner*** (cosmological evidence)
- **I**—***Intelligent** design requires a designer* (teleological evidence)

- **G**—*Moral law requires a **Giver** of this moral law*

Why the BIG acrostic? When presenting evidences for God, it is best to use the logical flow of thought. It is important to first establish that the universe had a beginning and is not eternal. Many scientists believe the beginning of the universe began with the Big Bang, hence our acrostic BIG. If the universe had a beginning, then logically something or someone must have caused it to begin. Next, this universe is seen to have extraordinary design. This design is too intricate and precise to have "just happened." This design seems to have come from an intelligent designer. The final evidence is to look within our hearts. Every person has a sense of what is fair, of justice and injustice, of a moral law. Every law requires a lawgiver, and a moral law requires a moral lawgiver. Let's look at each evidence.

B — Universe That Began Requires a Beginner

What may be known about God is plain to them, because God has made it plain to them. For since the creation of the world God's invisible qualities—his eternal power and divine nature—have been clearly seen, being understood from what has been made, so that men are without excuse.

Romans 1:19–20

When the apostles Barnabas and Paul heard of this, they tore their clothes and rushed out into the crowd, shouting: "Men, why are you doing this? We too are only men, human like you. We are bringing you good news, telling you to turn from these worthless things to the living God, who made heaven and earth and sea and everything in them.

Acts 14:14–15

Paul then stood up in the meeting of the Areopagus and said: "Men of Athens! I see that in every way you are very religious. For as I walked around and looked carefully at your objects of worship, I even found an altar with this inscription: TO AN UNKNOWN GOD. Now what you worship as something unknown I am going to proclaim to you. 'The God who made the world and everything in it is the Lord of heaven and earth and does not live in temples built by hands.'"

Acts 17:22–24

The evidence for "a universe that began requires a beginner" is as follows:

1. Everything that had a beginning had a cause.
2. The universe had a beginning.
3. Therefore the universe had a cause.

Let's examine these three points carefully.

1. *Everything that had a beginning had a cause.* This is the law of causality, which is the fundamental principle of science. The essence of science is to search for causes.

2. *The universe had a beginning.* Up until the time of Albert Einstein, the world of science believed the universe was eternal, and atheists and evolutionists had great comfort. But since Einstein, five scientific discoveries have come to light that prove the universe did have a beginning, in what scientists call the "Big Bang." The big bang theory will be seen to support the Genesis account for the beginning of the world rather than the evolutionary account.

Are we saying that we believe in the big bang theory? No, we don't believe in the big bang theory because it is a naturalistic explanation of the origin of the universe. But the evidence that the naturalists cite for the big bang is evidence for creation, thus we use the same evidence to show that there is a *supernatural* cause, not *natural* cause for the world.

For example, in discussing the scientific discoveries of NASA's satellites COBE and WMAP that support the big bang picture, George Will said, "Soon the American Civil Liberties Union, or People for the American Way, or some similar faction of litigious secularism will file suit against NASA, charging that the Hubble Space Telescope unconstitutionally gives comfort to the religiously inclined."[3]

But the word *evolution* and scientific debates make a lot of Christians queasy about apologetics. Who among us is a scientist and can refute evolutionary claims? Five scientific discoveries support the big bang theory, and the SURGE acrostic has been developed to share these points.[4] For our purpose, we will simply share the highlights of each point.

S — Second Law of Thermodynamics

Thermodynamics is the study of matter and energy. The second law of thermodynamics says the universe is running out of usable energy. One day the universe will simply run out of gas. What does this prove? If the universe had been running on its own energy from eternity, it would have been out of energy by now. But it has not, and so the universe must have begun in the distant (but not eternal) past. The universe, then, is not eternal but had a beginning.

The second law of thermodynamics is also known as the law of entropy, which says that nature tends to come to disorder. Buildings deteriorate over time, fruit decays, our bodies get older and feeble. This law says the universe is like a wound clock running down. If it is running down, then someone must have wound it up. Yet our world is still here, so the universe cannot be eternal, or we would have wound down (reached entropy) by now.

U— Universe Expanding

In 1927 Edwin Hubble (namesake of the space telescope) discovered that the light from distant galaxies was redder than it should be. Hubble concluded that it was redder because the universe was growing apart—in short, expanding! The light from the galaxies was changing because it was moving away from us. Furthermore, he found that the light was expanding in all directions, which means that it all came from a single point.[5] What does this prove? Scientifically, there once was nothing, and then all of a sudden, there was something—the universe suddenly came into being in what is known today as the "Big Bang." There was no time, space, or matter before the Big Bang, but all came into existence at that moment.

R — Radiation from the Big Bang

In 1965 two Bell Telephone Laboratory scientists discovered the radiation afterglow from the Big Bang. The light from the Big Bang is no longer visible, but the heat can still be detected. In 1948 scientists predicted that this radiation would exist if the Big Bang really did occur, and nearly twenty years later, it was discovered. This discovery confirmed that the universe is not eternal but had a beginning.

G — Great Galaxy Seeds

If the Big Bang had occurred, then scientists believed that we would see ripples in the temperature of the radiation discovered. In 1992 NASA's COBE satellite not only discovered the necessary ripples, but also found that the explosion and expansion of the universe were so precise that they allowed galaxy formation. Astronomer George Smoot, announcing COBE's findings, called these exact ripples the "machining marks from the creation of the universe" and the "fingerprints of the maker."[6] But that's not all COBE discovered. COBE took pictures of the ripples (literally pictures of the past because of the time it takes for light from distant objects to reach us), and these infrared pictures point to matter that would form the galaxies, or "seeds" of the galaxies as they exist today. Once again, that which should have occurred if the Big Bang was true was found.

E — Einstein's Theory of General Relativity

In 1916 Albert Einstein's calculations of his theory of general relativity revealed a definite beginning to all time, all matter, and all space. This discovery was the beginning of the end for the idea that the universe was eternal. Einstein found his conclusion "irritating," because he wanted the universe to be eternal and self-existent rather than reliant on any outside cause. But this theory has been proven and is one of the strongest supports for the universe having a beginning, which makes it evident that there was a beginning.

3. *Therefore, the universe had a cause.* Why is it important that the universe had a beginning? How is this evidence for God's existence? Well, the question of questions is what *caused* the Big Bang, or what (or who) caused the universe's beginning. Natural forces are ruled out because they were not the *cause* of the Big Bang but were *created* at the Big Bang. Since a cause cannot come into being after its effect, something *outside* of nature must have been the cause. But what could do this? Here is what Robert Jastrow, an astronomer and founder of NASA's Goddard Institute of Space Studies and an agnostic, had to say about the Big Bang and God:

> Now we see how the astronomical evidence leads to a biblical view of the origin of the world. The details differ, but the essential elements in the astronomical and biblical accounts of Genesis are the same: the chain of events leading to man commenced

suddenly and sharply at a definite moment in time, in a flash of light and energy.[7]

Later on in an interview discussing the evidence for the Big Bang and its consistency with the biblical accound in Genesis, Jastrow mused:

Astronomers now find they have painted themselves into a corner because they have proven, by their own methods, that the world began abruptly in an act of creation. . . . And they have found that all this happened as a product of forces they cannot hope to discover. . . . *That there are what I or anyone would call supernatural forces at work is now, I think, a scientifically proven fact.*[8]

One objection to note is that some would say if everything needs a cause, then God needs a cause too. Atheists point here to the law of causality, but when they do so, they misunderstand it. "The Law of Causality does not say that everything needs a cause. It says that everything that comes to be needs a cause. God did not come to be. No one made God. He is unmade. As an eternal being, God did not have a beginning, so he didn't need a cause."[9]

So the first evidence that Lin should have Ted consider is that the universe had a beginning, and this requires a cause (or Beginner).

What is the best way to use the BIG evidences with someone at work? Just think of Bill Gates, the founder and creator of Microsoft. No, we're not saying Bill Gates is God, and Microsoft certainly is not a piece of heaven! But nearly everyone in the workplace uses a computer with Microsoft Windows and Microsoft programs such as Word, Excel, Publisher, or PowerPoint. So this is a great point of comparison. With the B—*universe that began requires a Beginner*—it is best to talk about the time before there was a Microsoft Windows and only DOS.

Many of us can remember our first computers that used only DOS and the wonderful day we finally switched to Microsoft Windows. The point is that no one looks at Microsoft Windows and believes it is eternal. Even the teenage computer whizzes who have only known Microsoft believe that there was a time with no Microsoft and that one day Microsoft was born. Microsoft began because it had a beginner, namely, Bill Gates. If we can believe without question that a computer program like Microsoft had a beginning, then how much more should we believe that the universe had a beginning, especially with the SURGE evidence!

I — Intelligent Design Requires a Designer

The heavens declare the glory of God;
    the skies proclaim the work of his hands.
Day after day they pour forth speech;
    night after night they display knowledge.
There is no speech or language
    where their voice is not heard.

Their voice goes out into all the earth,
    their words to the ends of the world.
In the heavens he has pitched a tent for the sun,
    which is like a bridegroom coming forth from his pavilion,
    like a champion rejoicing to run his course.
It rises at one end of the heavens
    and makes its circuit to the other;
    nothing is hidden from its heat.

Psalm 19:1–6

Every house is built by someone, but God is the builder of everything.

Hebrews 3:4

The "intelligent design requires a designer" evidence is as follows:

1. Every design had a designer.
2. The universe has a highly complex design.
3. Therefore, the universe had a designer.

Let's examine these three points carefully.

1. *Every design had a designer.* This is obvious. Of course, if a design was designed, it must have been designed by a designer.

2. *The universe has a highly complex design.* Two relatively recent discoveries have been uncovered that prove the design of the universe—the anthropic principle and DNA. The anthropic principle says the universe is fine-tuned so that humans can exist. (*Anthropic* comes

from the Greek word for "man," *anthropos*.) Christian astronomer Hugh Ross has cited twenty-six different characteristics about the universe that enable it to sustain life and thirty-three characteristics about our galaxy, our solar system, and the planet Earth that are finely tuned to allow life to exist.[10] Many of the examples are highly technical, but let's look at a few.

- *Atmosphere*. Our atmosphere is perfectly designed for life. It is "just right" for us. Its size and corresponding gravity hold a thin—but not too thin—layer of gases that protect us and allow us to breathe. Oxygen makes up 21 percent of the atmosphere. But if the oxygen level were 25 percent, fires would continually erupt. If the oxygen level were 15 percent, humans would suffocate. If our planet were smaller, it couldn't support an atmosphere, as on Mercury. If it were larger, like Jupiter, the atmosphere would contain free hydrogen, which is poison for us. Earth is the only planet we know of that contains an atmosphere that can support human, animal, and plant life.

- *Distance*. Earth is at a "just right" distance from the sun and the other planets in our solar system. If we were closer to the sun, we would burn up. If we were farther away, we would freeze. Earth's slightly elliptical orbit means that we enjoy a quite narrow range of temperatures, which is important to life. The speed of Earth's rotation on its axis, completing one turn every twenty-four hours, means that the sun warms the planet evenly. Compare our world to the moon, where there are extraordinary temperature variations because it lacks sufficient atmosphere or water to retain or deflect the sun's energy.

- *Moon*. It is important that Earth has only one moon, not two or three or none, and that it is the "just right" size and distance from us. The moon's gravity impacts the movement of ocean currents, keeping the water from becoming stagnant.

- *Water*. Water itself is an important part of a "just right" world. Plants, animals, and human beings are made mostly of water, and we need it to live. One unique thing about Earth is the abundance of water in a liquid state. Water has surface tension. This means that water can move upward, against gravity, to bring liquid nutrients to the tops of the tallest plants. Everything else in the world freezes from the bottom up, but water freezes from the top down. Everything else contracts when it freezes, but water expands. This means that in winter, ponds and rivers and lakes can freeze at the surface but allow fish and other marine creatures to live down below.

As scientists understand our universe better, they notice that there is a fine-tuning of all these factors that make life possible. William Lane Craig says:

> In the last thirty-five years, scientists have been stunned to discover that the Big Bang was not some chaotic, primordial event, but rather a highly ordered event that required an enormous amount of information. In fact, from the very moment of its inception, the universe had to be fine-tuned to an incomprehensible precision for the existence of life like ourselves. And that points in a very compelling way toward the existence of an Intelligent Designer.[11]

The fact that we live on a "just right" planet in a "just right" universe is evidence that it all was created by a loving God.

DNA, the material of which our genes are made and the genetic material for every living thing on the planet, is another evidence of design. Naturalist Charles Darwin believed in a "simple cell." If you observe a creature with primitive-type eye cells and then another with a little more advanced vision, and another with even more advanced vision, and so on, you might draw the conclusion that eyes had evolved. Modern biochemists, however, now know that there is no such thing as a "simple cell"!

> A single DNA molecule, the building block of all life, carries the same amount of information as one volume of an encyclopedia. No one seeing an encyclopedia lying in the forest would hesitate to think that it had an intelligent cause; so when we find a living creature composed of millions of DNA-based cells, we ought to assume that it likewise has an intelligent cause.[12]

One of the startling discoveries about DNA is that it is a highly complex informational code, so complex that scientists struggle hard to decipher even the tiniest portions of the various genes in every organism. DNA conveys intelligent information; in fact, molecular biologists use language terms—code, translation, and transcription—to describe what it does and how it acts. Communication engineers and information scientists tell us that you can't have a code without a code maker, so it would seem that DNA is probably the strongest indicator in our world that there is an intelligent designer behind its existence.

Dr. Richard Dawkins, a professor of biology who writes books and articles praising evolution, says in his book *The Blind Watchmaker*, "Biology is the study of complicated things that give the appearance of having been designed for a purpose."[13] Even those who desperately fear the implications of design find design impossible to avoid.

3. *Therefore, the universe had a designer.* If you've ever seen Mount Rushmore, you know that the natural forces of wind and rain did not erode the rock into the shapes of four presidents' faces. It took the skilled hands of an artist—a designer.

William Paley, in the eighteenth century, posed this question: If you found an intricately designed watch lying in the sand, would you think it was made by someone and lost by someone, or would you think it just "came into being" over millions of years of exposure to the wind and the sand? Of course you would know that a watch demands a watchmaker. After establishing this, Paley said that the human eye is much more complex and sophisticated than any pocket watch. It is therefore reasonable to believe that the human eye is made by design and that a designer exists.

So the second evidence that Lin should have Ted consider is that the design of our universe requires a designer.

Let's go back to the BIG evidences and Bill Gates, the founder and creator of Microsoft. With the *I*—"intelligent design requires a designer"—when you look at Microsoft, you know that there is remarkably intelligent design in the software that affects appearance, operation, and results. But no one in their right mind would believe that Microsoft's intelligent design just happened or evolved over thirty years of computer parts rubbing against each other. No, everyone knows that the intelligent design of Microsoft required a designer, Bill Gates. Now if we can believe that Microsoft's intelligent design required a designer, then how much more should we believe that the intelligent design of the universe requires an intelligent designer!

G — Moral Law Requires a Giver of This Moral Law

Indeed, when Gentiles, who do not have the law, do by nature things required by the law, they are a law for themselves, even

though they do not have the law, since they show that the requirements of the law are written on their hearts, their consciences also bearing witness, and their thoughts now accusing,
now even defending them.

Romans 2:14–15

The moral law deals with what is good versus what is evil. Every
law that says we should do good and not evil has a moral lawgiver.
The moral law evidence is as follows:

1. Every law has a lawgiver.
2. There is a moral law.
3. Therefore, there is a moral lawgiver.

Let's examine these three points carefully.

1. *Every law has a lawgiver.* A moral law is a prescription—something we ought to do. But there is no prescription without a prescriber.
There is no legislation without a legislator.

2. *There is a moral law.* Within the heart of every man, woman, and
child, a law has been inscribed that drives our thoughts, our reactions,
and our decisions. It is called the moral law, a sense of morality that
we are born with and to which we hold others accountable. Consider
the following concepts.

Concept of Fairness

Where does the concept of fairness come from? Any parent who
ever raised children sooner or later heard them complain that something wasn't "fair." I remember my daughters as little children crossing
their arms, scowling, and saying, "Daddy, that's not fair!" (As teenagers they *still* say that!) Sue Bohlin of Probe Ministries says that she
was convinced of the existence of a moral God when her children,
without being taught, complained that something wasn't "fair." She
asks, "Why is it that no one ever has to teach children about fairness,
but all parents hear the universal wail of 'That's not fa-a-a-a-a-air!'"
She calls this the sense of "ought."[14]

Fairness is an internal awareness of how things should be, whether
it is with children who have to do their chores or people trying to save
the environment. Why should we save the environment? Why should
we fight prejudice or feed the starving? Because we "ought" to, that's

why. It's the right thing to do. But where did this sense of "ought," or fairness, come from? It comes from a moral law written in our hearts. Moral laws don't describe what is; they prescribe what ought to be. They tell us what we ought to be doing, whether we are doing it or not.[15]

C. S. Lewis was once an atheist because he thought that if there was a good and loving God, there would be no evil or injustice in the world. That is, until he thought about how he knew the world was unjust. He wrote, "[As an atheist] my argument against God was that the universe seemed so cruel and unjust. But how had I got this idea of just and unjust? A man does not call a line crooked unless he has some idea of a straight line. What was I comparing this universe with when I called it unjust?"[16] This realization of a standard of morality led Lewis out of atheism and ultimately to Christianity. In short, we can't say something is unjust unless we know what is just. Hence, if there is anything absolutely unjust anywhere, there must be an absolute moral lawgiver.

Concept of Values

Think about the fact that certain values are found in all human cultures. Murder is wrong in every culture. Lying and cheating and stealing are wrong. If evolution is true and we evolved from a primordial soup, then where did this sense of moral right and wrong (law) come from?

What do Enron, WorldCom, Adelphia, Global Crossing, ImClone, and Qwest and taking the fifth amendment bring to mind today? They demonstrate the desperate need for ethics. Ethics tells us that there is a right way to do something and a wrong way.

Concept of Accountability

Only people, not nature or animals, are judged as right and wrong. When a hurricane causes death and destruction, we don't judge it as "wrong." Animals are not judged wrong when they kill for food. Even when animals such as lions fight to establish social dominance, we don't say that is a wrong thing.

So why is it that we judge people on the basis of their actions? We hold people accountable for their actions because only people have the ability to make decisions based on what is right and wrong and understand the consequences of their actions.

Concept of Guilt

Guilt is another indicator of ultimate right and wrong. Koukl says about guilt:

> It's tied into our understanding of things that are right and things that are wrong. We feel guilty when we think we've violated a moral rule, an "ought." And that feeling hurts. It doesn't hurt our body; it hurts our soul. An ethical violation is not a physical thing, like a punch in the nose, producing physical pain. It's a soulish injury producing a soulish pain. That's why I call it ethical pain. That's what guilt is—ethical pain.[17]

Fairness, values, accountability, and guilt are all evidences of the moral law that is written on the heart of every person.

3. *Therefore, there is a moral lawgiver.* Where does fairness, that nagging sense of "ought," come from? The reason all human beings start out with an awareness of right and wrong and the reason we all yearn for justice and fairness is that we are made in the image of God, who is just and right. Romans 2:14–15 says that God has written this moral law in our hearts, as our conscience bears witness when we violate it. The reason we feel violated when someone does us wrong is that a moral law has been broken—and there can be no moral law without a moral lawgiver. Every time you say or feel, "That's not fair!" you are evidencing a moral lawgiver.

Where do values come from? The United States was founded on the concept that the moral law and values given by God are for every person. In the Declaration of Independence, Thomas Jefferson wrote that all men "are endowed by their Creator with certain unalienable rights." Jefferson believed that there was a moral law in that human rights are God-given and applicable to all people everywhere. Jefferson and the founding fathers understood that this moral law came from the moral Lawgiver—the "Creator." They believed that his moral law was the ultimate standard of right and wrong.[18]

What about accountability? We expect people to be held responsible for their actions, but if God doesn't exist, to whom are people accountable? Who can truly judge moral lawbreakers if not God? If God does not exist, then ideas of morality are foolish, transient, and cultural. In other words, these ideas are laws made by man and there is no reason to follow them. But if God does exist, he holds each of us accountable for our ethical decisions. Morality stems from the nature of God, and we are moral when we act in agreement with God and immoral when we act in rebellion against God.

Why is there guilt? Why do people make excuses for their immorality? Why are people overwhelmed by their failures in life? Because they recognize that they have violated the moral law and stand guilty before the moral Lawgiver.

The most common objection to the moral law and moral Lawgiver is that morality did not come from within but from without as a product of culture and societal pressure. You see, things aren't really wrong; these are just rules cultures have followed to live together. This is the basis for moral relativism. But consider the problems with this view.

- When the morals of two different societies collide (such as in war), which one is right and which is wrong? Germany thought that Hitler's approach was the right approach, but the United States and its allies did not. Are we right because we won the war or because Hitler's approach was immoral and a violation of the moral law of the moral Lawgiver?

- If morality is simply external and relative, then there can be no right or wrong, just different preferences. It's a preference like you enjoying vanilla ice cream and your friend enjoying chocolate. If there is no right or wrong, then tolerance is the answer. The only wrong is to judge others for being wrong! But think about this. Is homosexuality (violating God's standards of sexuality) wrong or just an alternate lifestyle? Is abortion murder or simply free choice? Is pedophilia an abomination, or is it acceptable depending on one's status? Are these simply changing cultural norms, or are they violations of the moral law? Think back to the Civil War era. Was slavery a cruel and unjust system, or was it a necessary way of life? To some whites in the South, slavery was necessary to run the plantations and support the economy of the Old South. It was their preference, and the abolitionists of the North had no right to judge them! But slavery was not the preference of the abused slaves; it was the law of the land. In reality, slavery was a violation of the moral law of the moral Lawgiver, and this led to the Civil War and eventually to Abraham Lincoln's Emancipation Proclamation.

Let's go back to the BIG evidences and Bill Gates. The G—"moral law requires a giver of this moral law"—can be likened to dealing with Microsoft programs; you know there are laws, or rules, governing how you use the software. Microsoft has built rules into the software that govern everything from how you can use their programs to how to communicate with other programs. They give you a warning before you make a mistake (such as exiting without saving a file), and they have even designed laws to keep you from making illegal copies. Now no one in their right mind would believe that Microsoft's intricate and sometimes hidden laws and rules just happened or evolved. No, everyone knows that the laws and rules of Microsoft were put in place by Microsoft's designer and lawgiver, Bill Gates. Now if we can believe that Microsoft's laws were put in place by Bill Gates, then how much more should we believe that the moral law that is written in our hearts requires a moral lawgiver!

So the final evidence that Lin should have Ted consider is that the design of our universe requires a designer. As Lin walks Ted through the BIG evidences, using Microsoft and Bill Gates as his point of comparison, Ted will begin to see clearly that to deny the evidence for the existence of God is to deny science, logic, and reason. This new knowledge will lay the groundwork for Ted to consider what God is like. Has God communicated to us? How can we communicate with him? Such questions will provide further opportunities for dialogue and sharing.

Summing It All Up

What kind of God does all this evidence point to? Well, the cosmological evidence shows that he must be a *supernatural power*, for he is a power beyond nature who brought the whole natural world into existence. Also, he must be a *super intelligence*, for he designed a supercomplex universe and human life. And he must be *morally perfect*, for he is the standard for all moral law. This is exactly what is meant by a theistic God.

BIG Evidences for God Checklist

B—Universe that Began Requires a *Beginner*
- S—*Second* law of thermodynamics
- U—*Universe* expanding

- R—*Radiation* from the Big Bang
- G—*Great galaxy* seeds
- E—*Einstein's* theory of general relativity

I—*Intelligent* Design Requires a Designer
- "Just right" atmosphere of the earth
- "Just right" distance of the earth from the sun
- "Just right" moon
- "Just right" water
- DNA makeup of the cell
- A watch requires a watchmaker

G—Moral Law Requires a *Giver* of This Moral Law
- Concept of fairness
- Concept of values
- Concept of accountability
- Concept of guilt

Digging Deeper on the Evidences for God

Geisler, Norman. *Baker Encyclopedia of Christian Apologetics.* Grand Rapids: Baker Books, 1999, 276–83.

Geisler, Norman, and Ron Brooks. *When Skeptics Ask.* Grand Rapids: Baker Books, 1990, 15–33.

Geisler, Norman, and Frank Turek. *I Don't Have Enough Faith to Be an Atheist.* Wheaton: Crossway, 2004, 73–112, 170–93.

Zacharias, Ravi. *Who Made God and Answers to Over 100 Other Tough Questions.* Grand Rapids: Zondervan, 2003.

7

Did Humans Evolve?

"Hey, interesting poster," Shari told Angie. Shari had popped her head into Angie's cubicle to discuss the details for the upcoming sales seminar they had to attend. Angie had a poster tacked to her cubicle wall that said:

To see how smart it is to leave God out of our thinking, look at this:
Frog + Princess's kiss = Handsome Prince
(a children's story no one believes)
Frog + Chance + Millions of years = Handsome Prince
(many people call this science)

"So I take it you don't believe in evolution," Shari quizzed.

"Well," Angie laughed, "the poster pretty much sums up the theory of evolution for me. Evolution has too many holes to believe in it—like we evolved from little amoebas or descended from apes. I think it takes more faith to believe in evolution than to believe that God created us."

"You know, I've recently heard about some of the problems with evolution," Shari said, "like fossil finds that one day are the 'missing link' and then the next day they're not. I've even read that scientists are abandoning evolution in droves. Tell me more about these 'holes' in the theory of evolution."

"Let's discuss that over lunch when we have more time," Angie offered.

Does the theory of evolution have any "holes"? Isn't the issue just religion versus science? Or is evolution a theory in crisis? Let's begin by defining evolution. Evolutionists claim that life began millions of years ago with simple single-cell creatures and then developed through mutation and natural selection into the vast array of plant and animal life that populates the planet. We humans came from the same ancestor as the ape.

But many biologists, biochemists, and other researchers (not just Christians) have begun to point out the holes of the theory of naturalistic evolution. Biochemist Michael Behe of Lehigh University writes:

> The result of these cumulative efforts to investigate the cell—to investigate life at the molecular level—is a loud, clear, piercing cry of "design!". . . . The conclusion of intelligent design flows naturally from the data itself—not from sacred books or sectarian beliefs. . . . The reluctance of science to embrace the conclusion of intelligent design . . . has no justifiable foundation. . . . Many people, including many important and well-respected scientists, just don't *want* there to be anything beyond nature.[1]

So what are the problems with evolution that even leading scientists are beginning to see? Evolution makes claims to knowing: (1) the origin of the universe, (2) the origin of life, and (3) the origin of new life-forms. We will examine these claims by using the acrostic U-LEAP, for this describes how a person must take a leap of faith to believe in evolution once the facts are examined. This acrostic could be called the "five nails in evolution's coffin." Let's walk through the U-LEAP concepts and see what they reveal about evolution.

U — Origin of the Universe

The first nail in evolution's coffin is that the theory is incapable of explaining the origin of the universe. We learned this by studying the SURGE discoveries of the Big Bang in chapter 6, which are evidences for the creation account of Genesis 1–2. Remember that we don't believe in the big bang theory because it is a naturalistic explanation of the origin of the universe. But the evidence that the naturalists cite for the big bang is evidence for creation, thus we use the same evidence to show that there is a *supernatural* cause, not *natural* cause for the world. Let's review them briefly for this point.

S—*Second law of thermodynamics*. This law says the universe is running out of usable energy. Since energy is still available, the universe must have begun in the distant (but not eternal) past. The universe, then, is not eternal but had a beginning. The second law of thermodynamics is also known as the law of entropy, which says the universe is like a wound clock running down. If it is running down, then someone must have wound it up, which means it had a beginning.

U—*Universe expanding*. Edwin Hubble discovered that the light from distant galaxies was moving away from us and expanding in all directions, which means that it came from a single point. This proves that there once was nothing, and then, all of a sudden, there was something—the universe suddenly came into being in what is known today as the "Big Bang." Time, space, and matter did not exist before the Big Bang; all came into existence at that moment.

R—*Radiation from the Big Bang*. The light from the radiation afterglow from the Big Bang is no longer visible, but the heat was detected in 1965. In 1948 scientists predicted that this radiation would exist if the Big Bang really did occur, and nearly twenty years later, it was discovered. This discovery confirmed that the universe is not eternal but had a beginning.

G—*Great galaxy seeds*. In 1992 the Big Bang was again confirmed when NASA's COBE satellite not only discovered the necessary ripples, but also found that the explosion and expansion of the universe were so precise that they allowed galaxy formation, or "seeds" of the galaxies as they exist today.

E—*Einstein's theory of general relativity*. Albert Einstein's calculations of his theory of general relativity revealed a definite beginning to all time, all matter, and all space. This discovery was the beginning of the end for the idea that the universe was eternal. This theory has been proven and is one of the strongest supports for the universe having a beginning, which makes it evident that there was a beginning.

Since the universe had a beginning, it must have had a beginner. Remember that the question of questions is: what *caused* the Big Bang, or what (or who) caused the universe's beginning? This beginning cause must be either a natural or a supernatural cause, but natural forces are ruled out because they were not the *cause* of the Big Bang but were *created* at the Big Bang. Since a cause cannot come into being after its effect, something outside of nature must have been the cause. And the only kind of cause beyond nature would, by its very nature, be a supernatural cause. So the evidence points to the fact that the beginner of the universe's beginning is none other than God. And since God is the beginner of the universe, naturalistic evolution is ruled out as a possibility for the origin of the universe. Hence, cosmic evolution is refuted by the evidence.

L—Origin of Life

The second nail in evolution's coffin is that the theory is incapable of explaining the origin of life, of how life can come from nonlife. If Darwinists can't explain where the first life came from, then what's the point of speaking about new life-forms? Macroevolution, if even possible, cannot begin without preexisting life.

Darwinists came up with another theory to explain the first theory, which is evolution! The new theory is called "spontaneous generation." Evolutionists say life generated spontaneously from nonliving chemicals by natural laws without any intelligent intervention. They claim a one-celled amoeba came together by spontaneous generation or without intelligent intervention in "primordial soup" on the primitive earth. In 1871 Darwin theorized that life emerged from chemicals reacting in a "warm little pond."[2] All life has evolved from that first amoeba without any intelligent guidance at all. This theory is succinctly summarized as "From the goo to you via the zoo"![3]

Let's look at some of the many problems with the theory of spontaneous generation.

There is no such thing as "simple" life. All life is complex, even a one-celled animal. For Darwinists, the first life must have generated spontaneously from nonliving chemicals. Darwin underestimated the problem of how life emerged because he thought that basic living matter—a one-cell organism—was quite simple. He didn't think it would be very difficult for life to evolve from nonlife, because the gap between the two didn't appear very great to him. In those days, they didn't have any way of seeing the complexity that exists within the membrane of the cell because they didn't have microscopes that could see things that small.

We now know that the first life, or any life, is anything but simple! This became known in 1953 when James Watson and Francis Crick discovered DNA, the chemical that encodes the instructions for building and replicating all living things. Each cell has a specified message or information that is called "specified complexity." "A single DNA molecule, the building block of all life, carries the same amount of information as one volume of an encyclopedia. The entire amoeba has as much information in its DNA as 1,000 complete sets of the *Encyclopedia Britannica*!"[4]

I recently read a report about a boy in Charleston, South Carolina, who found a message in a bottle that had floated down from Maine. The newspaper article described how the boy called the number written on the note and communicated with the note sender. Now, if a simple message jammed in a bottle requires an intelligent being, why doesn't a message a thousand encyclopedias long require one? Engineering professor Walter Bradley says, "When we see written language, we can infer, based on our experience, that it has an intelligent cause. And we can legitimately use analogical reasoning to conclude that the remarkable information sequences in DNA also had an intelligent cause. Therefore, this means life on earth came from a 'who' instead of a 'what.'"[5] In chapter 6, we saw that design requires a designer. Therefore, a cell with its complex design requires a designer.

Spontaneous generation has never been observed. This is true because no human was there to observe it. The development of the first life on earth was a one-time, unrepeated historical event. The principle of uniformity holds that causes in the past were like causes we observe today. If the message "Take out the garbage—Mom" requires an intelligent cause today, then any similar message in the past must also have required an intelligent cause. So when we study the first one-celled life, the principle of uniformity tells us that only an intelligent cause could assemble the equivalent of a thousand encyclopedias within that cell.

Spontaneous generation has not been duplicated. Scientists have been unable to combine chemicals in a test tube and arrive at a DNA molecule, much less life. In fact, all experiments designed to spontaneously generate life have failed. So scientists cannot do what we are told mindless natural laws have done. How can we believe that mindless natural laws could produce life when brilliant scientists cannot?

There is no explanation for the source of the nonliving chemicals, much less an explanation of life. Not only can scientists not account for the complexity of the cell with its DNA, they also can't explain where the proteins that DNA relies on to produce came from. So which came first, proteins or DNA? One must be in existence for the other to be made.

Time is allegedly the key for spontaneous generation to work. Darwin didn't have a good idea of how life arose in the first place. He thought that life naturally develops everywhere. People in his day thought maggots spontaneously developed from decaying meat. At the time Darwin's *Origin of Species* was published, Francesco Redi discovered that meat that was kept away from flies never developed maggots. Louis Pasteur claimed to destroy the concept of spontaneous generation by showing that air contains microorganisms that can multiply in water, which only gives the illusion of the spontaneous generation of life. Back in the 1920s, some scientists agreed with Pasteur that spontaneous generation doesn't happen in a short time frame, but they theorized that over billions and billions of years, it might really happen. That became the basis for the idea that nonliving chemicals can combine into living cells if given enough time.

There were many destructive forces present. Rather than organize, natural laws randomize and disorder, which is an aspect of the second law of thermodynamics. Suppose you dump red, white, and blue confetti out of an airplane a thousand feet above your house. Do you think it will form an American flag on your lawn? Probably not. The reason is that natural laws will mix up or randomize the confetti. Someone says, "We need to allow more time." All right, you now take the plane up to ten thousand feet to give the natural laws more time to work on the confetti. Will this additional time help the chances of forming the flag on your lawn? Actually, the additional time will make it worse, for this will give the natural laws more time to do what they do—disorder and randomize.

All of these problems with the theory of spontaneous generation led biologist Dean Kenyon, writing the foreword for Charles Thaxton, Walter Bradley, and Roger Olsen's book *The Mystery of Life's Origin*, to conclude, "The authors believe, and I now concur, that there is a fundamental flaw in all current theories of the chemical origins of life."[6] Cosmologist Allan Sandage said, "The most amazing thing to me is existence itself. How is it that inanimate matter can organize itself to contemplate itself?"[7] And Nobel Prize winner Sir Francis Crick said, "The origin of life appears to be almost a miracle, so many are the conditions which have had to be satisfied to get it going."[8]

Nevertheless, these facts haven't stopped evolutionists from trying to cover the reality that evolution cannot explain the origin of life. In fact, some of evolution's most persistent proponents have proposed some pretty weird theories. For example, Crick himself, the co-discoverer of DNA, proposed that the building block for life came from somewhere else in space. Fred Hoyle and N. C. Wickramasinghe suggested that particles of living cells could have reached the earth without being incinerated by the atmosphere. Crick and Leslie Orgel went even further by suggesting that an advanced civilization may have intentionally sent life spores to earth![9]

So are we to believe that the best answer some leading evolutionists can come up with to the question of the origin of life is aliens rather than God? No wonder Lee Strobel says that "the origin of life is the Achilles heel of evolution."[10] In brief, first life was either caused by purely natural forces or it is the result of intelligent intervention. But natural forces are known (uniformly) not to be the cause of the kind of specified complexity found in even a single living cell. Therefore, an intelligent being must have created it.

E—Evidence of Fossils

The third nail in evolution's coffin is that the fossil record, which was supposed to be the greatest supporter of evolution, has become its greatest weakness. Darwin himself was concerned about the lack of evidence among the fossils. He said, "Why then is not every geological formation and every stratum full of such intermediate links? Geology assuredly does not reveal any such finely graduated organic chain, and this, perhaps, is the most obvious and gravest objection which can be urged against my theory."[11]

In 1979 David M. Raup, the curator of the Field Museum of Natural History in Chicago, said:

> We are now about one hundred and twenty years after Darwin and the knowledge of the fossil record has been greatly expanded. We now have a quarter of a million fossil species, but the situation hasn't changed much. . . . We have even fewer examples of evolutionary transition than we had in Darwin's time.[12]

What does the fossil record show? It shows that in rocks evolutionists dated back some 570 million years, there is the sudden appearance
of nearly all the animal phyla, and they appear fully formed, "without
a trace of the evolutionary ancestors that Darwinists require."[13] It's a
phenomenon that points more to creationism than Darwinism! The
public has been duped into believing that there is a wealth of fossil finds that support evolution, but that is not the case. The media
trumpets a new "missing link," such as the archaeopteryx (an extinct
bird once thought to be a reptile-bird), but when it is found to be
false, they quietly hide the news in the back section of the paper, if
they mention it at all. Host of the nationwide radio program *The Bible
Answer Man* and director of the Christian Research Institute Hank
Hanegraaff has even come up with the word *pseudosaur* to describe
these supposed missing links. *Pseudo* means false and *saur* refers to
a dinosaur or reptile.[14]

Harvard evolutionist Stephen Gould has this to say about the
fossil record:

> The history of most fossil species includes two features par-
> ticularly inconsistent with gradualism: 1). Stasis. Most species
> exhibit no directional change during their tenure on earth. They
> appear in the fossil record looking much the same as when
> they disappear; morphological change is usually limited and
> directionless. 2). Sudden Appearance. In any local area, a spe-
> cies does not arise gradually by the steady transformation of its
> ancestors; it appears all at once and "fully formed."[15]

Gould points out that the fossil types appear suddenly and fully
formed with no change over time. These discoveries fit creation rather
than evolution! Author of *Icons of Evolution* Jonathan Wells writes,
"The fossil evidence is so strong, and the event so dramatic, that it has
become known as 'the Cambrian explosion,' or 'biology's big bang.'"[16]

Another problem with fossils is that they cannot establish ancestral relationships. Why is this important? Michael Denton, a
molecular biologist and physician, writes that "99 percent of the
biology of any organism resides in its soft anatomy, which is inac-
cessible in a fossil."[17] In other words, it's difficult to identify the
biological makeup of a creature just by looking at its fossil remains.
Why? Jonathan Wells states, "The fossil evidence is open to many
interpretations because individual specimens can be reconstructed
in a variety of ways, and because the fossil record cannot establish

ancestor-descendant relationships."[18] So when scientists say that a bone fragment belonged to a certain type of extinct animal, remember that the skeletal remains tell them only 1 percent of the biology of the creature, while they lack 99 percent of the soft tissue.

That leads us to another question. Darwinian evolutionists have long argued that similar structure between apes and humans is evidence of common ancestry (or common descent). Does similarity of structure prove a common ancestor or a common designer? To answer this question, just look at successive models of the airplane, from the one made by the Wright brothers to a modern spacecraft. Did each successive one evolve from the former? Or did an intelligent being intervene and create a new one? In a world governed by precise physical and chemical laws, there may be only a certain range of anatomical structures conducive to animals designed to walk on two legs.[19] Since we all have to live in the same world, shouldn't we expect some creatures to have some similar characteristics? Similarity and succession do not share common descent but a common designer.

As we have seen, the fossil record actually supports the case for creationism and harms the case for evolution. The evidence does not support the theory. One way to picture this is to see the Darwinist as a gunslinger at the OK Corral who walks into a fight and finds out, only too late, that his gun is empty!

A—Acts of God vs. Acts of Nature

The fourth nail in evolution's coffin is that the effect cannot be greater than the cause. Remember that the principle of uniformity holds that causes in the past were like causes we observe today. Science is a search for causes. Logically, there can be only two types of causes: intelligent and nonintelligent. Let's take the following quiz.

Item	Intelligent Cause	Nonintelligent Cause
1. The Grand Canyon had a(n) . . .		
2. The presidents on Mount Rushmore had a(n) . . .		
3. A sand dune had a(n) . . .		
4. A sand castle had a(n) . . .		

An eight-year-old could pass this quiz (hopefully you did as well)! The Grand Canyon had a nonintelligent cause because it was carved by an act of nature, while the figures of the presidents on Mount Rushmore obviously had an intelligent cause because they were crafted by the actions of someone with intelligence.

Let's say you are taking a walk on the beach and come across a sand castle next to a sand dune. The sand dune would have had a nonintelligent cause because it was made by an act of nature, while the sand castle would obviously have had an intelligent cause because it was made by someone with intelligence.

Now how can even an eight-year-old know this to be true? Because the effect is never greater than the cause. When considering how life came to be, there can be only two causes: intelligent (act of God) and nonintelligent (act of nature). Evolution wants us to believe the following.

Nothing produced something. This has never happened and never will! This theory violates the laws of science and the laws of logic, and even a child knows this. It is interesting that in a March 2001 Gallup Poll, two-thirds of Americans chose *creationism* over *evolution* when asked which of these two terms best describes human origins.[20] This is surprising when one considers that most of these Americans were indoctrinated in the theory of evolution while in school.

Why would they still choose creationism over evolution? We think it reveals not only their religious preference but also their sense that evolution is illogical. No scientific law allows something to evolve from nothing. If there was nothing in the universe to begin with, nothing could cause anything to appear. Evolutionists often try to duck this problem by saying that evolution is not concerned with the origin of life, only with how life progressed after it appeared. But if you can't get something from nothing, it is pointless to think you can get the greater from the lesser. Water doesn't rise any higher than its source on its own. Juggle the figures any way you like, but without a creator, you are not going to get anything, let alone everything.

Nonlife turned into life. Evolutionists want us to believe that some chemicals in the "warm little pond" spontaneously generated into a life-form. When confronted with the fact that this belief is illogical and improbable and has never been repeated by their greatest minds, their only defense is to use the word *chance*. Chance is not a force, and it never caused anything. Using chance as their only support is nothing more than ignorance being disguised as information. No scientific law can account for nonliving things coming to life. The soil in your garden didn't turn into the trees and flowers. They came from seeds, cuttings, or grafts from other trees and flowers.

Nonintelligent life produced intelligent life. As we saw earlier under the origin of life point, the cell with its DNA is incredibly complex. Since we know that design requires a designer (such as Mount Rushmore and the sand castle), we know that the design of the cell required a designer.

So when we consider the causes of the origin of the universe and the origin of life, we have only two choices: they were acts of God in that they showed intelligence or acts of nature in that they did not show intelligence. Since the effect cannot be greater than the cause, the answer has to be that the origin of the universe and the origin of life were acts of God. If we completed the quiz with questions 5 and 6, what would your answers be?

Item	Intelligent Cause	Nonintelligent Cause
5. The origin of the universe had a(n) . . .		?
6. The origin of life had a(n) . .		?

P—Preservation of Life-Forms

The fifth nail in evolution's coffin is that the life-forms have been preserved to remain within their own type without the drastic intermediate transitional states that evolution would require. Naturalistic evolutionists believe that the life-forms have evolved through natural selection. To see if this is possible, let's answer the following questions.

1. *What is the difference between macroevolution and microevolution?*

According to macroevolution, all life-forms (animals, plants, fishes, humans) have descended from the same ancestor (the first one-celled creature). This descent, or evolution, occurred by natural processes without any intelligent intervention. Darwinist Richard Dawkins refers to this as the "blind watchmaker," which means he admits the appearance of design but denies intelligent design.[21]

Everyone agrees that evolution has occurred in some fashion. To be sure, there are variations within the different species of plants and animals, as can be seen by the two hundred different breeds of dogs, cows being bred to improve milk production, and even bacteria adapting and developing immunity to antibiotics. This is called "microevolution." There is a vast difference between microevolution and macroevolution. Microevolution is an observed fact; macroevolution is not. Microevolution is adaptation within a type; macroevolution is transformation to another type. Darwin believed (as do evolutionists) that since we have observed microevolution (for example, the different breeds of dogs), this is evidence of macroevolution, in that everything, including these dogs, all came from the same simple cell.

2. *How did macroevolution supposedly work?*

From a single cell, many increasingly complex forms of life developed. But how could such changes take place? Evolutionists give two basic answers: mutations and natural selection.

Mutations are sudden changes in the genes of an organism resulting in some change in its outer or inner structure. These newly acquired characteristics are then inherited by following generations.

Natural selection is the process by which forms of life with these sudden changes survive because they are more suited for their environment. They are thus "naturally selected." This is also known as the "survival of the fittest." Better forms survive and weaker forms die out.

3. *Does artificial selection (such as the breeding of dogs) prove natural selection?*

Genetic limits say no. Genetic limits seem to be built within the basic types. Dog breeders always encounter genetic limits when they try to create a new breed of dog. No matter what they do, they have found that a dog always remains a dog! By the way, using dog breeding to support natural selection is invalid because one uses intelligence while the other does not. Even when using intelligence, evolution hits genetic walls, so how are we to believe that the blind Darwinian process could succeed?

Cyclical change says no. Not only are there genetic limits to change within types, but this change within types seems to be cyclical—that is, they don't change to new life-forms but stay within the same form. Although Darwin's finches had beaks that adapted to the weather, they always remained finches! Every time microevolution is seen, no new life-form is seen but only the same form.

Author and a leader in the intelligent design (ID) movement Philip Johnson says, "In other words, the reason dogs don't become as big as elephants, much less change into elephants, is not that we just haven't been breeding them long enough. Dogs do not have the genetic capacity for that degree of change, and they stop getting bigger when the genetic limit is reached."[22] As someone wisely asked, "If we evolved from monkeys, how come there are still monkeys?" False analogy says no. There is a huge difference between natural selection and intelligent breeding. The latter involves an intelligent being who plans the process and intervenes to assure the end he desires. Natural laws do not do this.

4. *Could the intermediate states survive?*

Intermediate forms would not survive transition. The organs of a creature are highly interdependent as are their uses. Evolutionists assert that birds evolved gradually from reptiles over a long period of time. This would require a transition from scales to feathers. How could these creatures survive while their scales were no longer scales but not quite feathers? They would not be able to swim or fly, and they would be easy prey on land, in water, and from the air. Furthermore, these transitional creatures would be extremely unlikely to find food for themselves. Nature destroys freaks; it doesn't protect them.

Darwin admitted, "If it could be demonstrated that any complex organ existed which could not possibly have been formed by numerous, successive, slight modifications, then my theory would absolutely break down."[23]

5. *What about the common DNA?*

Evolutionists say that evidence of common descent lies in the fact that all living things contain DNA. They think that the DNA similarity between apes and humans, which some say is 85–95 percent,[24] strongly implies an ancestral relationship. But does the similarity of DNA show a common *ancestor* or a common *creator*? Other studies show that the DNA similarity between humans and mice is also about 90 percent.[25] Steve Jones, a scientist and evolutionist, said on a radio program, "We also share about 50 percent of our DNA with bananas, and that doesn't make us half bananas, either from the waist up or the waist down."[26]

Study figure 7.1. Does similarity and progression prove that the kettle evolved from the teaspoon? Of course not! Similarity and pro-

Figure 7.1

gression do not always imply common ancestry, for in this case, we know they show a common creator or designer. This is true for real living things as well.

If we were to use this idea of similarities to determine which animal is most like us, we would come up with dire results. Take, for instance, our number of chromosomes (46). Two of our closest ancestors would be the tobacco plant (48) and the bat (44)! Let's go a bit further with this. Because the chromosomes in living matter are one of the most complex bits of matter in the known universe, it would seem logical to assume that organisms with the least number of chromosomes are the end result of millions of years of evolutionary experimenting to increase complexity in living organisms. Therefore, this would imply that we started from penicillium with only two chromosomes, slowly evolved into fruit flies (8), and after many more millions of years became tomatoes (12), and so on, until we reached the human stage of 46 chromosomes. Millions of years from now, if we're fortunate, we may become the ultimate life-form, a fern, with a total of 480 chromosomes!

One more thing on DNA: if all species share a common ancestor, we should expect to find the DNA protein sequences to be transitional from fish to amphibian and from reptile to mammal. But what we find is that the basic types are molecularly isolated from one another, which would seem to reject any type of ancestral relationship. There are no

Darwinian transitions, only distinct molecular gaps that evolutionists cannot explain.

We have learned that Darwinism fails to adequately explain the origin of the universe, the origin of life, the evidence of the fossil records, the acts of God versus acts of nature, and the preservation of the life-forms. So the acrostic U-LEAP is quite accurate, for it describes the leap of faith one must take to believe in evolution once the facts are examined.

What Difference Does It Make?

What has been the result of evolution? Michael Denton says that Darwinism "broke man's link with God" and then "sent him adrift in the cosmos without purpose."[27] He goes on to say: "As far as Christianity was concerned, the advent of the theory of evolution . . . was catastrophic. . . . The decline in religious belief can probably be attributed more to the propagation and advocacy by the intellectual and scientific community of the Darwinian version of evolution than to any other factor."[28]

Prominent evolutionist William Provine of Cornell University has said that if evolution is true, then there is no evidence for God, there is no life after death, there is no absolute foundation for right and wrong, there is no ultimate meaning for life, and people don't really have free will.[29]

But we have seen that evolution is not true! So that means there is evidence for God, there is life after death, there is an absolute foundation for right and wrong, there is ultimate meaning for life, and people really do have free will!

Why Do Scientists Still Believe in Evolution?

If evolution is so flawed, why don't more scientists believe in an intelligent designer? Walter Bradley, when asked this question, replied:

Many *have* reached that conclusion. But for some, their philosophy gets in the way. If they're persuaded ahead of time that there isn't a God, then no matter how compelling the evidence, they'll always say, "Wait and we'll find something better in the future." But that's a metaphysical argument. Scientists aren't more objective than anybody else. They all come to questions like this with their preconceived ideas.[30]

Darwinist Richard Lewontin of Harvard University says that his materialism "is absolute for we cannot allow a divine foot in the door."[31] There are at least four reasons for evolutionists trying to prohibit "a divine foot in the door":

1. By admitting God, Darwinists would be admitting that they are not the highest authority when it comes to truth.
2. By admitting God, Darwinists would be admitting that they don't have absolute authority when it comes to explaining causes.
3. By admitting God, Darwinists would risk losing financial security and professional admiration.
4. By admitting God, Darwinists would be admitting that they don't have the authority to define right and wrong for themselves.[32]

Since the evidence for the origin of the universe and life supports an intelligent designer rather than evolution, we can see that belief in Darwinism is more a matter of the will than the mind. We must dialogue with those who cling to evolution using scientific facts, logic, and reason if we are to see success. We must also realize that the majority of Americans really do not believe in evolution, and once we show them the evidence for God in the origin of the universe and life, they will be more open to considering his Son.

U-LEAP Evolution Checklist

U—Origin of the *Universe*
- Evolution is incapable of explaining the origin of the universe.
- The universe had a beginning as can be seen by its SURGE.
- Since the universe had a beginning, it must have had a beginner.

L—Origin of *Life*
- Evolution is incapable of explaining the origin of life.
- Evolution's theory, spontaneous generation, says that life was generated spontaneously

from nonliving chemicals without intelligent intervention.

- There is no such thing as simple life, as can be seen in the DNA of the cell.
- Spontaneous generation has never been observed or duplicated.
- Spontaneous generation does not explain the source of the chemicals there in the first place.
- Spontaneous generation does not account for the time needed or the destructive forces that would be present.

E—*Evidence* of Fossils

- The fossil finds do not support the theory of evolution.
- The fossil finds show stasis and sudden appearance, which support creationism.
- Fossils cannot establish ancestral relationships.
- Similarity of structure is evidence of a common designer, not common ancestry.

A—*Acts* of God vs. *Acts* of Nature

- The effect cannot be greater than the cause.
- Nothing cannot produce something.
- Nonlife cannot turn into life.
- Nonintelligent life cannot produce intelligent life.

P—*Preservation* of Life-Forms

- Microevolution (adaptation within a type) is an observed fact while macroevolution (transformation to another type) is not.
- Macroevolution would have to work through mutations and natural selection.
- Artificial selection (such as the breeding of dogs) does not prove natural selection because of genetic limits and cyclical changes.
- Intermediate states could not survive the transition.

- DNA similarity does not demonstrate common descent but rather a common creator.

Digging Deeper on Evolution

Geisler, Norman. *Baker Encyclopedia of Christian Apologetics*. Grand Rapids: Baker Books, 1999, 224–35.

Geisler, Norman, and Ron Brooks. *When Skeptics Ask*. Grand Rapids: Baker Books, 1990, 211–32.

Geisler, Norman, and Frank Turek. *I Don't Have Enough Faith to Be an Atheist*. Wheaton: Crossway, 2004, 73–112, 113–67.

Hanegraaff, Hank. *The Face that Demonstrates the Farce of Evolution*. Nashville: Word, 1998.

Strobel, Lee. *The Case for Faith*. Grand Rapids: Zondervan, 2000, 87–112.

Zacharias, Ravi, and Norman Geisler. *Is Your Church Ready? Motivating Leaders to Live an Apologetic Life*. Grand Rapids: Zondervan, 2003, 49–71.

8

If There Is a God,
Why Is There Suffering in the World?

"If there is a God, why is there so much suffering in this world?" Debby asked me (Randy) during a lunch meeting.

I was the sales manager for a medical equipment company, and one of my responsibilities was to travel and meet with each sales representative monthly. The purpose of the meeting was to evaluate, encourage, and train. Usually we would spend some time in the field, then we would meet over lunch for some good Southern food, sweet tea, and plenty of discussion. When in the field, our discussions were always about the business. But at lunch, our discussions always gravitated to spiritual things. Debby knew I was a Christian and always brought up spiritual questions that puzzled her.

Debby's path in life had been a rough one, mostly from her own poor choices, which she readily admitted. She had an illegitimate child at seventeen, married the child's father at eighteen, survived ten years of marriage to this physically abusive man, and now eight years later was living with another man. Her son was now becoming a major problem in that he was verbally abusing her. Yet during the past eight years, Debby had put herself through nursing school and had become a nurse and was now a good sales representative for our company. Debby told me that she looked forward to our meetings each month because she could ask me questions that she would never dare ask a minister.

"I have been struggling with this question for a long time. I am a good person. I love people, especially the elderly, which is why I find it easy to sell to them. I believe in God and even watch church on TV sometimes. But all through my life, it seems like God has abandoned me. I have had a very difficult life, some of it the result of my own choices. I've been knocked down so many times, I don't remember ever standing up. Still I try to get back up and do the right thing. But each time I am swatted down like a fly!" Debby said, wiping tears from her eyes with her napkin.

"I have stopped asking God why he has allowed me to endure such trouble, because he has never answered me. I know I am not the best person in the world, but I also know a lot of people worse than me who seem to have prospered. I was talking about this with my neighbor a few months ago, and she said that suffering in the world is evidence to her that God does not exist. She said that a good God would not allow all of the pain and suffering in this world, so either there is not a good God or there is no God at all. I disagreed with her, but lately I have been plagued by doubts over my neighbor's words. As a nurse, I saw so many people suffering with disease and pain. Now every day I see the elderly wasting away, unnoticed and uncared for by people." Debby paused to take a sip of some sweet tea. "If there is a God, why is there so much suffering in this world?"

The subject of pain and suffering is a large obstacle for spiritual seekers. Lee Strobel, for his book *The Case for Faith*, commissioned pollster George Barna to conduct a national survey in which he asked people, "If you could ask God only one question, what would that question be?" The number one answer was "Why is there pain and suffering in the world?"[1]

Like most people, I am no stranger to pain and suffering. I was born with a deformity (a cleft lip and palate), which meant surgery and years of speech lessons as well as ridicule from other kids. I had a godly mother but an abusive, ungodly father. As a child, I learned how to box simply to protect myself from my father's blows. Later, as a police officer, I worked many car accidents involving alcohol where the drunk who caused the accident emerged without a scratch but the innocent people in the other car were either killed or horribly mangled. As a pastor, I saw abuse in marriages, sexually abused children, articulate adults who gradually lost their minds to Alzheimer's, and people robbed of their loved ones by cancer. As a brother, I saw both my sister-in-law and sister lose a child at birth, and I saw my same sister give birth to her next son who was born with autism. As an American, I was horrified to watch the evil unleashed on our country on September 11, 2001.

The question I was now being asked by Debby is one I have been asked by many people. In fact, I have asked it myself from time to time. The question is, "Where is God?" As the smoke began to clear from the ruins of the World Trade Center, people began making some interesting statements about God. Some comments heard were: "God did not know this was going to happen. Evidently he was busy somewhere else doing other things." Or "God knew what was going to happen, but he could not or would not intervene. He just didn't care." Follow the logical results of such reasoning:

- God didn't know, so he is not *all-knowing*; thus he is not God— at least not the one in which Christians have traditionally believed.
- God couldn't stop it, so he is not *all-powerful*; thus he is not God.
- God didn't care, so he is not *loving*; thus he is not God.

Or it is put this way:

- If God is all-good, he would destroy evil.
- If God is all-powerful, he could destroy evil.
- But evil is not destroyed.
- Thus there is no God.[2]

Books have been written on this subject of suffering, but most people don't want a book—they just want an answer. We took the various answers given for suffering in this world and made the acrostic PAINS to help you remember these reasons. You can share this acrostic in one setting, or you can spend hours going over each point. Your setting and the person with whom you are dealing will determine your response. Let's look at how I walked Debby through the PAINS acrostic.

I said, "Debby, that is a great question and one I too have asked of God from time to time."

"Really?" she replied. "I'm surprised to hear that."

"It's true," I said. "In fact, most Christians have asked this very question of God. Even in the Bible, King David, as well as others, asked God this question.[3] Let's explore this question together. Okay? I'll share some reasons I think God allows suffering in this world, and then we'll discuss them."

"That would be great!" Debby replied.

I wrote on a napkin the four points stated above. "If God is all-good, he would destroy evil. If God is all-powerful, he could destroy evil. But evil is not destroyed. Thus there is no God." I told her that we would come back to these points later, and then I shared with Debby the five reasons for suffering.

Five Reasons for Suffering in This World—PAINS

P—*There Is a Purpose in Suffering*

The very question assumes there is a God, so let's start here. We know that since there is a God, he has allowed suffering for some reason. That means there is a purpose behind our suffering. Let's think about some possible reasons for suffering.

Suffering gets our attention. Suffering makes us look upward. C. S. Lewis said, "God whispers to us in our pleasures, speaks in our conscience, but shouts in our pains. It is His megaphone to rouse a deaf world."[4] Sometimes we look up in anger, but we are still looking in the right direction.

Suffering may be the consequences of our own actions. Sometimes, not always, our suffering is the result of our own wrong actions. Debby had sexual relations outside of the protection of marriage, which resulted in a baby. The consequences of that illicit sexual relationship are with her to this day. Yet she blamed God for her suffering, not herself.

Is our suffering God's fault or a result of our own poor choices? If I jump off a cliff and break my legs, can I complain to God because of the law of gravity? No, our actions have consequences, and many times our suffering comes from wrong choices. Let's say I decided to get drunk on the way home (Debby laughed because she knew I don't drink alcohol). Then I had a bad car accident and the rescue workers had to use the "jaws of life" to extricate me from my vehicle. My body was horribly mangled from the wreck, and the doctors had to amputate my leg. In the hospital room, I asked God to forgive me, and he did. Now, will my leg grow back? No, but I am forgiven by God! Nevertheless, I suffer irreparable consequences.

Suffering may bring about good. Sometimes good comes out of suffering. One of my favorite characters in the Old Testament is Joseph. Joseph's life was one of unjust suffering. His suffering began when his brothers sold him into slavery. Then he was put into an Egyptian jail because of a lie, and he stayed there for years, seemingly forgotten by God. Finally, he got out and was put into a position of power and had the opportunity to punish his brothers. But this is what he said to them: "You intended to harm me, but God intended it for good to accomplish what is now being done, the saving of many lives" (Gen. 50:20). Joseph did not mean that evil is somehow good. Rather, he meant that even in suffering, God is at work to bring about his good purposes in our lives.

Consider the terrorist attacks of 9/11. Using planes as bombs was a terrible evil, but God brought some good out of it, such as the rise of our national pride and increased respect for police and firefighters.

Even physical pain can be a good thing. Think of what would happen if we lost our pain senses tomorrow. We could step on a nail or burn our hand and never know it, allowing infection to set in. In fact, one doctor who worked in a leprosy clinic believes that leprosy deadens the nerve cells, which results in the loss of limbs.[5] So sometimes suffering can actually be good for us.

How about Job? "After Job had prayed for his friends, the LORD made him prosperous again and gave him twice as much as he had before. . . .The LORD blessed the latter part of Job's life more than the first" (Job 42:10, 12). James says of Job, "As you know, we consider blessed those who have persevered. You have heard of Job's perseverance and have seen what the Lord finally brought about. The Lord is full of compassion and mercy" (James 5:11).

One day we will know the purpose. In this life, we may never understand the reasons God allows us to suffer. In fact, Moses said, "The secret things belong to the LORD our God, but the things revealed belong to us and to our children forever, that we may follow all the words of this law" (Deut. 29:29). But when God's children get to heaven, they will know the purpose for their suffering. Is there a difference between our knowing the purpose of suffering and God knowing the purpose for it? Of course. What do you think it is? As a parent, I often withheld candy or something sweet from my children before supper or said no to their desires. Did this seem wrong to them? Of course it did, but I was doing what was best for them, even though they did not understand it at the time. One time I withheld candy from my daughter before supper and she said, "You're a bad daddy!" Now was I being a "bad" daddy or a "good" daddy? I was being a good daddy and actually showing love to my child by withholding certain pleasures that she thought she needed and deserved. I think this too is God's perspective.

Debby nodded and replied that this point made a lot of sense. "I understand now how suffering can lead to good results. But," she exclaimed, "why would God create a world filled with disease, poverty, and death in the first place?" I shared my next point with her.

A—We Are Living in Adam's World

I said, "Debby, let's play the pretend game of 'God for a Day.' Tomorrow when you wake up, you discover that you are God and you are going to create a brand-new world like this one but better. What kind of world would you create if you were God?"

"Well," Debby pondered, "it would be a world without suffering, accidents, disease, and death. No one would grow old. And it would be a world of amazing beauty, kindness, justice, and love. Everyone and everything would get along with each other."

"That sounds like a great world," I said as I wrote down her responses on a napkin.

If we were God, what a wonderful world we would create. Interestingly, the world Debby described—and she is representative of the majority of people—is *exactly* the kind of world God created! He created a world without suffering, accidents, disease, and death. No one grew old. And it was a world of amazing beauty, kindness, justice, and love. Everyone and everything got along with each other. God even looked at everything he had made and said it was "very good" (Gen. 1:31).

But there was one thing God created that Debby left out: free will. God created man and woman with the ability to choose to follow God or rebel against him. He created them with the ability to love him freely or to reject him wholly. God did not want robots that would serve his every whim because they had to or were simply programmed to do so. No, he wanted people who would love him freely and without condition.[6]

Adam and Eve chose to exercise their free will and rebel against God. That one act of sin is what is called "the fall." The result of

Adam and Eve's sin was that the earth was cursed and people were cursed as well (Gen. 3:14–19). Natural disasters such as tornadoes and hurricanes are the result of the fall. Human death is a result of the fall (Rom. 5:12), as are disease, murder, and other disasters. The worst result of the fall was that humankind was now separated from God (Gen. 3:23–24).

The result of the fall is that no one is innocent. Rabbi Kushner asked the wrong question: "Why do bad things happen to good people?"[7] According to the Bible there are no good people in God's eyes. Paul said that all of us have sinned and fallen short of God's glory (Rom. 3:23). Sin-infected creatures with free will make bad choices in life, which affect others. The overwhelming majority of evil in this world comes from the hand of human beings. If a woman is horribly raped, she is innocent. She is not at fault, but the rapist is guilty. There were children on those planes that were used as bombs on 9/11. The children were innocent, but the terrorists were guilty of murder.

We blame God for suffering in this world and yet most of the time it is our fault as humans for this suffering. Where was God when Hitler murdered thousands of Jews? He was there with them, but never forget that it was Hitler who did the killing, not God.

The sad truth of Adam's world is that all of us are sinners and all of us are guilty of causing suffering to others, in one form or the other. We are dying today of diseases that never existed two hundred years ago. We have polluted and abused our environment and die of cancer and other maladies and yet we blame God. We pollute our bodies with harmful food or overeating and die of heart attacks or obesity, and yet we insist it is God's fault. No one is truly innocent and yet we blame God.

"So," Debby said thoughtfully, "all of the bad things in this world are man's fault, not God's."

"You are absolutely right," I affirmed.

"So all of the time we blame God for suffering, we should be blaming ourselves? I never saw that before," Debby admitted.

I — Suffering Helps Us Identify

Suffering helps us to identify with others. People who have never suffered make terrible counselors. Suffering helps us to be aware of other sufferers, reach out to help them, plus the process heals both the one suffering and the one trying to help. Only those who have lost a child can understand that pain and the steps toward healing. My sister understands such pain because she lost her son. My sister understands the struggles of a child with autism as well as the joys in seeing him make progress. Debby could identify with abused women because she has been in abusive relationships.

In fact, the Bible says that one reason for suffering is that we can take the comfort we received from God through our trials and share it with someone else. "Praise be to the God and Father of our Lord Jesus Christ, the Father of compassion and the God of all comfort, who comforts us in all our troubles, so that we can comfort those in any trouble with the comfort we ourselves have received from God. For just as the sufferings of Christ flow over into our lives, so also through Christ our comfort overflows" (2 Cor. 1:3–5).

Dr. Charles Swindoll explained the passage this way:

Who can understand what it is like to sit alongside a friend or loved one who is dying from a terminal illness? Who knows the heartache of having a home split apart? What about someone to understand the loss of a child . . . or the misery of a teenager on drugs . . . or the anguish of living with an alcoholic mate . . . or a failure in school . . . or the loss of a business? Who on earth understands?

I'll tell you who—the person who has been through it wrapped in the blanket of God's comfort. Better than anybody else you, who have endured the stinging experiences, are the choicest counselors God can use.

This is one of the reasons why we suffer—to be prepared to bring encouragement and comfort to others who come across our path enduring a similar situation. Remember that!

Look back at the chain reaction. We suffer . . . God comes alongside to comfort . . . others suffer . . . we step alongside to comfort them. With God's arm firmly around my shoulders, I have the strength and stability to place my arm around the shoulder of another. Isn't this true? Similar experiences create mutual understanding.

Because of this we can confidently say that our troubling circumstances are never in vain. The bruises may hurt, but they are not without reason. God is uniquely preparing us for the comfort others will need. In one sense, we are all "preparing for the ministry." Our Father is preparing us to meet the deep, inner needs of others by bringing us through the dark places first.[8]

What we suffer develops within us the difference between sympathy and empathy. Sympathy is feeling sorry for someone while empathy is being able to understand the pain of another, to enter into a person's feelings, thoughts, and emotions. While I can feel sympathy for someone who has lost a spouse I cannot feel empathy since my wife is alive. But a widow or widower can identify with the pain of this loss and thus be the best counselor a grieving spouse needs.

"Well," Debby objected, "I still don't see why God couldn't have wiped out the really bad people like Hitler, Saddam Hussein, or Osama bin Laden before they killed so many people. If God knows criminals, rapists, and murderers are going to commit their crimes even before they do them, why doesn't he stop them?"

N—Neutralize the Sinners

Debby's question leads to the fourth point about suffering. God has provided governments to deal with the majority of evil in this world (Rom. 13:1–7). He has also provided the church to be a light in a dark world. And through the Bible, God tells us what it will take for us to be happy and holy.[9]

But think about Debby's question of why God doesn't just neutralize the really bad people of this world. For God to neutralize suffering in this world would mean that he would have to neutralize the source of suffering. As we have just seen, for God to neutralize the source of suffering, he would have to neutralize people! For as long as we are free to do evil, there will be evil. And if we are not free to choose good or evil, we are merely robots, not persons.

Now that is exactly what Debby was proposing. God could start with Hitler, Hussein, and bin Laden, the really bad sinners. But why should God stop there? He could then move down the line to the "medium sinners" and begin to neutralize rapists, serial killers, and pedophiles. But how could God stop there? What if someone robbed and murdered one of our children tonight? Shouldn't God kill that murderer as well? But then we have to consider this problem: have we ever really hated someone? We all have. Jesus said that we are not to murder, but if we hate someone in our heart, we are guilty of the same crime (Matt. 5:21–22). The Bible says that in God's eyes, if we break one commandment, we have broken them all (James 2:10). All have sinned, and none of us is innocent. For God to neutralize the world of suffering would mean he would have to wipe out the cause of suffering, and that would be all of us.

Debby let out a big sigh and in a deep southern drawl said, "I can see that my solution would damn me as well as the bad sinners."

"Yes, and it would damn me as well, Debby. But I'm glad you mentioned a solution, because there is a solution to the suffering in this world."

S—There Is a Savior

Every December 25 we celebrate Christmas, and Christmas marks the time when the Son of God came to earth to be a man. Consider what this means to our subject of suffering. Jesus walked this earth and suffered just like us. He knew what it was like to be hungry (Matt. 4:2), he did not have a home or possessions (Luke 9:58), he was ridiculed by others (Matt. 27:29), he wept when someone he loved died (John 11:35), he was betrayed by two close friends (Luke 22:47, 61), he was beaten and suffered pain (John 19:1–2), and he experienced injustice when he was put to death even though he was innocent (2 Cor. 5:21).

Now what does all of this mean? It means that Jesus understands our pain! The Bible says Jesus can sympathize with our sufferings because he has suffered (Heb. 4:15). He knows what we are going through, and because he does, he can help us.

So Jesus understands our pain and suffering; that's good. But honestly, when we are in pain, we need more than just an understanding friend—we need a solution! Jesus is the solution to our suffering. He overcame evil in this world (John 16:33). And he overcame sin, disease, and death when he arose from the grave on Easter Sunday morning (Luke 24:6–7). He offers to us that same overcoming power of the resurrection with which we can live our lives (Eph. 1:18–20).

Consider this: some evil has actually helped to defeat evil. Jesus being crucified on the cross was a great evil. But God allowed the evil of the crucifixion to overcome the greater evil of our sins. Moreover, Jesus will one day bring a new heaven and a new earth free of the effects of sin (Rev. 21:1).

Finally, Jesus will eventually bring justice to the world. Let's look again at the four points on Debby's napkin:

- If God is all-good, he would destroy evil. ("Destroy" here does not mean annihilate; it means to defeat or become victorious over.)
- If God is all-powerful, he could destroy evil.

- But evil is not destroyed.
- Thus there is no God.

Let's add one word and see what difference it makes:

- If God is all-good, he would destroy evil.
- If God is all-powerful, he could destroy evil.
- But evil is not destroyed . . . *yet*!
- Therefore God can and will destroy evil one day.[10]

Jesus will bring justice. Contrary to a popular adage, justice delayed is not justice denied. Eventual justice by God is ultimate justice—and ultimate justice is the best kind of all.

Debby nodded and smiled and said, "I never saw God in this way before. The doubts of my heart have been answered. I think I am going to start praying again."

"Debby," I said, "that's great. Now let me tell you how you can have the overcoming power of Jesus Christ in your life every day." I then shared the gospel with her, and she said that she had trusted in Jesus as a child but had strayed over the years. With that, we ended our lunch meeting and went our separate ways. The next month when I saw Debby, she asked me to write down the PAINS points for her so she could talk to her neighbor about God and suffering. Here was a convert to apologetics!

Why Suffering? Checklist

P—There Is a *Purpose* in Suffering
- It gets our attention.
- It is sometimes the consequences of our actions.
- It may bring about good.
- One day we will know the purpose.

A—We Are Living in *Adam's* World
- God created a perfect world with free will.
- Humans sinned and brought evil into the world.

I—Suffering Helps Us *Identify*
- One reason for suffering is to take the comfort God gave to us and give it to others.

  - Suffering makes the difference between
    sympathy and empathy.

N—*Neutralize* the Sinners
  - Should God wipe out the really bad sinners?
  - If he did, he would have to include us as well.

S—There Is a *Savior*
  - Jesus understands our pain and suffering.
  - Jesus overcame evil with the resurrection.
  - Jesus will one day bring a new heaven and
    new earth.
  - Justice delayed is not justice denied.

Digging Deeper on Pain and Suffering

Geisler, Norman. *Baker Encyclopedia of Christian Apologetics.* Grand
    Rapids: Baker Books, 1999, 219–24.

Geisler, Norman. *The Roots of Evil.* Eugene, OR: Wipf and Stock,
    2002.

Lewis. C. S. *The Problem of Pain*. New York: Macmillan, 1962.

Swindoll, Charles R. *For Those Who Hurt*. Grand Rapids: Zondervan,
    1977.

Tada, Joni Eareckson. *A Step Further*. Grand Rapids: Zondervan,
    1978.

Yancey, Philip. *Where Is God When It Hurts?* Grand Rapids: Zonder-
    van: 1977.

9

Are Miracles Possible?

"You're awfully quiet today," Kris said to Linda, her co-worker and friend. They were eating lunch together in the patio area outside their office building.

Linda replied, "I had a rough weekend. My mother called and asked me to stop for a visit. When I got there, she dropped a bombshell on me, telling me that she has terminal cancer."

"That's terrible," Kris exclaimed. "I am so sorry. What a bad weekend."

"Thanks, but it went from bad to worse," Linda said with her head bowed. "My mother, who is a Christian, once again tried to get me to convert. She told me, 'I probably have only six months to live. I want to see you again after I die.' Well, that was unfair pressure, and it made me mad. I blew up and said that I would never convert. My mother asked why, so I picked up her Bible, shook it at her, and said, 'This book that you have lived by and are now willing to die by is just a book of fairy tales. That's right, fairy tales. Moses parting the Red Sea, Elijah calling down fire from heaven, and then the stories of Jesus feeding five thousand people with some bits of fish and bread, walking on water, and then rising again from the grave—I mean, come on, Mom. No one believes in those things anymore. You may be willing to die a fool, but I refuse to live as one!' With that, I stormed out of the house and went to my apartment. I spent the rest of the weekend angry and crying. Angry at my mother for believing in a God who doesn't exist, and angry at this God for taking my mother if he *does* exist."

They ate their salads in silence, Linda embarrassed over her remarks and Kris praying for wisdom.

Finally, Kris spoke up. "Linda, we've been friends a long time, and I need to say that I think you made a statement to your mother that I don't believe is accurate. You said that no one believes in miracles anymore. But right now, even as we eat, hundreds of thousands of people all over this world, from farmers to CEOs to even scientists, believe in God and believe he can do miracles. In fact, every living U.S. president we have right now believes in God, the Bible, and miracles. Would you consider all of these people fools? Linda, if your mother is a fool for believing in miracles, then so am I, because I believe in miracles too. Now it may be that you have points for your position that I have never considered. But it may be that I have points for my view that you have never considered. Would you say that is possible?"

Linda shrugged and said, "I suppose that's possible."

"Linda, I've always known you to be intelligent, rational, and willing to listen to someone else's position with an open mind. Let me share why I believe miracles are possible."

In sharing our faith with unbelievers, establishing the credibility of miracles is second in importance only to the evidences for God. If a person like Linda believes that biblical miracles are just "fairy tales," then she will not believe the Bible is trustworthy, that Jesus is the resurrected Son of God, or that she needs Jesus to be her Savior. Establishing the existence of God lays the foundation for establishing the possibility of miracles. Establishing the possibility of miracles lays the foundation for establishing the credibility of the Bible and that Jesus is the Son of God and thus the only way to God. In short, a miracle is a special act of God, but there cannot be special acts of God unless there is a God who can act.

Kris's position is that miracles are the finger of God touching our world, much like a finger touching the surface of water in an aquarium. If you stick your finger into a fishbowl, what do the fish see? They see something intruding into their world. They see an impact as ripples are made from the intrusion, and they see something unnatural to them, for they know that the finger is not a part of their world (which is why they scatter). Using the FINGER acrostic, we will cover the possibility of miracles, the purpose of miracles, and the characteristics of miracles.

F—Feasible

Linda and others hold a conviction that miracles are not possible. The most powerful way to overcome this position is simply by showing the doubter that if God exists, then miracles are possible. To disprove that miracles are possible, one must prove that the existence of God is impossible. But no one has ever done that. To put it succinctly, evidence for miracles is everywhere because evidence for God is everywhere, as we saw in chapter 6. Thus there is good evidence for miracles. The greatest miracle of all—the creation of the universe out of nothing—has already happened. Could a God who created the entire universe out of nothing part the Red Sea? Bring fire down from heaven? Feed five thousand people? Walk on water? Raise the dead? Of course! As C. S. Lewis said, "If we admit God, must we admit Miracle? Indeed, indeed, you have no security against it. That is the bargain."[1]

The most important objection came from David Hume (1711–1776) and has had a widespread effect on our modern world, even on Linda. David Hume was one of the founders of the Enlightenment, which came to mean that humans supposedly became so enlightened (educated and advanced) that they could put their faith not in religion or superstitious beliefs like miracles but rather in reason and the truth founded by the scientific method. We like to summarize Hume's position as "If it's not repeatable, then it's not believable." Therefore, since miracles are not repeatable (they are rare and unique events), they are not believable. But let's think about that for a minute. The origin of the universe (the Big Bang) happened only once. The origin of life (whether by evolution or creation) happened only once. Hume's own birth happened only once. In fact, the entire history of the world is filled with rare, unrepeatable events.

Hume would say to a witness of Christ's resurrection that it never happened even though the witness was there. His reasoning? The normal way of things in this world is that when people die, they stay dead. So an event that is rare is not believable or possible. But what if you shot a hole-in-one (which is a rare event to be sure) and had twenty good witnesses to your shot? Hume's reasoning would not believe you or your witnesses unless you could tee up and do it five times in a row. But wait a minute. The issue is not whether an event is regular or rare but whether we have good *evidence* for the event. We should be wary of a line of reasoning that tells us to disbelieve what actually occurred. It seems that this obstinate disbelief in miracles is really a matter of the will rather than of the mind. This is evidence of a worldview predisposed against God and, as such, blind to any evidence for him.

The first and most important point to establish is that miracles are feasible. Miracles are feasible because of the evidence for the existence of God. It is probable that Kris would first need to walk Linda through the evidences for God to prepare her for believing in miracles.

I—Identify

Now we move to purpose. Why would God use miracles in this world? In chapter 6, we learned that there are three BIG evidences for God. God began the universe with the Big Bang (cosmological), God designed the universe with extraordinary precision (teleological), and God gave us a conscience (moral law). From these three evidences, we learn that this God is infinitely powerful and intelligent and is the ultimate standard of morality. Such a God would be expected to communicate with the creatures he has created. He has done that through creation (cosmological and teleological evidences) and conscience (moral evidence). But how could God reveal himself to more fully communicate his purpose and will for us?

There were no doubt many ways God could manifest himself to us, but he chose to do it through messengers (prophets) who could do miracles, like Moses (Exod. 4:1–3), Jesus (Acts 2:22–23), and the apostles (Heb. 2:3–4).

God's miracles would identify his messengers because his miracles are unusual and easily recognizable, and only God can do them. This is exactly what the Bible says happened. "How shall we escape if we ignore such a great salvation? This salvation, which was first announced by the Lord, was *confirmed* to us by those who heard him. God also testified to it by signs, wonders and various miracles, and gifts of the Holy Spirit distributed according to his will" (Heb. 2:3–4).

"A miracle is a special act of God that interrupts the normal course of events."[2] Natural laws describe what happens regularly in our world, while miracles describe what happens rarely by supernatural causes. Even Hume defined a miracle as being a rare event but then discounted it for being rare! But if the event was not "rare," it would not be a miracle. So through rare events called miracles, God has told the world which book or which person speaks for him. Miracles are acts of God that identify the word of God and the messenger of God. Of course, not every rare event is a miracle. There are unusual activities (like magic) that are merely odd and are only tricks. There are also rare natural phenomena (like eclipses). What distinguishes a true miracle as a special act of God is that it has the "fingerprints" of God on it.

What are these "fingerprints"? We will see shortly, but first we need to know what a miracle is not. Religious people talk about seeing and experiencing "miracles" every day. There are two ways to destroy the concept of miracles: one way is to deny them and the other way is to say that everything is a miracle. If everything is a miracle, then nothing is. There are natural events, providential events, and miracles. People (particularly Christians) commonly refer to *natural* events, wonders of nature, as "miracles." Certainly there are wonders of nature that cause us to marvel at God's handiwork, like the birth of a baby or the beauty of a flower. But those events are natural, not *super*natural. The Bible also describes some events that are beyond the nature we see every day. Those are supernatural. When we say we believe in miracles and refer to the birth of a baby or the beauty of a flower, we are illustrating the supernatural with the natural and denying the existence of anything beyond the natural. There are also *providential* events that are caused by God indirectly, not directly. With providential events, God uses natural laws to accomplish them. The fog at Normandy was providential because it helped to conceal the Allied attack against the Nazis. It wasn't a miracle, because it could be explained by natural laws, but God may have been behind it nonetheless. For it to have been a miracle, the bullets would have had to bounce off our soldiers' chests as they assaulted the beach.[3]

So a miracle is a supernatural act of an intelligent and good God who identifies his word and confirms his messenger as he communicates to us. A miracle serving as God's sign has to be unique, easily recognizable, and something only God can do.[4] What are the characteristics of a miracle? Is it a warm, fuzzy feeling? Surviving a scare with cancer? The Chicago Cubs winning the World Series? The nature of God illustrates what we should expect the nature of miracles to be. The following points help to identify this nature.

N—Noteworthy Power

God's infinite power was demonstrated by the instantaneous beginning of the universe. So a miracle would need to be an act of power that could not be explained naturally; otherwise it would not be a miracle. A miracle would be noteworthy, in that it would make people sit up and take notice that something unusual has happened. A miracle would also need to be an act of power that could not be duplicated by anyone other than God. Internal, unverifiable warm, fuzzy feelings would not qualify as an act of power noteworthy of God. Surviving cancer may be the result of our wonderful body's chemistry reacting to the disease or medical treatment or even a providential act of God, but this would not fulfill the purpose of verifying God's message or messenger and so would not be a miracle. The closest thing to a miracle in our day would be the Cubs winning the pennant! (Just kidding.)

Now a word of caution is necessary here. Many try to get the Bible off the hook by explaining away miracles as something other than supernatural occurrences of God's power. Some say that miracles are just myths rather than actual historical events. Others try to explain away the miracle by saying that the wind blew the Red Sea back in a spot shallow enough for the Israelites to cross. That approach is in opposition with the plain, normal interpretation of the Scriptures. Their point is that God isn't powerful enough to pull off these miracles. But as we have already seen, a God who created the world out of nothing would have no trouble splitting a sea so that his people could walk through on dry land (Exod. 14:22)!

G—Grid of Divine Claims

A miracle was the way God chose to identify his message and messengers. Thus each miracle would be connected with God's previous communications, the grid of divine truth claims. When Jesus performed miracles, it wasn't to impress or entertain. He wasn't like a stand-up comedian who said, "I've got a million of them," and then proceeded to share his miracles like jokes. No, his miracles were set in a specific context of communication from God, and they built upon each other as did the communications. If you plotted a path on a grid, you would see that each point is not independent but rather interdependent on the others to reveal the path's direction and conclusion. One point builds on another. Jesus's miracles were the same in that they were always connected to divine truth claims. The context of the resurrection, for example, was God communicating that this Jesus was indeed his one and only Son. This is important, for it was prophesied that the Messiah would be put to death (Psalm 22; Isaiah 53) and rise again from the grave (Ps. 16:10). Jesus continually claimed to be God's Son (as we will see in chapter 12) and even predicted his death and resurrection. The resurrection fit the grid of biblical communications (called prophecies) for the qualifications for the Messiah.

This is important as we consider the timing of miracles. Many people believe that miracles happened continually in Bible times. While the Bible is filled with miracles (about 250 of them), these are spread out over thousands of years, and most of them occur in three short spans of time—during the time of Moses, Elijah and Elisha, and Jesus and the apostles. Why during those times? Because during those times, God was giving new communication (revelation) and identifying his messengers with his truth. What about the rest of the time the Bible covers? Hundreds of years pass in the Bible when there are no recorded miracles from God. Why? Because there was no new word from God, and a miracle confirmed a new word from God. When we contemplate the timing of miracles, we remember 1 Samuel 3:1: "The boy Samuel ministered before the LORD under Eli. In those days the word of the LORD was rare; there were not many visions." Miracles were rare because the word of God was rare.

So far we have seen that biblical miracles were always given to identify God's message and messengers, were noteworthy acts of power, and were connected to divine truth claims. But there is more.

E—Exhibition of Design

The miracle of the creation of the world showed God's precise design for the universe to sustain life. A miracle would have to exhibit intelligent design, for such is the nature of God. Think of the feeding of the five thousand (a miracle recorded in all four Gospels). Is it a simple children's bedtime story or a miracle of intricate design? In Luke's account, we see the mind-blowing design of the miracle. The *timing* of the miracle: the disciples were sent out to minister on their own (as they soon would be on their own) and returned rejoicing. Herod, who had beheaded John the Baptist, was now seeking Jesus.

The *teaching* before the miracle: Jesus taught the crowds about the kingdom of God. Don't miss the connection between God's message and God's messenger here. The *testing* of the miracle: not of Jesus but of his disciples. They would have to learn to see with eyes of faith and not doubt. The *technical* aspects of the miracles: the Bible is very specific here and doesn't gloss over the details. Jesus had been teaching all day, and it was now late in the afternoon. They were in a remote place with no convenience stores around. Jesus had the five thousand men and their wives and children sit in groups of fifty. All they had were five loaves of bread and two fish. Jesus multiplied the food to feed everyone until they were full, using twelve baskets so that each disciple would experience the miracle personally. Talk about details! Finally, the *turning point* of the miracle: the people recognized that Jesus was a messenger sent from God, as did his disciples (Luke 9:20). Jesus followed this up by once again predicting his death and resurrection (Luke 9:22). Every miracle of God had extraordinary design and precision, just as we would expect of God.

R—Result in Moral Conviction

The final characteristic of a miracle from God is that it promotes moral conviction, a reflection of the moral nature of God. Since God is a moral being, he desires good, or moral, behavior in his creatures, which is one of the reasons he gave us the moral law that is written in our hearts (Rom. 2:14–15). A true miracle from God will result in a moral conviction that God has spoken and we should respond appropriately. As we saw in the miracle of the feeding of the five thousand, miracles had a "turning point," or result. The "turning point" of the feeding of the five thousand was that most of the people saw Jesus as more than just a man; they saw him as a messenger from God. Peter actually saw him as the "Christ of God" (Luke 9:20).

Are miracles supposed to produce faith? Sometimes miracles did produce faith, but sometimes they did not. Their purpose is to prompt faith, but it is not automatic. When Jesus raised Lazarus from the dead, some people believed, but the chief priests conspired to kill him (John 12:10–11). The same thing happened when Peter and John healed the lame beggar (Acts 4:16–17). Even Jesus said, "If they do not listen to Moses and the Prophets [the Bible], they will not be convinced even if someone rises from the dead" (Luke 16:31). Sometimes a miracle helped bring about faith in Christ; sometimes it revealed a person's unbelief in Christ. A moral law does not just *convince*, it also *convicts*. If someone was open to believing in Jesus, a miracle could help him decide more quickly. But if someone was closed to believing in Jesus (as were the Pharisees), no amount of miracles would create faith. The point is this: a miracle always resulted in a conviction about God's message and his messenger. A miracle was like drawing a line in the sand, and all who believed in Jesus crossed the line while all others walked away. The religious leaders' rejection of this message and the Messenger (Jesus) resulted in a negative moral conviction of their dark moral center. They tried to eradicate this conviction as they tried to eradicate Jesus. But everyone who witnessed a miracle was convinced that it was from either God or man.

Are Miracles for Today?

When discussing miracles, the question always comes up as to whether we could see miracles today. To answer that question, let's review what we have learned about miracles using the FINGER acrostic. We have learned that miracles are feasible. They identify God's message and messenger. They are demonstrated by noteworthy power. They are based on the grid of divine truth claims. They exhibit God's design. And they result in moral conviction. Since the Bible is true and complete (as we will see in chapter 10), God is not confirming any new message or messenger, so his purpose for miracles is not present today. I am not saying that God does not do miracles today, for he can do anything he wants when he wants. Remember that we discussed "acts of God" or "acts of providence" that may occur many times in our lives. But a miracle of God is something about which there can be no doubt. As we have written elsewhere:

> It's just that he [God] may not have a reason to publicly display his power the way he did during biblical times because all of the truths he wanted to reveal have already been revealed and confirmed. As with a house, the foundation only needs to be laid once. Biblical miracles were special acts of God that laid the foundation for his permanent revelation to mankind.[5]

So far we have learned that there is a God who has created humankind and that he has communicated to humankind his purpose and plan in writing, in a book. But is the Bible God's book? Is the Bible accurate or just a bunch of fairy tales told to deceive the masses? Our next chapter will help us decide.

Miracle FINGER Checklist

Miracles . . .

F—Are *Feasible*
- If God exists, then miracles are possible.
- God has performed the greatest miracle of all—the creation of the world—and can certainly move in his world with other miracles.

I—*Identify*
- God's message and messenger.
- Note the difference between natural events, providential events, and miracles.

N—Are Demonstrated by *Noteworthy* Power
- Noteworthy in that they cause people to notice something unusual.
- This power cannot be duplicated by anyone else.

G—Are Based on the *Grid* of Divine Truth Claims
- Miracles are connected to previous communications, the grid of divine truth claims.
- Miracles are rare and occur only when God is communicating to humans.

E—*Exhibit* Design
- Miracles have extraordinary design and precision.

R—*Result* in Moral Conviction
- Miracles result in a conviction that God has spoken, and we should respond appropriately.
- Miracles can convince and convict about God or Christ; this action depends on whether a person is open or closed to God.

Digging Deeper on Miracles

Geisler, Norman. *Baker Encyclopedia of Christian Apologetics*. Grand Rapids: Baker Books, 1999, 449–88.

———. *Miracles and the Modern Mind*. Grand Rapids: Baker Books, 1992.

Geisler, Norman, and Ron Brooks. *When Skeptics Ask*. Grand Rapids: Baker Books, 1990, 75–99.

Geisler, Norman, and Frank Turek. *I Don't Have Enough Faith to Be an Atheist*. Wheaton: Crossway, 2004, 198–217.

Lewis, C. S. *Miracles*. New York: Macmillan, 1947.

10

Can We Trust the Bible?

"Did you see the special on ABC last night about *The Da Vinci Code*?" Stephen asked as he popped his head into his co-worker's office. "They brought out some cool stuff about Jesus, Mary, and the Bible that I had never heard before."[1]

"No, I missed that program," Becky replied, "but I have heard some things about the book *The Da Vinci Code*.[2] What did they have to say?"

"Well, let's see." Stephen leaped into an office chair and gushed enthusiastically, "Elizabeth Vargas, the program's host, pointed out that first, Jesus was married and not single, and he had children with his wife. Then, the woman Jesus married was none other than Mary Magdalene who was—get this—not a prostitute but was supposed to be the future head of the church, not Peter. Third, there was this conspiracy by the Christian leaders to get rid of Mary and change the record of Jesus ever being married. Finally, Leonardo Da Vinci hid these truths in his works of art, such as his famous masterpiece *The Last Supper*. What do you think of that?" Stephen said with excited eyes.

Becky quickly prayed a silent prayer for wisdom and said, "Stephen, everyone loves a conspiracy theory, but they're normally nothing more than just that—a theory. Do you really believe that what you heard was fact or just part of a fiction book?"

"No, no," Stephen said with hands raised. "Becky, they have all this evidence that has been suppressed by the Christian church for years."

Becky leaned back in her chair and said, "Evidence. Like what?"

"Well," Stephen frowned and thought for a moment, "they had these experts on the program who said that the Bible is full of errors and holes, especially about Jesus and Mary and stuff. Take the errors with Jesus. The Da Vinci book said that Jesus was never thought to be divine until some church council decided to make him divine, but that was three hundred years after Jesus lived. He was just a man up until that time. But to keep the Christian religion going, they had to make Jesus into a god. Now the reason for the errors in the Bible is that the writers were covering up for the conspiracy that Jesus was not God but just a man. Why, did you know they said there were a lot more than just the four Gospels we have in our Bible, but the church had them destroyed because they were so controversial? All of these other gospels were destroyed, and everyone believed the lie of the Bible until a few years ago when one of these gospels—I think they said it was The Gospel of Thomas—was found. It was the smoking gun and blew this Bible conspiracy thing wide open!"

"Stephen," Becky replied, "recently I heard a speaker at church discuss *The Da Vinci Code*. Before you make up your mind and believe a fiction novel to be truth or a TV report to be fact, there is some evidence about *The Da Vinci Code* and the Bible that you need to be aware of."

"Okay, I'll quote you and say, 'Evidence, like what?'" Stephen smiled and leaned forward in his chair.

"Let's deal first with *The Da Vinci Code* book. Did you know it is full of errors? The thesis of the book is that there is a conspiracy, hidden by the Bible but found in Da Vinci's paintings, right?"

Stephen nodded affirmatively.

"Let's deal with the paintings first. Most reputable art historians dismiss the book's theory about Da Vinci's paintings as bizarre and groundless. These people are not theologians, but they know their paintings, more than a fiction writer would, I imagine. They're not trying to hide a conspiracy. They're just trying to eradicate ignorance about art. And they're saying that this book is fiction. Now, Stephen, without the code being in the paintings, there is no code."

"You know," Stephen said, "Elizabeth Vargas did mention to Dan Brown, the book's author, that most art experts dismissed his theories as bizarre and crazy."

"How did he respond to that?"

"Well, he just said that the art experts weren't looking at the pictures properly because they were programmed not to see the evidence."

"So," Becky said with eyebrows raised, "everyone else is blind but Dan Brown? That's convenient. Do you really believe that?"

"No." Stephen frowned. "I guess not. But what about the Bible being full of errors? They had a lot of evidence on that."

Becky looked away as she tried to remember any evidence for the credibility of the Bible . . . her Bible!

Just imagine what would happen if Becky had a resource guide for apologetics like *Bringing Your Faith to Work* in her desk. She could show that the Bible is trustworthy and use one word to cover the most important points. The word is REVEALER, since God is the one who has revealed himself to us, and that revelation was written down in his Word, which we call the Bible. The acrostic REVEALER covers eight key points of the veracity of Scripture.

R—Reports That Were Accurate

There are at least five reasons we know that the record of the New Testament is accurate: it includes historically confirmed descriptions, historically confirmed people, embarrassing details about the writers themselves, unlikely to be invented events, and divergent details.[3]

Historically confirmed descriptions. The book of Acts alone contains 84 facts that have been confirmed by historical and archaeological research.[4] Luke, the author of Acts, recorded details such as wind direction, water depths, various languages spoken on his travels, geographical details, industry descriptions, highlights of various towns visited, and even strange town names. No one seriously rejects the book's accuracy today. Now, if Luke's historical details are accurate, would his reports of thirty-five miracles in the same book be any less than accurate? Of course not. Let's go further. Should we not expect the same accuracy from Luke's Gospel? Absolutely. In fact, the Gospel of Luke has been confirmed to be accurate in its details. If Luke is telling the truth, then Matthew and Mark (who are telling the same story) must also be telling the truth. John was an eyewitness of Jesus's ministry, and we have 59 confirmed historical details from the Gospel of John.[5] Combined, we have at least 143 historically accurate details from just a few of the New Testament books that have been confirmed to be authentic.

Historically confirmed people. The New Testament records at least thirty real historical characters that have been confirmed by archaeology or non-Christian sources.[6] These documents mention Pilate, Caiaphas, Festus, Felix, and the entire Herodian bloodline. The Bible's descriptions of these people, of where they were and what they were doing, have all been confirmed by non-Christian sources as completely accurate.

Embarrassing details about the writers. One way historians can tell if an author was telling the truth is to test his words by "the principle of embarrassment," which assumes that if the author includes details that are embarrassing to him, they are true. Our natural tendency is to leave out things that make us look bad. Consider that the Bible's writers included such details as being intellectually slow (Mark 9:32; Luke 18:34; John 12:26), unfeeling and uncaring (Mark 14:32–41), rebuked by Jesus (Mark 8:33), cowards (Matt. 26:33–35), and doubters (Luke 24:11; John 20:25). If this were a made-up story, the writers would present themselves as heroes instead of zeroes!

Unlikely to be invented events. Closely related to embarrassing events, the New Testament writers recorded information about the resurrection they would not have written if they were making up the story. Consider that they said that *Jesus's body was buried in the tomb of Joseph of Arimathea*, a member of the Jewish ruling council that had just sentenced Jesus to death. Why portray an enemy in such a favorable light unless the detail was true? Why record a well-known individual (at the time) who easily could have been checked out unless the writer knew what Joseph would say?

Look also at *the first witnesses to Jesus's resurrection*. No, they weren't the apostles flying to the tomb with an *S* on their chests, but some women, one of whom had earlier been reported to have been demon-possessed. The brave men were hiding in fear while the weak women were going to the tomb. Furthermore, women at this time were not considered to be reliable legal witnesses, especially one who reportedly had been demon-possessed. If we were making up a story, we would be the heroes and would make sure that trustworthy witnesses were on hand.

Take into account also the *conversion of the priests*. Many priests in Jerusalem became believers in Jesus (Acts 6:7), but if this point were not true, it easily could have been checked out at the time of Luke's writing of Acts.

Finally, consider the *explanation of the Jews* for the empty tomb. Matthew says that his readers already know about the false Jewish explanation for the empty tomb (Matt. 28:11–15). If this false Jewish explanation were not true, Matthew's readers would know about it.

Divergent details. On the one hand, we see a remarkable unity of the Bible. On the other, some details seem to differ. For example, Matthew says there was one angel at the tomb of Jesus, while John says there were two. We will answer this supposed contradiction in chapter 11, but my point here is that the divergent details show there was no collusion among the writers of the New Testament. Why is that important? As a former police officer, I (Randy) know that suspects of a crime must be kept separate or they will polish up their story or alibi. One way to reveal a person's guilt is to catch that person lying from an accomplice's story. Not only suspects, but even witnesses to a crime should be kept separate, because if they compare notes, invariably their stories will agree and crucial facts will be lost, because no person sees the same story in the same way. The Gospels all agree on the same major fact—Jesus rose again from the dead. The writers recorded the same scene from different perspectives and added these complementary details to their account. Rather than polishing up their story, they told the truth as they saw it.

A book with these five characteristics has to be viewed as an accurate writing. The New Testament Gospels cannot have been invented, because they contain too many historically confirmed characteristics.

E—Eyewitnesses

As a police officer investigating a crime or accident, the first thing I did was search for eyewitnesses. I did not want hearsay evidence; I wanted to hear from people who saw the event unfold. Their testimony would tell me what really happened and would hold up in court. In fact, a witness in court is grilled by both the defense and the prosecution as to whether he or she actually could have seen the event transpire. If the person could and did, that person's testimony is accepted as fact. Peter, Paul, and John all claimed to be eyewitnesses, and Luke and the writer of Hebrews claim to have been informed by eyewitnesses. No hearsay evidence was presented, and these witnesses could (and did) tell where they were when the resurrection happened and what they were doing. Not only did the apostles claim to be eyewitnesses, but they boldly dared their readers to check them out.

- Listen to Peter: "We are all witnesses of the fact [the resurrection]" (Acts 2:32). "We are witnesses of this" (Acts 3:15). "For we cannot help speaking about what we have seen and heard" (Acts 4:20). "I appeal as a fellow elder, a witness of Christ's sufferings" (1 Peter 5:1). "We were eyewitnesses of his majesty" (2 Peter 1:16). Peter saw something, and he wanted everyone to know it.

- Hear what John said: "The man who saw it [referring to his witnessing the crucifixion] has given testimony, and his testimony is true" (John 19:35). "Jesus did many other miraculous signs in the presence of his disciples, which are not recorded in this book" (John 20:30). "That which was from the beginning, which we have heard, which we have seen with our eyes, which we have looked at and our hands have touched—this we proclaim concerning the Word of life. The life appeared; we have seen it and testify to it, and we proclaim to you the eternal life, which was with the Father and has appeared to us. We proclaim to you what we have seen and heard, so that you also may have fellowship with us. And our fellowship is with the Father and with his Son, Jesus Christ" (1 John 1:1–3). John wanted his readers to know, "I was there. I heard Jesus, I saw Jesus, and I even touched Jesus. He is real!"

- Listen to what Paul wrote: Paul was appearing before King Agrippa and sharing his testimony. Governor Festus challenged Paul on his conclusions, so Paul threw the challenge back at their feet. He told them that the events of Christianity, including the resurrection, were "not done in a corner" and had not "escaped [the king's] notice" (Acts 26:24–28). Only a witness who knew that these events were true and well known would have taken such an approach. In 1 Corinthians 15:3–8, Paul cited fourteen eyewitnesses whose names are known: the twelve apostles, James, Peter (Cephas), and Paul himself. Furthermore, he mentioned an appearance by Jesus to more than five hundred others at one time. Paul wrote 1 Corinthians between AD 55 and 56, some twenty-five years after the resurrection. By naming these eyewitnesses, most of whom would still be alive, Paul was challenging the church to check out the facts.

- Luke said he investigated eyewitnesses before he wrote his Gospel: "Many have undertaken to draw up an account of the things that have been fulfilled among us, just as they were handed down to us by those who from the first were eyewitnesses and servants of the word" (Luke 1:1–2).
- The author of Hebrews told where he got his information: "How shall we escape if we ignore such a great salvation? This salvation, which was first announced by the Lord, was confirmed to us by those who heard him" (Heb. 2:2).

The weight of the eyewitness evidence is overwhelming. "But wait a minute," someone may protest. "Of course they say they were eyewitnesses. But how do we know that is true?" Already we have seen the amazing accuracy of these writers, which has been verified by secular scholars. If Luke was never in Perga, how would he have known the correct destination for a ship coming from Cyprus (Acts 13:13)? Or how would he have known the proper port of Attalia that travelers would use (Acts 14:25)? Only eyewitnesses would know the details and include them in their writings.

But there is one more key evidence that supports that these writers were eyewitnesses. They all *died* for their story. If they had made up the story of the resurrection, they certainly would have recanted before being crucified (Peter), stoned (James), or beheaded (Paul). But no one did. Eleven of the twelve were martyred for their faith (John was exiled to the Greek island of Patmos). Why would anyone die for a lie?

Chuck Colson, former aide to President Nixon, went to prison over the Watergate scandal. He said that it took only two weeks for someone to "crack" and turn against the president and none of Nixon's aides was facing torture or execution. But none of the Eleven cracked or made a deal with the authorities.[7]

Supreme Court Justice Anthony Scalia said in a speech delivered at the Mississippi College School of Law that since the New Testament writers had nothing to gain and everything to lose, we ought to believe what they said about the resurrection. "It is not irrational to accept the testimony of eyewitnesses who had nothing to gain. . . . The [worldly] wise do not believe in the resurrection of the dead. So everything from Easter morning to the Ascension had to be made up by groveling enthusiasts as part of their plan to get themselves martyred."[8] While many people (such as Muslim terrorists) will die for a lie they think is truth, no right-thinking person will die for what he or she *knows* is a lie. These were eyewitnesses, and we must listen to their testimony!

V—Verified Predictions

"The Bible is the only book in the world that has precise, specific predictions that were made hundreds of years in advance and that were literally fulfilled."[9] In J. Barton Payne's *Encyclopedia of Biblical Prophecy*, he lists 1,817 predictions from the Bible, 1,239 from the Old Testament and 578 from the New.[10] The Old Testament has 71 predictions about the first coming of the Christ—predictions about his ancestry, his birthplace, his virgin birth, the precise time he would be born, and so on. Jesus fulfilled every one! Plus, the Bible has 95 predictions about Christ's second coming. Let's look at a couple of examples:

- *Psalm 22.* Verse 16 says his hands and feet would be pierced; verse 14 says his bones would be out of joint; and verse 18 describes the casting of lots for his garments. Obviously these verses are predicting the crucifixion, yet they were written hundreds of years before crucifixion was even used as a method of execution.
- *Isaiah 53:2–12.* These verses foretell twelve aspects of the passion of the Christ that all were fulfilled. He would be rejected, be a man of sorrow, live a life of suffering, be despised by others, carry our sorrows, be smitten and afflicted by God, be pierced for our transgressions, be wounded for our sins, suffer like a lamb led to the slaughter, die with the wicked, be sinless, and intercede for transgressors.

The prophecies Jesus literally fulfilled are even more amazing when one considers that he had no control over most of them. For example, he could not arrange his ancestry, the city of his birth, or the time of his birth. Yet these prophecies were written two hundred to four hundred years before he was born. No book besides the Bible has such a great number of fulfilled and verified prophecies.

E—Early Copies

At least nine contemporaries who were eyewitnesses of New Testament events recorded their observations. Let's talk about what we *don't* have. The New Testament was written from around AD 50 to 80, while the eyewitnesses were still alive. But we don't have the original New Testament writings; we only have copies of the original manuscripts. Is this unusual? Not at all, for we have no original manuscripts for any significant literature from the ancient world. We have reconstructed New Testament books into their original form by comparing the surviving copies of the manuscripts.

Is there a reason God didn't preserve the originals? One possibility is that God's Word could be better protected through copies than through the original documents. If the originals were in someone's possession, that person could change them, hide them, destroy them, or turn them into relics of the church to be worshiped. But with copies in various locations, no one person could alter them, hide them in a monastery, wipe them out, or worship them.[11]

Is the lack of the originals a problem? Absolutely not, when we consider what we *do* have. We have more manuscripts and earlier manuscripts of the New Testament than of any other ancient document held to be viable today. Consider the following.

More manuscripts. Some 5,700 handwritten Greek manuscripts of the New Testament are still in existence. Furthermore, there are more than 9,000 manuscripts in other languages (e.g., Syriac, Coptic, Latin, Arabic). Some of these nearly 15,000 manuscripts are complete Bibles; others are books or pages, and a few are fragments. Nothing else from the ancient world comes even close! *The Iliad* by Homer has only 643 manuscripts, while most ancient works have only a dozen manuscripts. Yet no one doubts the veracity of these works.

Earlier manuscripts. The New Testament has manuscripts written soon after the originals. The earliest undisputed fragment is the John Rylands fragment dated at AD 117–138.[12] Even earlier are nine disputed (by critics) fragments dating from AD 50 to 70, found with the Dead Sea Scrolls. So the time gap between the original and first surviving copy is twenty-five years. *The Iliad* has the next shortest gap at five hundred years; while most other ancient works are a thousand years or more from the original. The oldest manuscripts containing complete New Testament books are from AD 200, and a manuscript with all of the Gospels and most of the New Testament survives from AD 250. A manuscript containing the whole New Testament survives from about AD 325. If these manuscripts were all scholars had, they could reconstruct the original New Testament with great accuracy.

The evidence is that we have manuscripts some twenty-five years removed from the original New Testament. By the second century, we have complete books and most of the New Testament as well as the exhaustive quotes of the church fathers. The church fathers of the first few centuries made more than 36,000 citations from the

New Testament, which includes every verse except eleven! How accurately do all these manuscripts compare with one another? The copies are 99.5 percent accurate, and the half percent in question does not affect a single doctrine of the Christian faith.[13] So the New Testament we have today is the same that was written down nearly two thousand years ago.

A—Archaeology

Archaeology supports the Old Testament. Thousands of archaeological finds have confirmed the Old Testament record. Recent discoveries have confirmed King David's reign, the existence of the patriarchs (Abraham, Isaac, and Jacob), the cities of Sodom and Gomorrah, the Jewish captivity, an Assyrian king, the tunnel into Jerusalem during David's reign, a single language of the world at one time, the Hittites, and the site of Solomon's temple, to name a few. Half a century ago, archaeologist William F. Albright declared, "There can be no doubt that archaeology has confirmed the substantial historicity of the Old Testament tradition."[14]

Archaeology supports the New Testament as well. As seen under the points "Reports that Were Accurate" and "Eyewitnesses" earlier in the chapter, the New Testament has been proven to be extremely accurate. Roman historian Colin J. Hemer says that archaeology has confirmed not dozens, but nearly a hundred details from the biblical account of the early church. Small details have been corroborated, such as the way the wind was blowing, how deep the water was a certain distance from shore, what kind of disease the inhabitants of a certain island had, and even the names of local officials. The historian Luke provided nearly a hundred details about Jesus and the history of the church, and he has never been proven wrong. His books were written within one generation of eyewitnesses who were still alive and could have corrected him if details were false. No other religious book from the ancient world has that kind of substantiation.[15]

L—Length of Time

Lately we have heard from people who claim that the Holocaust never occurred. Why is this happening now? Because most of those who were eyewitnesses have died. Yet because we have written eye-witness testimony to the horrors of the Holocaust, those trying to revise history are not being successful. How does this relate to the accuracy of the Bible? Since the major works of the New Testament are the accounts of eyewitnesses and are written within two genera-tions of the events, they definitely would not be legend or myth. Why? Research shows that a myth cannot begin to crowd out historical facts while the eyewitnesses are still alive.[16] Within two generations, eyewitnesses would still be around to correct the errors of those at-tempting to revise history (as seen with the Holocaust). How does the writing of the New Testament documents relate to the time of Jesus's death and resurrection?

All New Testament books were written before AD 100 (about seventy years after Jesus's death). How do we know this? Three early church fathers—Clement, Ignatius, and Polycarp—quoted passages out of twenty-five of the twenty-seven books in the New Testament.[17] Clem-ent was in Rome (c. AD 95), and Ignatius (c. 107) and Polycarp (c. 110) were hundreds of miles away in Smyrna, so for the New Testa-ment to have circulated to these places by then would mean that the New Testament would have had to been written by AD 95–100 at the latest. But let's go earlier!

Most if not all of the New Testament books were written before AD 70 (about forty years after Jesus's death). How do we know this? Jerusalem's temple and city were destroyed in AD 70, but no New Testament book explicitly mentions this destruction. Indeed, the first three Gospels mention the temple's destruction as a future event (cf. Matthew 24; Mark 13; and Luke 21). Many scholars believe the apostle John wrote his books (John; 1, 2, 3 John; and Revelation) well after AD 70 (c. AD 85–90), which may account for his not explicitly referring to the event. The destruction of the city of Jerusalem (where the church was born) and the temple (the former center of religious life for most Christians at this time) would have had the same effect on them that the World Trade Center being destroyed by Muslim terrorists had (and is still having) on our country. Can you imagine a New York author describing life in New York and never mentioning 9/11? That would be likely only if the book was written *before* September 11, 2001. The same holds true for the New Testament being written before AD 70. But let's go earlier!

Many New Testament books were written before AD 62 (about thirty years after Jesus's death). How do we know this? One key leader of the New Testament was the apostle Paul—author of thirteen New

Testament books—who was executed by the Roman emperor Nero. Now, Luke is the author of the book of Acts and Paul is its main subject, yet nowhere in Acts is the death of Paul mentioned. Obviously, this narrative of Paul's ministry had to have been written *before* his death. Luke records the deaths of two Christian martyrs (Stephen and James the brother of John), but when Acts ended, Paul and James the brother of Jesus were still living.

Church fathers such as Clement of Rome and others, writing in the late first century, state that Paul was executed during the reign of Nero, which ended in AD 68.[18] And we know from the historian Josephus that James was killed in AD 62. So the book of Acts had to have been written before AD 62! Furthermore, the Gospel of Luke had to have been written before Acts, because Luke's Gospel was an earlier book written to the same recipient of Acts, Theophilus. Thus it had to have been written by AD 60 or earlier, because the time required for the events of Acts would have taken at least two to three years.

Paul, writing between AD 62 and 65, quoted Luke 10:7 and called it "Scripture" (1 Tim. 5:18). So Luke's Gospel had to have been in circulation long enough for both Paul and Timothy to know Luke's Gospel and regard it as Scripture. The Gospel of Mark must have been written in the AD 50s, because Luke said he got his facts for his Gospel by checking with eyewitness sources (Luke 1:1–4). Most scholars believe that Mark's Gospel was one of Luke's eyewitness sources. So far we have seen that we have recorded eyewitness testimony written between twenty-five and thirty years after Jesus's death, burial, and resurrection. But let's go earlier!

Some New Testament books were penned in the AD 50s, with sources as early as the 30s (a few years after Jesus's death). How do we know this? Even liberal scholars believe that Paul wrote his first letter to the church of Corinth between AD 55 and 56.[19] This means that the church was in existence and celebrating Jesus's resurrection (one key theme of 1 Corinthians) within twenty-five years of its occurrence. But in 1 Corinthians 15:3–8, Paul records an early church creed that even liberal scholars date right back to the resurrection—from eighteen months to less than eight years after the event.[20] If ever there was a place that a legend of the resurrection could not occur, it was Jerusalem, because the Jews and the Romans would have produced the body or bones of Jesus, and that would have put Christianity in the tomb.

E—External Sources

Do we have any external sources—sources outside the Bible—that refer to the existence of Jesus or the veracity of the New Testament? Yes, multiple first-century, non-Christian sources mention Jesus. There are twelve known non-Christian writers who mention Jesus within 150 years of his life. We will examine these twelve sources in chapter 12 as we ask, "Is Jesus the Son of God?" But it is important to note two things about these twelve sources. First, they are secular in nature and not pro-Christianity. In fact, all of them are anti-Christian. Second, these outside sources describe the existence of a man named Jesus and give remarkable data concerning his life that match the Bible report accurately.

We have more external sources that prove the veracity of the New Testament. The early church fathers—men of the second and third centuries such as Justin Martyr, Irenacus, Clement of Alexandria, Origen, Tertullian, and others—quoted the New Testament so often (36,289 times) that all but eleven verses of the New Testament can be reconstructed from their quotations.[21] By comparing the New Testament copies with the church fathers' quotations, we can be sure we have the original text.

R—Reliable Translations

There is a common misconception that our English Bible is at the end of a long series of translations and retranslations of the original and has lost its reliability. Where did our translations come from? After the New Testament was written, it was copied by men who were professionally trained copiers. Then those copies were copied, and so on until the invention of the printing press around AD 1500. As mentioned under the point "Early Copies," we still have about 5,700 of those early copies. Some are just fragments, others are complete books, but none of them are translations from one language into another. They are copies made in the same language—Greek. In addition, there are about 9,000 other copies that were made into different languages (mostly Latin). All copies can be compared to reproduce an accurate Greek New Testament. The English translations we have today come directly from the Greek—the same language in which the New Testament was written.

Do We Believe *The Da Vinci Code* or the Bible?

The Da Vinci Code makes the Bible seem like a late (fourth century) invention of evil men, full of conspiracy and empty of truth.
By contrast, the facts show the Bible was written by good men in the
first century. We have seen through the REVEALER acrostic that *The
Da Vinci Code* is the book of fairy tales, not the Bible! As someone
has said, "What the Bible says, it is true, so what the Bible says, we
should do." But aren't there errors or discrepancies in the Bible,
such as whether one or two angels were at Jesus's tomb? How do we
answer such questions? Our next chapter will help us.

Bible REVEALER Checklist

R—*Reports* That Were Accurate
- Historically confirmed descriptions
- Thirty historically confirmed people
- Embarrassing details about the writers
  themselves
- Unlikely to be invented events
- Divergent details

E—*Eyewitnesses*
- The writers claim to be eyewitnesses or
  informed by eyewitnesses.
- The writers willingly died for what they knew
  to be true.

V—*Verified* Predictions
- The Bible has 1,817 predictions in it.
- The Old Testament has 191 predictions
  concerning the Christ, and Jesus fulfilled
  every one of them.

E—*Early* Copies
- We have more manuscripts.
- We have earlier manuscripts.

A—*Archaeology*
- Archaeology supports the Old Testament.
- Archaeology supports the New Testament.

L—*Length* of Time

- It takes more than two generations for a myth to develop, because eyewitnesses are still alive.
- All New Testament books were written before AD 100 (about seventy years after Jesus's death).
- Most, if not all, New Testament books were written before AD 70 (about forty years after Jesus's death) while witnesses were still alive.
- Many New Testament books were written before AD 62 (about thirty years after Jesus's death) while many eyewitnesses were still living.
- Some New Testament books were penned in the AD 40s and 50s, with sources from the 30s (a few years after Jesus's death), when most eyewitnesses were still on the scene.

E—*External* Sources

- There are ten known non-Christian writers who mention Jesus within 150 years of his life.
- The early church fathers quoted the New Testament so often (36,289 times) that all but eleven verses can be reconstructed from their quotations.

R—*Reliable* Translations

- There are 5,700 copies of the New Testament in the original Greek and 9,000 copies in other languages.
- Our English translations today come directly from the Greek language.

Digging Deeper on the Trustworthiness of the Bible

Blomberg, Craig. *The Historical Reliability of the Gospels.* Leicester: Inter-Varsity, 1987.

Bruce, F. F. *Jesus and Christian Origins Outside the New Testament.* Grand Rapids: Eerdmans, 1974.

————. *The New Testament Documents: Are They Reliable?* Grand Rapids: Eerdmans, 2003.

Geisler, Norman. *Baker Encyclopedia of Christian Apologetics* (Grand Rapids: Baker Books, 1999), 91–102.

Geisler, Norman, and Ron Brooks. *When Skeptics Ask*. Grand Rapids: Baker Books, 1990, 141–61, 179–209.

Geisler, Norman, and Frank Turek. *I Don't Have Enough Faith to Be an Atheist*. Wheaton: Crossway, 2004, 222–97, 355–76.

Habermas, Gary. *The Verdict of History*. Nashville: Nelson, 1988.

11

Are There Errors in the Bible?

"I can't believe the Bible is without error," Ken told Cheryl as they were doing inventory for their shoe store. "You say that you believe the Bible is true and its stories and message are for today, but I have heard about all these errors in the Bible that make it seem more like a 'holey' Bible, you know, full of holes, than a 'Holy Bible!'"

Ken laughed, but Cheryl winced. Cheryl and Ken were co-managers of a retail store in a mall and had worked together for five years. During those years, Cheryl had witnessed to Ken many times, and he had been asking more questions about Christianity as of late.

"Name one," Cheryl asked. (This is an excellent response, for the burden of proof is on the critic of the Bible rather than on the Bible. Most of the time people can't come up with a good example, but be prepared with an explanation just in case they do.)

"Name one," Ken mumbled thoughtfully. "Okay, I have more than one. In the Old Testament, where did Cain get his wife? If there were just Adam and Eve and their sons, Cain and Abel, and Cain killed Abel, how did Cain find a wife? And in the New Testament, what about the number of angels at Jesus's tomb? Doesn't one writer say there was one while another writer says there were two? Those examples sound like errors to me."

"Ken, remember the conference we went to on counterfeit money last month?" Cheryl asked. "We learned that genuine money has all kinds of security features that distinguish it from counterfeit money: the portrait is clear and not flat; the Federal Reserve and Treasury seals are distinct and sharp; the border is clean and unbroken; the serial numbers are distinctive and evenly spaced and have the same ink as the Treasury seal; and finally, the paper used has red and blue fibers embedded in it. Then we used some new tools to test our money to see if it is genuine or not: ultraviolet light can reveal the special marks made with fluorescent ink that identify whether the money is authentic or not. And then there are the pens our company bought for the cash registers to mark suspicious-looking bills with a yellow mark. If the mark remains yellow, that means it is authentic; if the mark turns brown, that means it is suspect."

"What does all that have to do with the Bible?" Ken asked puzzled.

"Well, with money, there are some procedures to follow in examining a bill to see if it is genuine or not. We are to examine the portrait, the seals, the watermark, the paper, and so on," Cheryl explained. "It's the same with the Bible. I recently learned that there are some principles and procedures to follow in examining a supposed error or difficulty to see if the Bible is genuine or not. Those principles and procedures are found in the acrostic UNBROKEN. They will guide us in determining if the Bible contains errors or if there are explanations for the verses in question."

Do Bible difficulties (*difficulties* is a more accurate word than *error*) exist? Yes, but the difficulty lies with our understanding the Bible passage rather than with the Bible passage being untrue. Augustine wisely noted, "If we are perplexed by any apparent contradiction in Scripture, it is not allowable to say, 'The author of this book is mistaken'; but either the manuscript is faulty, or the translation is wrong, or you have not understood."[1] Let's approach this subject logically: (1) God cannot err (Titus 1:2; Heb. 6:18); (2) the Bible is God's Word (John 10:34–35); (3) therefore the Bible cannot contain error. If it does, then the Bible cannot be the Word of God. We chose the word UNBROKEN for this acrostic because it affirms to all that though the Bible has been attacked as untrustworthy for centuries, the critics always walk away defeated while the Bible remains unscathed. Let's walk through the UNBROKEN principles, applying them to suggested Bible difficulties.

When Dealing with Supposed Errors, Remember . . .

U—*Unexplained Is Not Unexplainable*

No one can fully explain all the Bible difficulties. But don't assume that what has not yet been explained will never be explained. Applying this principle to Ken and Cheryl, just because Ken doesn't understand the verse in question doesn't mean the verse is wrong. Just because he doesn't have an answer for a biblical question doesn't mean there is no answer!

We are to do what scientists do when they face a difficulty in science: dig for an explanation. As scientists begin the process of digging into an unknown problem, they uncover the hidden answers. Scientists, for example, once had no natural explanation for meteors, eclipses, tornadoes, hurricanes, and earthquakes. But they were patient and knew there had to be answers, so they set about to discover them.

Likewise, with the Bible, we cannot assume that a discrepancy is a contradiction. Rather, we must begin digging to uncover the hidden answers, because they are there. This is the foundational principle for dealing with Bible difficulties. For example, critics once thought that Moses could not have written the first five books of the Bible because there was no writing in Moses's day. Now we know that writing was in existence a couple of thousand years or more before Moses. Again, critics once said that the Bible was wrong in referring to the Hittite people, since they were totally unknown to historians. Now all historians know of their existence by way of their library that was found in Turkey. So we can have confidence that the biblical difficulties that have not yet been explained have an explanation and that we need not assume there is a mistake in the Bible.

Okay, what about Cain's wife? And were there one or two angels at Christ's tomb? Are there answers for Ken's questions? Yes, and the answers are given under the "Top Ten Lists of Bible Questions" found later in this chapter. Only investigation yields answers. But how do we investigate a passage of Scripture properly? The following principles will guide us.

N—*Don't Neglect the Context*

One of the most common mistakes of critics is to take a text out of its proper context. As the adage goes, "A text out of context is a pretext." A person using this errant procedure can prove anything from the Bible, which is why there are so many cults today. For example, the Bible says, "There is no God" (Ps. 14:1). Of course, the context is, "The fool has said in his heart, 'There is no God.'" Likewise, many fail to understand the context of Jesus' statement "Give to him who asks you" as though one had an obligation to give a gun to a small child who asked or nuclear weapons to Saddam Hussein just because he asked. There was a Christmas card published one year that had the Bible verse, "And they that dwell upon the earth shall rejoice over them, and make merry, and shall send gifts one to another" (Rev. 11:10 KJV). What a wonderful verse for the Christmas season until you read the rest of the verse. The verse concludes with "because these two prophets tormented them that dwelt on the earth." The context of chapter 11 describes the two witnesses who were testifying about God to the sinful world (their preaching was the "torment" of the two witnesses), then the Beast came and killed them, and everyone in the world saw their dead bodies for three and a half days. That is why the people were so happy and giving gifts. Failure to understand that meaning is determined by the context is probably the chief error of those who find fault with the Bible.

B—Book with Human Writers and Characteristics

With the exception of small sections like the Ten Commandments, which were "inscribed by God" (Exod. 31:18), the Bible was not verbally dictated. The writers were not secretaries of the Holy Spirit or living "tape recorders." They were human composers employing their own literary styles and idiosyncrasies. These human authors sometimes used human sources for their material (Josh. 10:13; Acts 17:28; 1 Cor. 15:33; Titus 1:12). In fact, every book of the Bible is the composition of a human writer—about forty of them in all. The Bible also uses different *human literary styles*, from the mournful meter of Lamentations to the exalted poetry of Isaiah, from the simple grammar of John to the complex Greek of the book of Hebrews. Scripture also manifests *human perspectives*. David speaks in Psalm 23 from a shepherd's perspective. Kings is written from a prophetic vantage point, and Chronicles forms a priestly point of view. Acts manifests a historical interest and 2 Timothy reveals a pastor's heart. Writers speak from an observer's standpoint when they write of the sun rising or setting (Josh. 1:15). They also reveal *human thought patterns*, including memory lapses (1 Cor. 1:14–16), as well as human emotions (Gal. 4:14). The Bible discloses specific *human interests*. For example, Hosea possessed a rural interest, Luke a medical concern, and James a love of nature.[2] But like Christ, the Bible is completely human yet without error. Forgetting the humanity of Scripture can lead to falsely impugning its integrity by expecting a level of expression higher than that which is customary for a human document.

R—*Research Difficult Passages in Light of the Clear*

Some passages of Scripture are hard to understand. The Bible never contradicts itself, and neither should your interpretation. Sometimes the difficulty is due to their obscurity. At other times, the difficulty is due to the fact that passages appear to be teaching something contrary to what some other part of Scripture is clearly teaching. When faced with a difficult passage, always investigate what is said not only in the context but also in other passages about the subject in question. For example, James appears to be saying salvation is by works (James 2:14–26), whereas Paul clearly teaches that it is by grace (Rom. 4:5; Eph. 2:8–9; Titus 3:5–7). In this case, James should not be understood as contradicting Paul. Paul is speaking about justification *before God* (which is by faith alone), whereas James is referring to justification *before men* (who cannot see our faith, but only our works).

Another example is found in Philippians 2:12 where Paul says "work out your salvation with fear and trembling." On the surface, this verse appears to be saying that salvation is by works. However, this idea is flatly contradicted by a host of Scriptures that clearly affirm that "it is by grace you have been saved, through faith—and this not from yourselves, it is a gift of God—not by works, so that no one can boast" (Eph. 2:8–9). And "to the man who does not work but trusts God who justifies the wicked, his faith is credited as righteousness" (Rom. 4:5). Also, "he saved us, not because of righteous things we had done, but because of his mercy" (Titus 3:5). When this difficult statement about "working out our salvation" is understood in the light of these clear passages, we can see that it does not mean that we are saved by works. What it means is found in the very next verse. We are to work salvation *out* because God's grace has worked it *in* our hearts. In Paul's words, "It is God who works in you to will and to act according to his good purpose" (Phil. 2:13).

O—*Original Text Is without Error*

When critics do come upon a genuine mistake in a manuscript copy, they make another fatal error: they assume it was in the original inspired text of Scripture. They forget that God uttered only the original text of Scripture, not the copies. Therefore, only the original text is without error. Inspiration does not guarantee that every copy of the original is without error. Therefore, we are to expect that minor errors are to be found in manuscript copies. But, again, as Augustine wisely noted, when we run into a so-called error in the Bible, we must assume one of two things—either the manuscript was not copied correctly or we have not understood it rightly. What we may not assume is that God made an error in inspiring the original text.

While present copies of Scripture are very good, they are not without error. For example, in the King James Version, 2 Kings 8:26 gives the age of King Ahaziah as twenty-two, whereas 2 Chronicles 22:2 says forty-two. The later number cannot be correct, or he would have been older than his father. This is obviously a copyist error, but it does not alter the inerrancy of the original.

Several things should be observed about these copyist errors:

1. The errors are in the copies, not the originals. No one has ever found an original manuscript with an error in it.
2. The errors are minor (often in names or numbers) and do not affect any doctrine of the Christian faith.
3. These copyist errors are relatively few in number.
4. Usually by the context, or by another Scripture, we know which of two readings is in error. For example, Ahaziah (see above) must have been twenty-two, not forty-two, since he could not have been older than his father.
5. Even though there are copyist errors, the entire message can still come through. For example, if you received a letter like this (see below), would you understand the whole message? And would you collect your money?

"#OU HAVE WON THE FIVE-MILLION-DOLLAR *READER'S DIGEST* SWEEPSTAKES."

Even though there is a mistake in the first word, the entire message comes through: you are five million dollars richer! And if you received another letter the next day that read like this, you would be even surer.

"Y#U HAVE WON THE FIVE-MILLION-DOLLAR *READER'S DIGEST* SWEEPSTAKES."

Actually the more mistakes of this kind there are (each in a different place), the surer you are of the original message. This is why scribal mistakes in the biblical manuscripts do not affect the basic message of the Bible. So, for all practical purposes, the Bible in our hands, imperfect though the manuscripts are, conveys the complete truth of the original Word of God.

K—*Knowledge of Literary Devices*

An inspired book doesn't have to be composed in one, and only one, literary style. Human beings wrote every book in the Bible, and human language is not limited to one mode of expression. So there is no reason to suppose that only one style or literary genre was used in a divinely inspired book. The Bible reveals a number of literary devices. Several whole books are written in *poetic* style (e.g., Job, Psalms, Proverbs). The Synoptic Gospels are filled with *parables*. In Galatians 4, Paul utilizes an *allegory*. The New Testament abounds with *metaphors* (e.g., 2 Cor. 3:2–3; James 3:6) and *similes* (cf. Matt. 20:1; James 1:6); *hyperboles* may also be found (e.g., John 21:25; 2 Cor. 3:2; Col. 1:23), and possibly even *poetic figures* (Job 41:1). Jesus employed *satire* (Matt. 19:24 with 23:24), and *figures of speech* are common throughout the Bible.

It is not a mistake for a biblical writer to use a figure of speech, but it is a mistake for a reader to take a figure of speech literally. Obviously when the Bible speaks of the believer resting under the shadow of God's "wings" (Ps. 36:7), it does not mean that God is a feathered bird. Or, when the Bible says God "awakes," as though he were sleeping (Ps. 44:23), it is a figure of speech indicating God's inactivity before he is aroused to judgment by human sin.

E—*Everyday, Nontechnical Language*

To be true, something does not have to use scholarly, technical, or so-called scientific language. The Bible is written for the common person of every generation, and it therefore uses common, everyday language. As we have said repeatedly, this book is specifically designed not for the theologian or philosopher but for the man and woman in the workplace. Rather than use technical words like *teleological*, we use *intelligent design*. The use of nontechnical language is not wrong but is directed to a different audience. The use of observational, nonscientific language is not *un*scientific; it is merely *pre*scientific. The Scriptures were written in ancient times by ancient standards, and it would be anachronistic to superimpose modern scientific standards on them. However, it is no more unscientific to speak of the sun "standing still" (Josh. 10:12) than to refer to the sun "rising" (Josh. 1:15). Contemporary meteorologists still speak daily of the time of "sunrise" and "sunset." For more information on the scientific accuracies of the Bible, see question 5 under the "Top Ten List of Old Testament Questions" found later in this chapter.

N— *Narrative That Includes the Good, the Bad, and the Ugly*

It is a mistake to assume that everything contained in the Bible is commended by the Bible. While the whole Bible is true (John 17:17), it records some lies—for example, Satan's (Gen. 3:4; cf. John 8:44) and Rahab's (Josh. 2:4). Inspiration encompasses the Bible fully and completely in the sense that it records accurately and truthfully even the lies and errors of sinful beings. A narrative describes events as they occur, which may include some good things, some bad things, and some ugly things! I (Randy) remember hearing the late atheist Madalyn Murray O'Hair in a debate, and she blasted the Bible for being a work of horror and untrue because it contained the story of Tamar, David's daughter, being raped by her brother, Amnon (2 Sam. 13:14). As a teen of thirteen, I remember agreeing with her that this was a horrible story, but I also had some other thoughts. First, if *I* were writing the Bible, I would not have included this story, but God did. This made the Bible *more* believable to me because of the human tendency to make ourselves look like heroes and not zeroes (the principle of embarrassment as we saw in chapter 10). Second, O'Hair said that for the Bible to be the Word of God, it would have to be filled with love, peace, and stories about puppy dogs and butterflies, not the horrible stories of rape, murder, and wars. I actually laughed, because I thought, *Who would* need *a book about puppy dogs and butterflies?* The purpose of Scripture is to show the results of sin and our need of a Savior. The rape of Tamar reveals the depravity of humans quite well, which reveals our need for Jesus. So the truth of Scripture is found in what the Bible reveals, not in everything it records. Unless this distinction is held, one may incorrectly conclude that the Bible teaches immorality because it narrates David's sin (2 Sam. 11:4), that it promotes polygamy because it records Solomon's sin (1 Kings 11:3), or that it affirms atheism because it quotes the fool as saying, "There is no God" (Ps. 14:1).

This chapter would not be complete without a brief look at some of the most common questions (often mistakenly called errors) of the Bible. Remember, while there are good questions, we have good answers. The questions below are the most common ones I have heard over the years, ten about the Old Testament and ten about the New Testament. These questions are listed according to the order in which they are found in the Bible and not according to the number of times they are asked. If your question is not listed here, then the best resource available is *When Critics Ask*, a book of more than eight hundred pages of questions from critics and doubters about the Bible.[3] Its format is user-friendly in that it lists the questions from Genesis to Revelation in the order they are found.

As you read the "Top Ten Lists of Bible Questions," please note how each question is related to a well-known Bible story (the New Testament questions are all from the Gospels). There are two groups who claim the Bible is in error—the critics and the doubters. The *critic* likes to dig into the Bible, finding minute conflicting details and believing he or she has found an error. The critic will proclaim victory until shown how the details of this supposed conflict are not conflicting but rather have an explanation. The *doubter*, on the other hand, has heard the Bible and knows its major stories but has some questions about things in these stories that don't seem to make sense. The doubter will not move closer to faith until the questions are resolved. The following list can help. Knowing whether you are dealing with a critic or a doubter will help you know how to respond.

Top Ten Lists of Bible Questions

Top Ten List of Old Testament Questions

1. *Where did Cain get his wife (Gen. 4:1–5:5)?*
This question is a favorite for skeptics, because they think that if Cain could find a wife, there must have been other "races" of people

on the earth who were not descendants of Adam and Eve. If this were true, it would be a stumbling block in accepting the creation account in Genesis and its record of only one man and woman at the beginning of history—a record on which many Old and New Testament doctrines depend.

The answer is that Cain married his sister or possibly his niece. The skeptics overlook the *time* element, for the Bible says that Adam "had other sons and *daughters*" (Gen. 5:4). Adam lived 930 years (v. 5) and started having children when he was 130. A man can have a lot of children in 800 years! Cain could have married one of his many sisters or a niece who grew into adulthood. A brother marrying a sister was not forbidden until much later (Lev. 18:9).[4] But doesn't Genesis 4:16–17 say that Cain went to the land of Nod and found a wife? No, the text says that Cain "knew" or had sexual relations with his wife and she conceived a son there.

2. *How could Noah's ark hold hundreds of thousands of species (Gen. 6:14–7:23)?*

The Bible says that Noah's ark was only 45 feet high, 75 feet wide, and 450 feet long (Gen. 6:15). Noah was told to take two of every kind of unclean animal and seven of every clean animal (6:19; 7:2). But scientists estimate there are a million species of animals. Where would Noah put them all?

The answer is that first, the modern concept of "species" is not the same as a "kind" in the Bible. There are probably only several hundred "kinds" of land animals that were taken into the ark, and the sea animals would remain in the sea, and many species could have survived in egg form. Second, we seem to forget that the ark was huge and compared in size to a modern ocean liner! The ark had three stories (Gen. 6:16), which tripled its available space to a total of over 1.5 million cubic feet! Third, Noah could have taken babies or smaller versions of some larger animals. The point is that there was plenty of room available for all the animals, food for the trip, and the eight humans aboard.[5]

3. *How could the sun stand still (Josh. 10:12–14)?*

During Joshua's battle with the kings of the Promised Land, God gave Israel the power to overcome their enemies. As the battle waged on, Joshua sought the Lord to cause the sun to stand still so they would have sufficient daylight to destroy all of their enemies. How could the sun stand still for a whole day?

Remember that the Bible uses everyday, nontechnical language to describe events. The sun may not have actually stopped but *appeared* to do so. It is not necessary to conclude that the earth's rotation was halted completely. Joshua 10:13 says that the sun "delayed going down about a full day." This could mean that the sun's rotation was not completely halted but rather retarded to such a degree that the sun did not set for a whole day. Or it is possible that God caused the light of the sun to refract from the cosmic heavens so it could be seen a day longer. Finally, as we saw in chapter 9, God, the Creator of the universe and everything therein, can intervene when and where he wills. Since he created the sun and its rotation, he can certainly halt it for one day and prevent any catastrophic results. Verse 14 says, "There has never been a day like it before or since, a day when the LORD listened to a man. Surely the LORD was fighting for Israel!" Sounds like a miracle, doesn't it?[6]

4. *What kind of God would allow Jephthah to offer his daughter up as a burnt offering (Judg. 11:29–40)?*

This question was one of Madalyn Murray O'Hair's favorite to show that either the Bible is full of bad things or the God of the Bible is a bad God. I heard her say, "You can't have it both ways. It's either one or the other!" The question she brings up is that just before Jephthah went into battle, he made a vow to the Lord that if God granted him victory, he would offer God the first thing that came out of his house as a burnt offering (Judg. 11:31). When Jephthah returned, the first thing out of his house to greet him was his daughter, and the Bible says that Jephthah made good on his vow. How could God allow Jephthah to do this and look upon it favorably?

Earlier we learned that when faced with a difficult Bible question, we should research difficult passages in light of the clear. The clear passages state that human sacrifice is an abomination to the Lord (Lev. 18:21; 20:2–5; Deut. 12:31; 18:10), so he would never allow Jephthah to make this kind of sacrifice or look with favor upon it. Also, we are sure that Jephthah, a man who sought after God, would have known of the law against human sacrifice and never would have considered it. So the clear passages tell us that he did not put his daughter to death to fulfill a vow to the Lord.

Well then, what was the sacrifice that upset Jephthah and his daughter so (Judg. 11:35, 37–38)? The sacrifice was that she would be offered to the Lord much as Hannah offered her son Samuel (1 Sam. 1:11, 22, 28). Not only would she be given to the Lord, but she would live the rest of her life in virginity (Judg. 11:37–39). This was very upsetting to his daughter, for it meant no marriage and no children. And it was upsetting to Jephthah because his daughter was an only child and fulfillment of the vow would result in no grandchildren and the end of his lineage. We have no evidence that Jephthah killed his daughter. Such action is clearly forbidden in Scripture (Exod. 20:13).

5. *Is the Bible wrong in matters of science?*

Whenever the Bible is accused of being wrong in matters of science, we think of Rodney Dangerfield exclaiming, "I don't get no respect!" While it is true that the Bible uses everyday, nontechnical language and was not written to be a textbook on science, this does not mean that the Bible is wrong on matters of science. The Bible is extraordinarily accurate in its descriptions and understanding of the world in which we live, and it provided scientific facts before they were even known by scientists. For example:

- the roundness of the earth (Isa. 40:22)
- the suspension of the earth in nothing (Job 26:7)
- the innumerable number of stars (Gen. 15:5; Jer. 33:22)
- the existence of valleys in the oceans (2 Sam. 22:16)
- the existence of springs and fountains in the seas (Gen. 8:2; Prov. 8:28)
- the existence of ocean currents (Ps. 8:8)
- the hydrologic cycle (Job 26:8; 36:27–28; Eccles. 1:6–7)
- the law of entropy (Ps. 102:22–27)
- the vast extent of the universe (Isa. 55:9)
- the nature of health, sanitation, and sickness (Leviticus 12–14)
- the importance of blood to the body (Lev. 17:11)

These facts are not stated in the technical jargon of modern science, of course, but in terms of the basic world of humankind's everyday experience. Nevertheless, they are completely in accord with the most modern scientific facts. It is ironic that it took hundreds and hundreds of years before modern humans discovered what was already in the Bible. It is time for the Bible to get "some respect"!

6. *How could God allow the witch of Endor to raise Samuel from the dead when God condemned witchcraft (1 Sam. 28:7–25)?*

The Bible severely condemns witchcraft, and those who practiced it during Old Testament times were to receive capital punishment (Exod. 22:18; Lev. 20:6, 27; Deut. 18:9–12; Isa. 8:19). Saul knew this and put all the witches out of Israel, but then he went to the witch of Endor to contact the dead prophet Samuel. The witch brought

Samuel back from the dead, thereby showing the power of witchcraft over the dead, even God's servants.

The probable answer is that the witch did not bring Samuel back from the dead, but God himself did to rebuke Saul. Evidence for this is that Saul was rebuked for his sin (1 Sam. 28:16–19); the witch herself was surprised by the appearance of Samuel from the dead (v. 12); witchcraft is condemned in this passage (v. 9); God sometimes speaks in unusual ways (cf. Baalam's donkey, Numbers 22); and Samuel truly seems to have appeared from the dead, rebuked Saul, and uttered a true prophecy (v. 19).[7]

7. *How could Solomon have so many wives when God condemns polygamy (1 Kings 11:1)?*

First Kings 11:3 says that Solomon had seven hundred wives and three hundred concubines. But the Bible warns against having multiple wives (Deut. 17:7) and violating the principle of monogamy—one man for one wife (cf. 1 Cor. 7:2). How is this possible?

Monogamy is God's standard for the human race, and God punished those who practiced polygamy (Gen. 2:21–25; 1 Kings 11:1–13). God prohibited a multiplicity of wives (Deut. 17:17). Paul said each person should have only one spouse (1 Cor. 7:2). God only permitted, not commanded, polygamy, as he did divorce, not because it was his desire, but because of the hardness of men's hearts (Deut. 24:1; Matt. 19:8). Every polygamist in the Bible, including David (1 Chron. 14:3) and Solomon, paid dearly for their sins.[8]

8. *How could a prophet of God curse forty-two children who were then killed by bears just because they called him "baldy" (2 Kings 2:23–24)?*

As Elisha was going up to Bethel, he was confronted by some "little children" (KJV) who mocked him by saying, "Go up, you baldhead!" Elisha then placed a curse on them, and immediately two bears came out of the woods and mauled forty-two of them. How could a man of God do this over such a minor offense?

First, this was no minor offense. These youth were mocking God's prophet, his mouthpiece to his people. With their words "go up," they were saying that if he really was a prophet of God, he should prove it by going up to heaven as Elijah did. Calling him "baldhead" could have been a reference to lepers who shaved their head to look for sores. So they were saying that Elisha was a powerless prophet and a detestable outcast. This mocking was dangerous, for as it cast doubt on God's messenger, it cast doubt on God's message.

Second, they were not "little children" but young men more comparable to a street gang. The original Hebrew word is best translated "young men" as in the NIV. So the life of the prophet was endangered by their number, their disrespect, and their intention to harm him. Finally, remember that it was God, not Elisha, who took their lives.[9]

9. *How could Esther participate in a pagan, immoral beauty contest (Esther 2:1–18)?*

Esther was selected by God as his instrument to deliver Israel from evil at the appointed time (Esther 4:14). So how could Esther, as a devout Jew, take part in a pagan pageant and become part of King Xerxes's harem?

Esther may not have had any choice about being part of the display of beautiful women before the king. Esther was "taken to the king's palace" (Esther 2:8), which seems to indicate that she was drafted into the service of the king, rather than having volunteered. Furthermore, there is no record that the participants in the pageant had to do anything immoral to be in the contest. Knowing Esther's character as revealed in the book, we can be sure she would have refused to do anything contrary to God's law. Finally, once chosen by the king, Esther was compelled to belong to his court. But it was the providence of God that brought Esther to this place at precisely the appropriate moment. We can be sure that God would have protected the purity of Esther as his chosen tool.[10]

10. *Can a sensible person really believe that a man was swallowed by a fish (book of Jonah)?*

Many critics laugh when they hear the story of Jonah: "It's a whopper of a tale!" Is there any evidence that this story really happened, or is it just an imaginary story or an allegory designed to communicate a message?

First, the story of Jonah is factual, because we have learned that if God exists, then miracles (as with Jonah) are possible. Second, the story of Jonah is mentioned in the historical book of 2 Kings (14:25). Third, the story of Jonah is considered factual by Jesus himself (Matt. 12:40). The point Christ was making was that if a person refuses to believe the story of Jonah being in the belly of the fish, then that person will not believe in the death, burial, and resurrection of Jesus. Jesus here was affirming that his death, burial, and resurrection would be as factual as the story of Jonah was. Furthermore, Jesus went on to mention the significant historical details of the events of Jonah. Finally, we have archaeological confirmation of a prophet named Jonah whose grave was found in northern Israel. And some ancient coins have been found with an engraving of a man coming out of a fish's mouth.[11]

Top Ten List of New Testament Questions

1. *Why was it all right for the Magi to follow the stars when the Bible condemns astrology (Matt. 2:2)?*

The Bible condemns astrology (Lev. 19:26; Deut. 18:10; Isa. 8:19), yet God blessed the wise men (Magi) and seemed to even guide them with the stars to show the birthplace of Christ.

First, astrology is a belief that the study of the arrangement and movement of the stars can *foretell* events whether they be good or bad. Second, the star (singular) in the biblical story was to *announce* the birth of Christ, not to *foretell* it. God gave the star to the Magi to let them know that the Christ child had already been born (Matt. 2:16). Third, there are other instances in the Bible in which the stars and planets are used by God to reveal his desires. The stars declare God's glory (Ps. 19:1–6); creation reveals his existence (Rom. 1:18–20) and will be affected at the return of Christ (Matt. 24:29–30). So the star guiding the Magi was not used to *predict*, but to *proclaim* the birth of Christ.[12]

2. *Why is there a mistake in the order of Christ's temptations in the wilderness (Matt. 4:5–10; Luke 4:5–12)?*

Matthew's order of the temptations is: (1) turn stones into bread; (2) jump from the pinnacle of the temple; and (3) receive all the kingdoms of the world. But Luke's order of temptations is: (1) turn stones into bread; (2) receive all the kingdoms of the world; and (3) jump from the pinnacle of the temple. Why are these temptations given in different sequence?

Remember that divergent accounts do not equal discrepancies. Let it be noted at the outset that there is no disagreement over whether the temptations happened or over what they involved. The different sequences may be that Matthew introduces these temptations *chronologically* while Luke lists them *climactically*, or topically. Matthew may be listing them as they really happened, and Luke may be listing them to express the climax he wanted to emphasize. We see this possibility because Matthew 4:5 begins with the word "Then" while verse 8 begins with the word "Again." In Greek these words suggest a more sequential order of the events. But in Luke's account, verses 5 and 9 each begin with a simple "And" (see NASB). The Greek in Luke's account doesn't necessarily indicate a sequential order of events.[13]

3. *How could hell be a place of darkness when flames (which are supposed to be in hell) give off light (Matt. 8:12)?*

Jesus described hell as a place of "outer darkness" (Matt. 8:12; cf. 22:13; 25:30). But the Bible also describes hell as a place of fire (Rev. 20:14) and unquenchable flames (Mark 9:48). But fire and flames give off light. How can hell be utterly dark when there is light there?

Both "fire" and "darkness" are powerful figures of speech to describe the unthinkable reality of hell. It is like fire because it is a place of destruction and torment. It is like outer darkness because people are lost there forever. While hell is a literal place, not every description should be taken literally. Powerful figures of speech are used to describe this terrible place so we can grasp its horror. We have seen that literary devices such as figures of speech are used in the Bible, such as God having "wings," or God being "asleep." There are figures of speech used to describe the eternal destiny of the lost that, if taken literally, contradict each other. For example, hell is depicted as an eternal garbage dump (Mark 9:43–48), which has a bottom. But it is also portrayed as a bottomless pit (Rev. 20:3). Each is a vivid description of a place of everlasting punishment.[14]

4. *If Jesus was crucified on Friday, how could he have been in the grave three days and three nights (Matt. 12:40; John 19:14)?*

Christ rose on Sunday (Matt. 28:1), but he said that he would be "three days and three nights in the heart of the earth" (Matt. 12:40). If Jesus was crucified on Friday, how could he have been in the tomb for three days and three nights when he rose on Sunday only two days later? Many people question the accuracy of the Scriptures on this very issue, so it is an important one to answer. They say, "Obviously, Jesus is wrong here. And if Jesus is wrong here, he may be wrong other places as well, so how can I trust him?" This is a good question.

The Gospel accounts show that Jesus was crucified and buried on Friday before sundown (which is the beginning of the next day for the Jews), and was resurrected on the first day of the week, which is our Sunday, before sunrise. This puts Jesus in the grave for part of Friday, all of Saturday, and part of Sunday. In other words, he was in the tomb two full nights, one full day, and part of two days. Since this is clearly not three full twenty-four-hour days, do we have a problem of conflict with the prophecy of Jesus in Matthew? Now, to explain away this problem, some say that Jesus was crucified on

Thursday or even Wednesday. They do this to try to explain the three days and three nights. But it is not a problem when we understand the following.

- *That Jesus was raised* on *the third day, not after it.* Jesus is recorded as saying, "The Son of Man must . . . be killed and *after* three days rise again" (Mark 8:31), and "he must be killed and *on* the third day be raised to life" (Matt. 16:21). These expressions are used interchangeably. In fact, most references say that the resurrection occurred *on* the third day. Also, Jesus said in John 2:19–20 that he would be raised up "in three days" (not the fourth day). And after the Pharisees told Pilate of the prediction of Jesus, "After three days I will rise again" (Matt. 27:63), they asked for a guard to secure the tomb "until the third day" (v. 64). If they had not thought that "after the third day" was interchangeable with the "third day," the Pharisees would have asked for a guard for the fourth day.
- *The Jewish reckoning of a "day."* The Jews believed any part of a period was considered a full period. Any part of a day was considered as a complete day (cf. Esther 4:16; 5:1; Ps. 1:2). The Babylonian Talmud (Jewish commentary) relates that "The portion of a day is as the whole of it." The Jerusalem Talmud (so designated because it was written in Jerusalem) says, "We have a teaching. A day and a night are an Onah and the portion of an Onah is as the whole of it." An Onah simply means "a period of time." The Jewish day began at 6:00 p.m. It is believed that they so reckoned time this way because in the week of creation, the first day began with a darkness that was turned into light; and thereafter each twenty-four-hour period was identified as "the evening and the morning"—in this order (Gen. 1:5, 8, et al.).[15]

The "three days and three nights" in reference to Christ's period in the tomb can be calculated as follows: (1) Christ was crucified on Friday. Any time before 6:00 p.m. on Friday would be considered one day and one night. (2) From 6:01 p.m. on Friday to 6:00 p.m. on Saturday would be the second day and night. (3) From 6:01 on Saturday until Jesus was resurrected on Sunday would be the third day and night. From a Jewish point of view, it would make three days and three nights from Friday afternoon until Sunday morning.

Even today we often use the same principle in reference to time. For example, many couples hope their child will be born before midnight on December 31. Why? If the child is born at 11:59 p.m., the child will be treated by the IRS as being a dependent 365 days and 365 nights of *that* year. This is true even if 99.9 percent of the year has elapsed. So there is no problem here with Jesus's prediction.

5. *How many blind men did Jesus heal—one or two (Matt. 20:29–34; Mark 10:46–52; Luke 18:35–43)?*

Matthew says that Christ healed two men, but Mark says that only one man was healed (10:51–52). Is this a contradiction that confirms the charge of an error?

Mark does mention one person getting healed, but that doesn't mean that there were not two as Matthew says there were. How do we know this? Mark does not say only one blind man was healed. Matthew says there were two, and where there are two, there is one every time! Further, Mark mentions the name of the one blind man, Bartimaeus, showing that he is concentrating on the one who was personally known to him. There is no error here, only two different perspectives of the same event.[16]

6. *Did Judas die by hanging or by falling on rocks (Matt. 27:5; Acts 1:18)?*

Matthew informs us that Judas hanged himself. But Luke says that "he burst open in the middle and all his entrails gushed out" (Acts 1:18). Once again, these accounts differ, but they are mutually complementary. Judas hung himself exactly as Matthew says he did. The account in Acts simply adds that Judas hanged himself on a tree over the edge of a cliff, and his body fell on sharp rocks below. Then his intestines gushed out just as Luke (the doctor) vividly describes.[17]

7. *What did the centurion really say about Christ on the cross (Matt. 27:54; Mark 15:39; Luke 23:47)?*

The problem is that Matthew records the centurion as saying, "Surely he was the Son of God," and Mark says, "Surely this man was the Son of God," but Luke records the words of the centurion as, "Surely this was a righteous man!" A critic once pointed out this possible error by saying that Luke was the only one telling the truth, while Matthew and Mark were embellishing the story of Jesus, making him into something no one else believed. I challenged him by saying that since he believed Luke was telling the truth, we should see what else Luke's Gospel had to say about Jesus. He declined and said I was trying to avoid the error. Well, is this an error or not?

The answer is that the centurion may have said both statements. His words don't have to be limited to one phrase or sentence. Because the Gospel of Luke was portraying Christ as the perfect man, Luke may have chosen this phrase rather than the ones used by Matthew and Mark. Since Matthew's and Mark's statements are nearly identical, we can be sure the centurion said this. Since Luke was a precise, detail-oriented, and accurate historian (as we saw in chapter 10), we can be certain that the centurion also spoke this statement. Finally, we must keep in mind what the centurion had witnessed during the preceding six hours as Christ hung on the cross. Finally, at the end, Christ with a loud voice gave up his life and an earthquake occurred. It is very probable that the centurion said a lot of things at this time, including these two statements![18]

8. *Were there one or two angels at Christ's tomb?*

Matthew 28:5 refers to the "angel" at the tomb after Jesus's resurrection, but John says "two" angels were there (John 20:12). Which account is right?

Just because two or more accounts of the same event differ, they are not necessarily mutually exclusive. The reports in these passages are not contradictory. We have already learned the infallible mathematical rule that easily explains this problem: wherever there are two, there is always one. Matthew did not say there was only one angel. He probably focused on the angel who spoke while John referred to how many angels they saw. One has to add the word "only" to Matthew's account to make it contradict John's. Once again, the problem is not with what the Bible actually says, but with the critic who adds to it.[19]

9. *Did Christ appear to the women first or to the disciples (Matt. 28:9)?*

Both Matthew and Mark list women as the first ones to see the resurrected Christ. But Paul says that Peter (Cephas) was the first one to see Christ after the resurrection (1 Cor. 15:5). Which account is correct?

Jesus appeared first to Mary Magdalene, then to the other women, and then to Peter. Paul, in 1 Corinthians, was not giving a complete list, but only the important ones for his purpose. Since only a man's testimony was considered legal or official in the first century, Paul would only list Peter and not the women in his defense of the resurrection.[20]

10. *Did Luke make a mistake when he mentioned a worldwide census under Caesar Augustus (Luke 2:1)?*

Luke refers to a worldwide census under Caesar Augustus when Quirinius was governor of Syria. However, according to the records of ancient history, no such census took place.

Until recently, critics have said that Luke made an error in his assertion of a census here that actually took place in AD 6 or 7. But recent scholarship has reversed this perspective, and it is now widely held that an earlier census took place just as Luke records. First, a census was the chief means to tax a subjugated people, so it would certainly take place. Second, registrations of this kind took place every fourteen years. Third, a census in these antiquated times was a massive project that took several years to complete. Today in the United States we take a census every ten years and the results are not known until years later. It is quite likely that a census began in 8 or 7 BC but may not have begun in Palestine until some time later. Fourth, it was not unusual to require people to return to the place of their birth or to the place where they owned property. Luke's account fits the regular pattern of census taking, and its date would not be unreasonable. Luke simply provides us with a reliable historical record of an event not recorded elsewhere.[21]

So we have seen that the Bible is trustworthy in all that it records. When we hear about the attacks the critics have launched against the Bible over the years, we are reminded of the following poem:

The Anvil? God's Word

Last eve I passed beside a blacksmith's door
And heard the anvil ring the vesper chime.
Then looking in, I saw upon the floor
Old hammers, worn with beating years of time.
"How many anvils have you had," said I,
"To wear and batter all these hammers so?"
"Just one," said he, and then, with twinkling eye,
"The anvil wears the hammers out, you know."
And so, thought I, the anvil of God's word,
For ages skeptic blows have beat upon;
Yet though the noise of falling blows was heard,
The anvil is unharmed . . . the hammer's gone.

Author unknown[22]

UNBROKEN Bible Checklist

Guidelines When Examining Difficult Passages

U—*Unexplained* Is Not Unexplainable
- Don't assume a discrepancy is a contradiction.
- Rather than remain in ignorance of the verse, choose to investigate the verse.

N—Don't *Neglect* the Context
- A text out of context is a pretext.
- This is probably the chief error of those who find fault with the Bible.

B—*Book* with Human Writers and Characteristics
- The biblical writers were human composers employing their own literary styles.
- The Bible uses human literary styles, human perspectives, and human thought patterns, and it discloses human interests.

R—*Research* Difficult Passages in Light of the Clear
- The Bible never contradicts itself, and your interpretation should not do so either.
- When faced with a difficult passage, always investigate what is said in other verses.

O—*Original* Text Is without Error
- While there are some mistakes in the manuscript copies, this does not mean the mistakes are a part of the original inspired text of Scripture.
- By comparing manuscript copies and external sources of Scripture, the entire message of Scripture comes through.

K—*Knowledge* of Literary Devices
- The Bible is not composed in one and only one literary style.
- The Bible uses literary devices such as poetic style, parables, allegories, metaphors, similes, hyperboles, and even satire.

E—*Everyday*, Nontechnical Language
   • The Bible is written for the common person
   and uses common, everyday language.
   • The Scriptures were written in ancient times,
   and we cannot impose our modern standards
   on them.

**N—*Narrative* That Includes the Good, the Bad,
and the Ugly**
   • Just because something is contained in
   Scripture doesn't mean it is commended by
   Scripture.
   • A narrative is a record of what occurred, and
   this includes the good, bad, and ugly.

Digging Deeper on Errors in the Bible

Archer, Gleason. *An Encyclopedia of Biblical Difficulties*. Grand Rapids: Zondervan, 1982.

Geisler, Norman. *Baker Encyclopedia of Christian Apologetics*. Grand Rapids: Baker Books, 1999, 74–80.

Geisler, Norman, and Thomas Howe. *When Critics Ask*. Grand Rapids: Baker Books, 1992.

Geisler, Norman, and Frank Turek. *I Don't Have Enough Faith to Be an Atheist*. Wheaton: Crossway, 2004, 370–74.

Haley, John. *An Examination of Alleged Discrepancies in the Bible*. Grand Rapids: Baker Books, 1951.

12

Is Jesus the Son of God?

"Hey Steve, do you believe all that stuff in the Bible about Jesus being God?"

"Yes, Ben, I do," Steve answered as they talked during their lunch break at the investment firm where they worked.

"Well," Ben said with his mouth full of his sandwich, "I just can't buy that. I'm Jewish, you know, but I have visited a lot of different churches just to see what others believe. The conclusion I've come to is that Jesus was a good, moral teacher who said some great things. He was a very wise man when you consider when and where he grew up. But I think Jesus just borrowed his teachings, like loving your enemies and peace not war, from Buddha. He heard the teachings of Buddha somehow and made them a part of his sermons. I mean, how do we know that isn't true?" Ben concluded with eyebrows raised.

While most people believe in God (only about 13 percent of Americans are atheists or agnostics)[1], the subject of Jesus generally elicits debate. Tim LaHaye, coauthor of the best-selling Left Behind series, says, "Almost everyone who has heard of Jesus has developed an opinion about Him. That is to be expected, for He is not only the most famous person in world history, but also the most controversial."[2] Many today believe that Jesus is the Christ, the risen Son of the living God. But others find it hard to accept the idea that a rural Jewish carpenter could have been the Creator of the world. They prefer to believe less sensational theories about him. For example:

- *Jesus is a man who achieved great things.* Among the groups who hold to this view is the Church of Jesus Christ of Latter-

day Saints—the Mormons. They teach that Jesus was a created
being and the elder brother of Lucifer.[3]

- *Jesus is a created being who was given the status of second-in-command.* According to the Jehovah's Witnesses, Jesus is "a god, but not the Almighty God, who is Jehovah."[4] Instead, they say that Jesus is "a created individual" who "is the second greatest personage of the universe."[5]

- *Jesus is a man no better than we are.* "It is plain that Jesus is not God Himself."[6] These words of Sun Myung Moon clearly spell out the view of his Unification Church. Its teaching is that Jesus's value is no greater than that of any other man. Those who follow Moon's theology say that Jesus's work was a failure.

- *Jesus's existence began at his conception.* One group that teaches this idea is The Way International. In their reinterpretation of biblical instruction, they hold that "Jesus Christ's existence began when he was conceived by God's creating the soul-life of Jesus in Mary."[7]

- *Jesus is a prophet and messenger of God.* According to the tenets of Islam, "Jesus . . . was only a messenger of Allah" (Sura 4:171 from the Qur'an). They also say he was a sinless prophet who never achieved the greatness of the prophet Muhammad.

- *Jesus is less than most people think he is.* Those who embrace agnosticism or atheism often have a low view of Jesus. Some cannot find it in themselves to place Jesus on as high a plane as such past notables as Buddha or Socrates. Bertrand Russell, a famous apologist of the atheistic viewpoint, writes, "I cannot myself feel that either in the matter of wisdom or in the matter of virtue Christ stands quite as high as some other people known to history."[8]

- *Jesus is a great moral teacher.* Some people don't reject all of Jesus's work on earth, though they do reject his claims to deity. William Channing of the Unitarian Church said, "Christ was sent to earth as a great moral teacher rather than as a mediator."[9]

- *Jesus is a mystic medium.* New Age thinkers consider Jesus to be a guide to self-actualization. In this regard, Jesus would be seen as a channel—one of many ancients who give New Age adherents a "glimpse" at the past. Through previous incarnations, they contend, he attained a level of purity that is achievable by all.

- *Jesus is a projection of our needs.* Some feel that the only reason Jesus has reached great heights of importance is that humans need someone like him to fall back on. Carl Jung, a famous Swiss psychologist and psychiatrist, said that Jesus is "our culture hero who, regardless of His historical existence, embodies the myth of the divine man."[10]

We learned earlier that the law of noncontradiction says contrary claims cannot be true at the same time. In other words, someone has to be right and someone has to be wrong in his or her opinion of Jesus. And truth can only be known as it corresponds to the facts. So what are the key facts of what we know about Jesus? We have put these key facts about Jesus into the acrostic CROWNED because Jesus was *"crowned* with glory and honor" (Heb. 2:9).

C—Claims

Jesus made extraordinary claims about himself.

Claimed to be Yahweh. Jesus called himself the "I AM" (John 8:58), giving himself the highest and holiest name of God—the name by which God identified himself to Moses in Exodus 3:14. Without a doubt, Jesus claimed to be God. The Jews who heard this claim by Jesus had no doubt that he was claiming to be God, and they tried to stone him for it (John 8:59).

The "I am" claims. Seven times the apostle John recorded the "I am" claims of Jesus. It is significant to note that these claims were the same claims could only be fulfilled by God himself. They were claims no ordinary person could ever dare to make, but Jesus could make them because they are true and because he is God.

- *"I am the bread of life"* (John 6:35; cf. Exod. 16:15). Bread represents sustenance and life. Only God is the Life-giver.
- *"I am the light of the world"* (John 8:12; cf. Ps. 27:1; Micah 7:8; John 1:4, 5; 1 John 1:5). The light of the world is God. He illuminates our life.
- *"I am the door"* (John 10:9 NASB). Jesus claimed to be the only way to God and the only way of salvation, saying, "I am the door; if anyone enters through Me, he will be saved" (John 10:9 NASB). Jesus claimed exclusivity here. He is the only way

to gain salvation, and only by believing in him does one have eternal life in heaven with God (see Acts 4:12).

- *"I am the good shepherd"* (John 10:11). Jesus knew what it meant to claim to be the Good Shepherd. He gave himself the role of God clearly portrayed in the Old Testament, the Shepherd of his people (Ps. 23:1; Ezek. 34:15–16, 23). The people hearing Jesus would have known full well that this was a claim of deity and messiahship.
- *"I am the resurrection and the life"* (John 11:25). This is another clear claim that Jesus is God, for only God can give life (1 Sam. 2:6; John 5:25–26). Jesus proved this claim by raising people from the dead (Luke 7:14–15; 8:54–55; John 11:43–44).
- *"I am the way, the truth, and the life"* (John 14:6). Jesus said he was the only way to God. "No one comes to the Father except through me" (John 14:6). Once again he claimed to be the exclusive way to God.
- *"I am the true vine"* (John 15:1, 5). Jesus continued this claim by saying, "You are the branches. If a man remains in me and I in him, he will bear much fruit; apart from me you can do nothing" (John 15:5). The apostle Paul said of believers in Jesus that "in him we live and move and have our being" (Acts 17:28). He is the true source of our life. Without him, we would wither and die.

Jesus also claimed:

- *To be equal with God* (John 10:30–33). Once again the Jews tried to stone Jesus because he claimed to be God (v. 33).
- *To be the Messiah* (Mark 14:61–64). When asked, "Are you the Christ (Greek for Messiah)," Jesus said, "I am. And you will see the Son of Man sitting at the right hand of the Mighty One and coming on the clouds of heaven." At this, the high priest tore his robe because of Jesus's blasphemy.
- *To be worthy of worship* (Matt. 8:2; 9:18; 14:33; 15:25; 20:20; John 9:38; 20:28).
- *To be equal in authority with God* (John 5:22, 26–29).
- *To be the object of prayer like God* (John 14:13–14; 15:7).
- *That Scripture spoke of him* (John 5:39).
- *That to know Jesus is to know God* (John 8:19; 14:8–9).

When faced with Jesus's claims to being God, critics raise several objections:

Jesus was not considered divine until much later. As we saw in chapter 10, *The Da Vinci Code* makes its own claim that Jesus was never thought to be divine until the fourth century and that his claims to divinity were part of a conspiracy. But as we saw earlier, we have manuscripts written some twenty-five or thirty years after the resurrection of Jesus that record all of the claims of Jesus mentioned above. Furthermore, the church fathers' quotations of these Scriptures confirmed Jesus's claims. So to say that Jesus never claimed to be God and that humans made up a story about him hundreds of years later is to ignore the evidence.

Jesus never claimed to be divine. Critics say that Jesus's claims are in his followers' writings, but Jesus never actually said them. Instead, the disciples made them up. But even outside sources, such as the historian Josephus, knew of Jesus's claims to deity. Josephus served as the historian for the Roman emperor Domitian during the first century. Writing in his *Antiquities of the Jews*, Josephus, who was not a Christian, discussed Jesus and said that people referred to him as the "Messiah" and that he "was called Christ."[11] For a mere legend about Jesus claiming to be the Messiah to have gained the circulation and impact it had (so that even Josephus knew about it) without one shred of basis in fact, is incredible. For this to have happened would be as fantastic as someone in our time writing a biography of the late John F. Kennedy and in it saying he claimed to be God, to forgive people's sins, and to have risen from the dead. Such a wild story would never get off the ground because there are still too many people around who knew Kennedy.

We are reminded of the vice-presidential debate in 1988 between Dan Quayle and Lloyd Bentsen. To demonstrate his ability to be vice president, Quayle said, "I have as much experience in the Congress as Jack Kennedy did when he sought the presidency." Bentsen sharply replied, "Senator, I served with Jack Kennedy. I knew Jack Kennedy. Jack Kennedy was a friend of mine. Senator, you're no Jack Kennedy."[12] The point is that eyewitnesses would not allow wrong things to be said about someone they knew whether it was Kennedy or Jesus. The legend theory does not hold water because even the enemies of Jesus knew of his claims to be divine.

Well then, why wasn't Jesus more obvious in his claims to be God? Even though Jesus made many claims to be God (as we have seen), some critics say that Jesus could have done a lot more to prove his claims to deity. There are some possible reasons he did not.

First, to be an example and glorify the Father. If Jesus pulled rank ("Hey, leave me alone . . . I'm God, you know") every time he got into trouble, he would not be an example for us when we are suffering, nor would he be the model of humility (1 Peter 2:21–25).

Further, to allow people to draw their own conclusions (as he did with parables). In John 6, Jesus fed the five thousand with the loaves and fish. The result was that the people knew he was the Prophet and tried to force him to become their king, so Jesus fled (vv. 14–15). He went to the other side of the lake, and the people followed. Jesus chastised them for not believing in him but only wanting their bellies filled (v. 26). Their need was not their physical hunger but their spiritual deficit and need of Jesus as their Savior (vv. 27–29). Miracles and claims can actually blind people from the truth that they need to repent and believe in Jesus.

Sure, Jesus claimed to be divine, but was he? What if Jesus were mistaken in his claims? C. S. Lewis responded to this question well when he said that since Jesus claimed to be God, he couldn't be just a great moral teacher because great moral teachers know better than to claim to be divine. Since Jesus claimed to be God, there are only three possibilities: Jesus was a liar, a lunatic, or the Lord.[13]

Jesus was a liar. If Jesus claimed to be God but knew he was not, this would make him a liar. He would not be a good, moral teacher as Ben told Steve but rather a bad, immoral deceiver who should be shunned, not revered. He was nothing more than a con artist who should have been arrested. Well, he was arrested, which brings up the question of why he would die without recanting unless he thought he was telling the truth. That leads to the next option.

Jesus was a lunatic. Maybe Jesus thought he was God but really wasn't. He would not be a good, wise teacher like Ben thought but rather a sad, demented babbler. One problem with this possibility is that Jesus uttered some of the most profound sayings ever recorded. Another problem is that everyone—even his enemies—claimed that Jesus was a man of integrity who taught the truth (Mark 12:14). Finally, his closest friends would have known that Jesus was mentally unbalanced and would not have died for a crazy man. That leaves us with the only possibility left . . .

Jesus is Lord. Explaining the claims of Jesus to someone like Ben forces them to move beyond the warm, fuzzy feelings people usually feel for Jesus and to the edge of a cliff. Was Jesus really the Lord? At this point, people need more than just claims to convince them.

Jesus made some grandiose claims to be God and the Messiah, but did he back them up? That leads us to our next point.

R—Résumé

Everyone in the business world is familiar with a résumé. A résumé is a form job applicants use to show that they are qualified for a certain job opening because their background and skills fulfill the job requirements. As we saw in chapter 10, there are 191 Old Testament prophecies about the coming of the Christ. To be the Messiah, Jesus would have to fulfill every one, and he did. Keep in mind that these prophecies were written hundreds of years before Jesus was born in Bethlehem. Even the most liberal critics admit that the prophetic books were completed about four hundred years before Christ, and the book of Daniel by about 167 BC. There is good evidence to date most of these books earlier, with some of the psalms and earlier prophets dating from the eighth and ninth centuries BC.[14]

The following chart lists just fourteen of the prophecies only Jesus fulfilled:

Prophecy	Reference	Fulfillment
Human race (woman)	Genesis 3:15	Luke 2:7; Galatians 4:4
Ethnic group (Abraham)	Genesis 12:1	Matthew 1:1
Tribe (Judah)	Genesis 49:10	Matthew 1:2; Luke 3:23, 33
Dynasty (David)	2 Samuel 2:7; Jeremiah 23:5–6	Matthew 1:1
Deity	Isaiah 9:6	Matthew 1:23
Born in Bethlehem	Micah 5:2	Matthew 2:5; Luke 2:4–7
Virgin born	Isaiah 7:14	Matthew 1:23
Heralded by a messenger	Isaiah 40:3; Malachi 3:1	Matthew 3:1–2
Perform miracles	Isaiah 35:5–6	Matthew 9:35
Cleanse the temple	Malachi 3:1	Matthew 21:12
Rejected by Jews	Psalm 118:22	Matthew 27:22
Crucified	Isaiah 53:12	Matthew 27:38
No bones broken	Psalm 34:20	John 19:33–36
Rise from the dead	Psalm 16:10; Isaiah 53:11	Matthew 28:6

Some explanations have been offered to try to explain away how Jesus fulfilled these prophecies down to the last detail.

Wrong interpretation. Many rabbis today say that some of these prophecies (such as Isaiah 53) are not messianic but were referring to the entire nation of Israel. Up until the time of Christ, however, Jewish interpreters taught that Isaiah 53 spoke of the Jewish Messiah. "Therefore I will give him a portion among the great, and he will divide the spoils with the strong, because he poured out his life unto death, and was numbered with the transgressors. For he bore the sin of many, and made intercession for the transgressors" (v. 12). Only after early Christians began to show how Jesus fulfilled this prophecy did the Jews move the interpretation to refer to the suffering Jewish nation.[15]

Coincidental fulfillment. Was it possible that Jesus was just one of many throughout history who coincidentally fit the prophetic fingerprint? What are the odds? Well, someone did the math and said the probability of just eight of these prophecies being fulfilled by one man is one chance in one hundred million billion. That number is millions of times more than the total number of people who have walked the planet![16]

Intentional fulfillment. While Jesus could have maneuvered his life to fulfill some of the prophecies, many of them would have been beyond his control, such as his ancestry, place of birth, method of execution, bones remaining unbroken, and soldiers gambling for his clothing.

Fabricated fulfillment. The Gospel writers did a public relations work for the persona of Jesus by changing details of his life to match up with the prophecies. Don't forget that there were multiple eyewitnesses around when the Gospel accounts were being circulated who would have challenged the rendering. Besides, why would the Gospel writers willingly die for a lie they fabricated? And while the Talmud refers to Jesus in derogatory ways, it never claims that the fulfillment of these prophecies was false.[17]

The miraculous fulfillment of these ancient prophecies is one of the most powerful arguments in confirming Jesus's claims to be the Messiah and God. His résumé is impeccable and untouchable!

O—One-of-a-Kind Life

Jesus proved his claims to be God and the Messiah not only by fulfilling the messianic prophecies, but also by his one-of-a-kind life.

John 3:16 says, "For God so loved the world that he gave his *one and only* Son. . . ." His "one-of-a-kind" life was proven by the fact that he was sinless, he performed miracles, and he uttered words like no one before or since him.

Consider his *sinless life*. Jesus himself said, "Which one of you convicts Me of sin?" (John 8:46 NASB). If any of us said that, our spouse and children or friends could easily share their list, but no one could say anything about Jesus. Moreover, his disciples who lived with him for three years, night and day, claimed that Jesus was sinless.

- Peter said that Jesus was an "unblemished and spotless" lamb (1 Peter 1:19 NASB) "who committed no sin, nor was any deceit found in His mouth" (1 Peter 2:22 NASB).
- John said of Christ, "In Him there is no sin" (1 John 3:5 NASB).
- Paul wrote that Jesus "knew no sin" (2 Cor. 5:21 NASB).
- The writer of Hebrews made the same point by claiming that Jesus was "without sin" (Heb. 4:15 NASB).

Even Jesus's enemies could not find fault with him. When the Pharisees searched for dirt on Jesus, they could find none (Mark 14:55). Furthermore, they admitted that Jesus taught "the way of God in accordance with the truth" (Mark 12:14). Even Pilate could not find Jesus guilty of anything (Luke 23:22). To live a sinless life does not prove deity (though only Jesus has managed to do it), but to claim to be God and offer a sinless life is another matter. It proves he was not lying when he said he was God.

Consider his *miraculous life*. Jesus turned water to wine (John 2:7–10), walked on water (Matt. 14:25), multiplied bread (John 6:11–13), opened the eyes of the blind (John 9:6–11), made the lame to walk (Mark 2:3–12), cast out demons (Mark 3:11), healed the multitudes of all kinds of sickness (Matt. 9:35), including leprosy (Mark 1:40–42), and even raised the dead to life on several occasions (Mark 5:35–42; Luke 7:11–15; John 11:43–44). When asked if he was the Messiah, he used miracles as evidence to support the claim, saying, "Go back and report to John what you hear and see: The blind receive sight, the lame walk, those who have leprosy are cured, the deaf hear, the dead are raised, and the good news is preached to the poor" (Matt. 11:4–5). Jesus's miracles verify his claim to be God.

"Wait a minute," someone may say. "These stories of miracles are just fairy tales." But we have learned so far that we live in a theistic world (chap. 6), so miracles are possible (chap. 9). Moreover, the New Testament is a reliable historical document of Jesus and his life (chaps. 10 and 11). Therefore we have no reason to doubt the miracles in the life of Jesus.

Consider his *marvelous words*. Reflect on the simplicity and the profundity of the Beattitudes from Jesus' Sermon on the Mount.

> Blessed are the poor in spirit: for theirs is the kingdom of heaven. Blessed are they that mourn: for they shall be comforted. Blessed are the meek: for they shall inherit the earth. Blessed are they which do hunger and thirst after righteousness: for they shall be filled. Blessed are the merciful: for they shall obtain mercy. Blessed are the pure in heart: for they shall see God. Blessed are the peacemakers: for they shall be called the children of God. Blessed are they which are persecuted for righteousness' sake: for theirs is the kingdom of heaven. Blessed are ye, when men shall revile you, and persecute you, and shall say all manner of evil against you falsely, for my sake. Rejoice, and be exceeding glad: for great is your reward in heaven: for so persecuted they the prophets which were before you.
>
> Matthew 5:3–12 KJV

Reflect on the beauty of the Lord's Prayer.

> After this manner therefore pray ye: Our Father which art in heaven, Hallowed be thy name. Thy kingdom come. Thy will be done in earth, as it is in heaven. Give us this day our daily bread. And forgive us our debts, as we forgive our debtors. And lead us not into temptation, but deliver us from evil: For thine is the kingdom, and the power, and the glory, for ever. Amen.
>
> Matthew 6:9–13 KJV

Jesus's parables revealed him as the greatest teacher who ever lived. Most people today know something about the good Samaritan (Luke 10), the prodigal son (Luke 15), and the lost sheep (Luke 15:4–7). Jesus is also known as the "quotable Jesus" because so many people know something that Jesus said. Some examples are: "Do not judge, or you too will be judged" (Matt. 7:1). "Then you will know the truth, and the truth will set you free" (John 8:32). "What good will it be for a man if he gains the whole world, yet forfeits his soul? Or what can a man give in exchange for his soul?" (Matt. 16:26). "Give not that which is holy unto the dogs, neither cast ye your pearls before swine" (Matt. 7:6 KJV). Who hasn't heard John 3:16: "For God so loved the world that he gave his one and only Son, that whoever believes in him shall not perish but have eternal life"?

No one else has ever come close to the wisdom, grace, freshness, and style of the teacher Jesus. Certainly not Buddha, not Socrates, and not Muhammad. If Steve could help Ben compare the teachings of Jesus to the teachings of Buddha, Ben would know that Jesus did not need to borrow from Buddha. How could a simple peasant, a lowly carpenter with no education, speak as Jesus did if he were not God? When the temple guards were sent to arrest Jesus while he was speaking, they returned empty-handed. When asked why, they declared, "No one ever spoke the way this man does" (John 7:46). To that we say, "Amen!"

W—Witness by Outside Sources

Remember the example in chapter 3, when Doug said to Mike, "If you can give me one piece of evidence for Jesus *outside* the Bible, I'll listen to one piece of evidence about Jesus from the Bible"? Mike had nothing to say because he didn't know about the wealth of evidence for the existence of Jesus from outside the Bible, which we call external sources. In addition to the eyewitness materials of the Gospels that have verified accuracy and have been confirmed by archaeology, there are also twelve known non-Christian writers who mention Jesus within 150 years of his life. Josephus, the Roman historian, has already been mentioned. By contrast, over the same 150 years, there are only nine non-Christian sources who mention Tiberius Caesar, the Roman emperor at the time of Jesus![18]

As a former police officer, I (Randy) can tell you how important a good witness is. There is the *friendly* witness—this witness is as useless as the references on a résumé who tell you that a person can walk on water! There is the *impartial* witness—like Joe Friday of Dragnet, "Just the facts, Ma'am, just the facts." This witness has no reason to lie, so if he says something good about the accused, this will be a strong witness. Then there is the *hostile* witness—one who is opposed to the defendant. If an attorney can get a hostile witness to admit to *any* good about the accused, this will carry a lot of weight with the jury.

Twelve key outside (non-Christian) sources mention Jesus within 150 years of his life. They are witnesses who are hostile to Christianity, and they include trusted historians, government officials, Jewish sources, and Gentile sources. For a chart and summary of these twelve outside sources as well as their statements, see appendix D. The material in this appendix is an excellent resource for anyone who doubts the existence of Jesus of Nazareth!

What can we learn from these neutral non-Christian sources about Jesus? Piecing together all twelve non-Christian sources, we see that:

- Jesus lived during the time of Tiberius Caesar.
- He lived a virtuous life.
- He was a wonder-worker.
- He had a brother named James.
- He was acclaimed to be the Messiah.
- He was crucified under Pontius Pilate.
- He was crucified on the eve of the Jewish Passover.
- Darkness and an earthquake occurred when he died.
- His disciples believed he rose from the dead.
- His disciples were willing to die for their belief.
- Christianity spread rapidly as far as Rome.
- His disciples denied the Roman gods and worshiped Jesus as God.[19]

The story line about Jesus from these non-Christian sources lines up exactly with the New Testament! In light of this evidence, how could anyone deny that Jesus existed? And how could anyone deny the veracity of the New Testament when these non-Christian sources affirm the core truths of it? So we know that Jesus claimed to be God and the Messiah, and these claims are proven by his outstanding résumé of fulfilled prophecies, his one-of-a-kind life, and the testimony of outside sources.

I was talking with a person at work who, like Doug, did not believe that a man named Jesus actually existed. He felt that Jesus was a fairy tale, just a myth, not someone to be taken seriously. So I shared the summary of the twelve outside witnesses for the existence and person of Jesus. Then I stated, "This *myth* left footprints!"

N—Nailed to the Cross

Since skeptics have no good answer for the empty tomb, their tactic has been to try to back up one step and say that Jesus never died. Muslims do not believe that Jesus died on the cross, for the Qur'an says that he only pretended to be dead (Sura 4:157–59). Orthodox Muslims have long held that God made someone else look like Jesus, and this person was mistakenly crucified as Christ. The leading contender for this person is Judas.[20] Ahmadiya Muslims believe that Jesus actually fled to India, and in Srinagar, Kashmir, there's a shrine that supposedly marks his real burial place.[21] During the nineteenth century, a new explanation for the empty tomb arose. This was the "swoon theory," in which Jesus did not die on the cross but merely swooned from exhaustion or drugs and was revived by the cool, dark air of the tomb.[22]

Let's see why the swoon theory just can't stand on its feet: First, both enemies and friends believed Jesus was dead. The Jews believed Jesus was dead, and Jesus's friends believed it. The Romans, who were professional executioners and experts at crucifixion, also believed it. Evidence of a crucifixion was found in 1968, when the remains of a first-century crucifixion victim were found in a Jerusalem cave. The heel bone of this man had a seven-inch nail driven through it, and his lower arms showed evidence of nails as well.[23] Second, Jesus was embalmed in seventy-five pounds of bandages and spices. How could Joseph of Arimathea and Nicodemus (John 19:40) have mistakenly embalmed a living Jesus? Third, even if everyone was wrong about Jesus being dead when placed in the tomb, how could such a badly injured and bleeding man still be alive thirty-six hours later? If you want a visual description of the physical horrors of the crucifixion, see the Mel Gibson film *The Passion of the Christ*. After seeing that film, try to imagine Jesus living in a cold, damp tomb without any medical attention for thirty-six hours! Fourth, even if Jesus did survive the cold, damp, dark tomb with no medical attention, how could he unwrap himself, move the two-ton rock up and away from the inside of the tomb, get by the crack Roman guards (who would have been killed for allowing such an escape), and then convince the scared, scattered, skeptical, cowardly disciples that he had triumphed over death? If all of this did happen, the disciples would have rushed Jesus to a trauma unit! Fifth, don't forget that non-Christian, unsympathetic writers clearly affirmed that Jesus died by crucifixion.

Jesus died by crucifixion just as the Bible describes. Consider the facts about Jesus's death:

- Sweat drops of blood in Garden of Gethsemane—hermatidrosis (Luke 22:44)
- Beaten before Caiaphas (Matt. 26:67)
- Beaten before the Romans with a cat-o'-nine-tails (Matt. 27:26, 30; Mark 15:15)
- Made to carry his own cross (John 19:17)
- Crucified with spikes through wrists and feet; asphyxiation (Mark 15:25)
- Nature of his wounds (whipping, crucifixion, and spear in side) ensured death (Matt. 27:26, 35; John 19:34–35)
- Death witnessed by his mother, friends, and closest disciple (John 19:25)
- Romans, professional executioners, certified him as dead (Mark 15:44–45; John 19:33–35)
- Double-checked by Pilate to confirm death (Mark 15:43–45)
- Buried (Matt. 27:58–60)
- Burial in tomb of Joseph of Arimathea (a member of the Sanhedrin) never denied by the Jews (John 19:38–42)
- Death recorded by non-Christian writers from the first and second centuries (e.g. Josephus, Tacitus, Thallus, Lucian, Phelgon, and the Jewish Talmud)
- Death verified by modern medical authorities in light of historical evidence. In an article in the *Journal of the American Medical Society*, Dr. William D. Edwards and others concluded: "Clearly, the weight of historical and medical evidence indicates that Jesus was dead before the wound to his side was inflicted and supports the traditional view that the spear, thrust between his right rib, probably perforated not only the right lung but also the pericardium and heart and thereby ensured his death. Accordingly, interpretations based on the assumption that Jesus did not die on the cross appear to be at odds with modern medical knowledge."[24]

We have seen that the Messiah was prophesied to die on the cross (Isa. 53:2–12) and that Jesus fulfilled that prophecy. But a question we hear a lot is why the cross was necessary. Lee Strobel asked Dr. Alexander Metherell, who had extensively studied the historical,

archaeological, and medical data concerning the death of Jesus of
Nazareth, this question: "Jesus intentionally walked into the arms
of his betrayer, he didn't resist arrest, he didn't defend himself at his
trial—it was clear that he was willingly subjecting himself to what
you've described as a humiliating and agonizing form of torture. And
I'd like to know why. What could have possibly motivated a person
to agree to endure this sort of punishment?"

Metherell replied:

> Jesus knew what was coming, and he was willing to go through
> it, because this was the only way he could redeem us—by serving
> as our substitute and paying the death penalty that we deserve
> because of our rebellion against God. That was his whole mis-
> sion in coming to earth. . . . So when you ask what motivated
> him, well . . . I suppose the answer can be summed up in one
> word—and that would be *love*.[25]

E—Empty Tomb

Jesus claimed to be God and the Messiah, and he proved these claims
by his outstanding résumé of fulfilled prophecies, his one of a kind life,
the testimony of outside sources, and his death on the cross because
of his love for us. Now we move to the most essential point that while
Jesus died and was buried in a tomb, three days later that tomb was
empty. Sensational crimes involving missing people or bodies unexpect-
edly showing up dominate the news from time to time. But as Strobel
says, "Rarely do you encounter an empty tomb. . . . The issue with Jesus
isn't that he was nowhere to be seen. It's that he *was* seen, alive; he *was*
seen, dead; and he *was* seen, alive once more."[26]

Consider the evidence that Jesus rose from the grave:

- A crack Roman guard was posted at the tomb, and a seal was
  set on the stone. To break this seal warranted the punishment
  of death (Matt. 27:64–66).
- On Sunday morning, the tomb was empty, and no one could
  produce a body (Matt. 28:6).
- The stone was rolled away, and the guards were knocked un-
  conscious (Matt. 28:2–4).

- The Jews admitted the tomb was empty and created the cover-up story that the disciples had stolen the body of Jesus (Matt. 28:11–15).
- Angels were present who told the good news that Jesus had risen from the dead (Matt. 28:4–7).
- Jesus made twelve different physical appearances over forty days to more than five hundred people.

Consider the order of the twelve appearances of Christ:[27]

Persons	Saw	Heard	Touched	Other Evidence
1. Mary Magdalene (John 20:10–18)	X	X	X	Empty tomb
2. Mary Magdalene and other Mary (Matt. 28:1–10)	X	X	X	Empty tomb (empty tomb and grave clothes also in Luke 24:1–12)
3. Peter (1 Cor. 15:5) and John (John 20:1–10)	X	X		Empty tomb, grave clothes
4. Two disciples (Luke 24:13–35)	X	X		Ate with him
5. Ten apostles (Luke 24:36–49; John 20:19–23)	X	X	X**	Saw wounds, ate food
6. Eleven apostles (John 20:24–31)	X	X	X**	Saw wounds
7. Seven apostles (John 21)	X	X		Ate food
8. All apostles (Matt. 28:16–20; Mark 16:14–18)	X	X		
9. 500 brethren (1 Cor. 15:6)	X	X*		
10. James (1 Cor. 15:7)	X	X*		
11. All apostles (Acts 1:4–8)	X	X		Ate with him
12. Paul (Acts 9:1–9; 1 Cor. 15:8)	X	X		

*Implied   **Offered himself to be touched

Can we go so far as to state that the empty tomb is a historical fact? Consider the following.

1. *Hostile sources admit that the tomb was empty.* Ancient historians Tacitus and Suetonius both imply that the tomb of Jesus was empty. Tacitus stated that Christ was put to death under Pontius Pilate, but then a "mischievous superstition" (the resurrection?) started in Judea and made its way even to Rome. Suetonius said that persecuted Christians were spreading "a new and mischievous religious belief."

The Jewish sources acknowledged the empty tomb. Ancient historian Josephus notes that the disciples believed in Jesus's resurrection. Josephus recorded the disciples' belief and did not dispute it. The Toledeth Jesu acknowledged the empty tomb but tried to explain it away by saying the body of Jesus was secretly moved to a second tomb. Justin Martyr and Tertullian both confirm the circulation of the lie that the disciples stole Jesus's body to explain away the empty tomb as found in Matthew 28:11–15.

Gentile sources acknowledged the empty tomb as well. Phlegon (b. ca. 80) stated that Jesus arose after death, exhibited the marks of his punishment, and showed how his hands had been pierced by nails. Roman government official Pliny the Younger described Christianity as an "excessive superstition" and a "contagious superstition," which may refer to the Christian belief and proclamation of the resurrection of Jesus. Mara Bar-Serapion wrote to his son that the Jews executed their wise King but that he lived on (either a reference to his teachings or the empty tomb).

2. *No ancient sources assert that the tomb still contained the body of Jesus.* This argument from silence is strong since this comes from sources hostile to Christianity, and their report further corroborates the New Testament accounts of the resurrection. If any of these ancient hostile sources believed that the tomb of Jesus was *not* empty, they surely would have said so.

3. *The proximity of the empty tomb.* Jesus taught in Israel, was crucified, and was buried in Jerusalem under Pontius Pilate. How could Christianity have survived in this geographical location, based on the premise of the resurrection, if the tomb had not been empty?

The Jewish leaders had a motive and the means to get such evidence if it were available. This is the *last* place Christianity could have been established if the tomb was not empty.

In summary, based on the evidence admitted by documents from hostile sources, the absence of contrary data, and the important information concerning the resurrection message in Jerusalem itself, there is strong support for the empty tomb based on ancient extrabiblical sources *alone*.[28] For more information on what these extrabiblical sources had to say about Jesus, see the non-Christian sources in appendix D.

As the appearances show, Jesus was seen alive, he was seen dead, and then he was seen alive once more. Nearly all people agree that Jesus was buried and that his tomb was empty three days later. But how could it be empty? Critics have come up with their own unique theories to explain away the empty tomb. Some of their theories or objections are as follows.

Hallucinations. When certain people are really devastated by a loss of someone they loved, sometimes they see this person in the form of a hallucination (however, this condition is very rare). The disciples had recently lost Jesus whom they loved, and the appearance accounts are nothing more than a recorded description of hallucinations. This theory has two flaws: (1) Hallucinations, like dreams, are not experienced by groups, but only by individuals. Over a forty-day period, Jesus appeared a number of different times and on a number of different occasions to a number of different people. Hallucinations are generally experienced by paranoid or schizophrenic individuals, and that certainly does not describe the disciples, nor could it be true of all of those who were eyewitnesses of Jesus's appearances.[29] (2) Let's assume that all of the disciples had this hallucination and proclaimed Jesus was risen from the dead. All the Jewish and Roman authorities had to do to stop this movement was to carry Jesus's dead body from the tomb, put it on a cart, and parade it through the streets of Jerusalem. That would stop the hallucinations and the movement of Christianity! Remember that these authorities dearly wanted to stop Christianity, and if they could have produced his body, they would have.

The disciples stole Jesus's body. The earliest Jewish response to the resurrection was not to deny the empty tomb but to explain it away by saying that Jesus's disciples stole his body in the night. Are we to believe that the disciples, who now were hiding in fear for their lives, had enough courage to go to the tomb, overpower the Roman guards, break the seal, and cart away the body of Jesus? And for what? To proclaim him risen when they knew he was not? Remember that the disciples paid the ultimate price for this message of resurrection—their own deaths!

Witnesses went to the wrong tomb. The women and the disciples simply went to the wrong tomb and, finding it empty, declared that

Jesus had risen from the dead. But wouldn't Joseph of Arimathea know where his tomb was? Wouldn't the soldiers who were guarding it know? And wouldn't the Pharisees, who would have loved to produce the dead body of Jesus for all to see, know where Jesus was buried?

Moreover, if the disciples went to the *wrong* tomb, this statement assumes that there was a *right* tomb—the place where Jesus lay entombed. How do we then explain the appearances of a resurrected Jesus twelve different times? The empty tomb was not what convinced most of the disciples; the appearances of Jesus are what changed them forever.

Judas was substituted for Jesus. As mentioned earlier, many Muslims believe that Judas, not Jesus, was actually crucified on the cross. But there is no evidence for such a mix-up; the authoritative source for this theory (the Qur'an) came more than six hundred years after the fact. This would require us to believe that everyone (disciples, Roman guards, Pilate, Jews, Jesus's family and friends) was mistaken about who was killed on the cross. Are we supposed to believe that Jesus's enemies would have allowed a switch at the last moment? If Jesus wasn't killed, then why was the tomb of the man who was killed empty, and how did he do it? Furthermore, the non-Christian witnesses were all wrong when they referred to Jesus being crucified on the cross.

The New Testament writers copied pagan resurrection myths. This theory and the discrepancy theory are the ones most commonly heard in the workplace. Skeptics say that the resurrection is a myth because the New Testament writers just copied supposed resurrection stories of mythical characters like Marduk, Adonis, and Osiris. We have already seen, however, that the events of the New Testament are not myth but are based on evidence supported by eyewitnesses, archaeology, and outside sources.

This myth idea cannot explain away why the tomb is empty. And it cannot negate the witness of the non-Christian sources. Surely the unsympathetic sources would have cited the comparison between the two resurrection accounts if they thought the New Testament was copying from pagan myths. Finally, no Greek or Roman myth spoke of the literal incarnation of a monotheistic God into human form by way of a virgin birth, followed by his death and resurrection.[30] The parallel of a dying and rising god does not appear until AD 150, more than one hundred years after the origin of Christianity.[31]

The discrepancies in the resurrection accounts mean the whole story is discredited. Skeptics say that there are so many differences in the resurrection accounts that the whole story is thrown into question. If the writers couldn't get the details straight—such as how many angels were at the tomb—how could they get anything else straight? We learned in chapter 11 that discrepancies are not contradictions but rather something that must be investigated. We saw in chapter 10 that the various differences in the Gospel accounts negate the charge of collusion. But are the differences so serious that they take away from the resurrection story? Of course not, for every one can be explained. As we saw in chapter 11 concerning the number of angels at the tomb, where there are two, there is always one! Matthew simply focuses on the angel who spoke while John refers to the number of angels he saw. For answers to other supposed discrepancies about the resurrection story, check out the answers in the book *When Skeptics Ask*.[32]

So the tomb really was empty. What does this all mean? Jesus made some grandiose claims to be God and the Messiah, but could he back up these claims? We examined his outstanding résumé of all of the prophecies he completely fulfilled; his one-of-a-kind life, which was sinless and full of miracles and wonderful words; the testimony of outside sources that confirm his existence, claims, crucifixion, and resurrection; and his death on the cross because of his love for us. Most important, we have seen that the tomb in which he was placed was empty three days later, just as he predicted. The only probable explanation for the tomb being empty is that Jesus rose again from the dead and proved his claim to be God and the Messiah. As someone has said: "The tomb of Buddha—occupied; the tomb of Muhammad—occupied; the tomb of Jesus—empty. You do the math!"

D—Demonstrated Results

Historian Kenneth Scott Latourette said, "As the centuries pass the evidence is accumulating that, measured by His effect on history, Jesus is the most influential life ever lived on this planet. That influence appears to be mounting."[33] Author Martin J. Scott wrote, "The influence of Jesus on mankind is today as strong as it was when He dwelt among men."[34] Noted historian Philip Schaff observed, "That ministry [of Jesus] lasted only three years—and yet in these three years is condensed the deepest meaning of the history of religion. No great life ever passed so swiftly, so quietly, so humbly, so far removed from the noise and commotion of the world; and no great life after its close excited such universal and lasting interest."[35]

In recent years, many people have claimed to be the Messiah, including Jim Jones, David Koresh, and most recently, Rev. Sun Myung Moon. On March 23, 2004, more than a dozen lawmakers attended a ceremony at the Dirkson Senate Office Building in Washington, D.C., to honor Sun Myung Moon. A crown was placed on his head by Rep. Danny Davis (D-Ill.), and Moon spoke, claiming that he was "sent to Earth . . . to save the world's six billion people. . . . Emperors, kings and presidents . . . have declared to all Heaven and Earth that Reverend Sun Myung Moon is none other than humanity's Savior, Messiah, Returning Lord and True Parent."[36] He first announced he was the Messiah in 1990.

When someone claims to be the Messiah, those to whom the claims have been made should see results.

- *Jim Jones's demonstrated results*. He founded his church in 1977. He later claimed at various times to be God, Buddha, and Lenin. In 1978 at Jones's command, 914 people (including Jones) committed suicide or were murdered. The group is now defunct.
- *David Koresh's demonstrated results*. He led a shootout on February 28, 1993, that left ten people dead: four agents from the Bureau of Alcohol, Tobacco and Firearms and six of his followers, the Branch Davidians. Fifty-one days later, on April 19, 1993, Koresh and seventy-four followers, including twenty-one children, were killed when their compound burned to the ground. His errant claims to be Jesus and the Messiah had not only religious but national reverberations that last to this day, for investigations were made of the federal agents and then Attorney General Janet Reno. Timothy McVeigh chose the second anniversary of the fire as the date to blow up the federal building in Oklahoma City, killing 168 people in 1995.
- *Rev. Sun Myung Moon's demonstrated results*. He is the leader of a deviant cult. He received an eighteen-month prison sentence in 1982 for tax fraud and conspiracy to obstruct justice. For more information about the results of Sun Myung Moon's teachings, go to the Watchman Fellowship's website at www.watchman.org.

What are the demonstrated results of Jesus's claims to be the Messiah and the fulfillment of these claims? Consider the effect on his disciples, on time, and on missions throughout the centuries.

The demonstrated results Jesus's claims had on his disciples:

- They abandoned their long-held sacred beliefs and practices, such as the animal sacrifice system, the supremacy of the law of Moses, strict monotheism from worshiping one God to also worshiping Jesus as God, observation of the Sabbath, and belief in a conquering Messiah.[37] Moreover, it wasn't just the New Testament writers who made this change—thousands of Jerusalem Jews, including Pharisees, converted to Christianity.
- They adopted radical new beliefs, such as observing Sunday as the new day of worship, baptism as a new sign of the new covenant, and communion as an act to remember Christ's sacrifice for their sins.
- They did not deny their testimony under persecution or threat of death. Even though they could have saved themselves by recanting, no one did. Eleven out of the twelve were martyred for their faith (the only survivor was John, who was exiled to the Greek Isle of Patmos). Why would they have died for a lie? "It was the appearances of Jesus that turned [the disciples] from scared, scattered, skeptical cowards into the greatest peaceful missionary force in history."[38]

The demonstrated results of Jesus are with us to this day. Think about how we *reckon time*. The abbreviation BC stands for "Before Christ" and AD is Latin and stands for *Anno Domini* ("in the year of the Lord"). The *Anno Domini* dating system is the only system in everyday use in the Western Hemisphere and the main system for commercial and scientific use in the rest of the world. It was developed by a monk named Dionysius Exiguus (a Scythian) in Rome in 525, as an outcome of his work on calculating the date of Easter. One man stands as the divider of the centuries in our world, and that man is Jesus Christ.

The demonstrated results of Jesus can be seen in the church's spread throughout the ages. While many in our world today look with disdain at the missionary spread of the church, they must admit that the spread of Christianity has resulted not only in churches, but also in hospitals, leprosy clinics, orphanages, schools, better treatment of women, and surprisingly, freedom of religion. Look at the United States, which was founded on the principle of freedom of religion. Now compare the United States with a Muslim country and try to find that same freedom!

"But religion has sparked so many wars!" This is a common objection to Christianity heard in the workplace. But the same could be said for politics. Politics can't be eliminated from society; we can only try to find the right political formula. And neither can we eliminate our spiritual needs; we can only find the right religion. A good start would be to find one committed to a leader who said, "Blessed are the peacemakers"; "Love your enemies"; "Bless those who curse you"; and "Turn the other cheek."

If you check the facts, atheists easily hold the record for mass killings—for example, Lenin, Stalin, Mao. War is horrible, and yet by sheer numbers the slaughter of millions by these atheists dwarfs anything done in religious wars.

I was talking to a college student recently who said, "Religion has caused more suffering, wars, and violence than any other cause."

I asked her to give me the number of people killed.

She said, with the Crusades and a few other religious wars she might have heard of, maybe a million deaths. (Some experts used to teach that the Thirty Years' War in Germany caused eight million deaths, but modern experts have proved that it was more like two hundred thousand; and in fact, the population of Germany actually increased during that war.)

I shared with her that most of the people who have died as a result of war have done so in the twentieth century and that most of the killing was done in the name of secular (not religious) beliefs. I then asked her who was the worst murderer of them all.

She said, "That's easy—it was Hitler."

"Nope," I said. "He's only number three. Try again."

She wrinkled her brow and guessed Stalin, and I said that most experts place him at number two with twenty million killed.

"The one who wins top prize as the number one murderer in history is Chairman Mao, with an estimated forty million. Notice that the top two were Communists and Hitler was a radical disciple of Social Darwinism. All of these are based on atheistic beliefs, not religious beliefs."

She didn't know what to say.

When looking for the cause of war, try greed, selfishness, pride, hate, unforgiveness—the very opposite to Jesus's teachings.

"But what about the Crusades?" This is another objection often brought up to oppose the positive results of Jesus on others. Most people, especially atheists, do not know the history behind the Crusades to properly evaluate them. September 11, 2001, might give us a different perspective on the Crusades. The founder of Islam was Muhammad, and he and his followers were rejected at first. It wasn't until Muhammad led several successful military conquests between 622 and 630 that his popularity grew. He forced people to convert by using the sword and led raids and shared the booty with his followers. Christianity began as a peaceful faith, while Islam began as a military faith. In the early days of Christianity, one might have been killed for becoming a Christian; in the early days of Islam's growth, one might have been killed for not becoming a Muslim! The Crusades did not begin until nearly 1100, more than a thousand years after the origin of Christianity. The Muslims had captured the Holy Land and were destroying sites and artifacts important to Christianity and forcing Christians to convert to Islam or die. The primary reason for the Crusades was to rescue Christians being tortured by Muslims and to take back the land the Muslims had previously seized by military conquest from the Christians.

So we have seen that Jesus made claims to be the Messiah and God in the flesh, and he proved it for all to see. The impact of Jesus the Christ has been summed up in the following essay titled "One Solitary Life":

Here is a man who was born in an obscure village, the child of a peasant woman. He grew up in another village. He worked in a carpenter shop until He was thirty. Then for three years He was an itinerant preacher.

He never owned a home. He never wrote a book. He never held an office. He never had a family. He never went to college. He never put His foot inside a big city. He never traveled two hundred miles from the place He was born. He never did any of the things that usually accompanies greatness. He had no credentials but Himself. . . .

While still a young man, the tide of popular opinion turned against Him. His friends ran away. One of them denied Him. He was turned over to His enemies. He went through the mockery of a trial. He was nailed upon a cross between two thieves. While He was dying, His executioners gambled for the only piece of property He had on earth—His coat. When He was dead, He was laid in a borrowed grave through the pity of a friend.

Nineteen long centuries have come and gone, and today He is a centerpiece of the human race and leader of the column of progress.

I am far within the mark when I say that all the armies that ever marched, all the navies that were ever built; all the parliaments that ever sat and all the kings that ever reigned, put together, have not affected the life of man upon this earth as powerfully as has that one solitary life.[39]

In Matthew 16:13, Jesus asked his disciples who people thought he was. After receiving various inaccurate replies, he looked at his disciples, the ones who knew him better than anyone else, and said, "But what about you? Who do you say that I am?" (v. 15). That same question he asks all of us. May we give the same answer as Peter: "You are the Christ, the Son of the living God" (v. 16).

Once we know who Jesus is, how are we to respond to him? Our next chapter will show us that since Jesus is who he says he is, he is the only way to God.

CROWNED Evidences Checklist

C—*Claims*
- Jesus claimed to be the Messiah.
- Jesus claimed to be God in the flesh.

R—*Résumé*
- There are 191 prophecies in the Old Testament about the coming of the Christ.
- Jesus fulfilled every one of them.

O—*One-of-a-Kind* Life
- Jesus lived a sinless life.
- Jesus did many miracles.
- No one ever spoke like Jesus.

W—*Witness* by Outside Sources
- Some try to deny that a man named Jesus ever lived, died on a cross, or was reported to have risen from the dead.
- We know of twelve non-Christian writers who mentioned Jesus within 150 years of his life.
- The picture they portray of Jesus lines up exactly with that of the New Testament.

N—*Nailed* to the Cross
- Some people use the mistaken person theory or the swoon theory to try to deny that Jesus ever died.
- We know that Jesus died on the cross because of the physical effects of the crucifixion and

because the Jews never denied Jesus was dead
and non-Christian writers attest to his death.
* The cross was necessary to give us access to
God.

E—*Empty* Tomb
* Consider the evidence that Jesus rose from
the grave.
* Consider the twelve appearances of Jesus.
* Recognize that no one has come up with an
adequate theory to explain the empty tomb
except that Jesus arose!

D—*Demonstrated* Results
* We can see the results in the lives of Jesus's
disciples.
* Our dating system is based on Jesus's birth.
* Nothing or no one has impacted life on this
earth more than this one solitary life.

Digging Deeper on Jesus as the Son of God

Buell, Jon. *Jesus: God, Ghost or Guru?* Grand Rapids: Zondervan,
1978.

Geisler, Norman. *Baker Encyclopedia of Christian Apologetics.* Grand
Rapids: Baker Books, 1999, 127–50, 381–85.

Geisler, Norman, and Ron Brooks. *When Skeptics Ask.* Grand Rapids:
Baker Books, 1990, 101–40.

Geisler, Norman, and Frank Turek. *I Don't Have Enough Faith to Be
an Atheist.* Wheaton: Crossway, 2004, 221–74, 300–354.

Habermas, Gary. *The Historical Jesus.* Joplin, MO: College Press,
1996.

Strobel, Lee. *The Case for Christ.* Grand Rapids: Zondervan, 1998.

Zacharias, Ravi. *Jesus Among Other Gods.* Nashville, TN: Word,
2000.

13

Is There Only One Way to God?

"I can't believe those Southern Baptists are so arrogant!" Laura steamed. "It's bad enough they have churches on every corner, and now this."

"What's got you so steamed up?" I (Randy) asked my business friend as four of us sat down for lunch overlooking a marsh in Charleston, South Carolina.

"Didn't you see Friday's paper?" she spat. "There was an article in it telling how the Southern Baptists have decided to try to convert Muslims and are sending food to Iraq in boxes with Bible verses in Arabic on them. It went on to say that they also believe that Jews need to accept Jesus or be doomed. Who do they think they are, God or something?"

The fact is I *had* read the June 20, 2003, newspaper article "Southern Baptists Vow to Preach to Muslims." Laura's recollection was almost a verbatim account of the article, which I had read with great interest. My interest stemmed from the fact that I know and appreciate the heart of the Southern Baptist Convention (the largest Protestant denomination in the world). Its passion for evangelism is what motivates and drives it, from evangelistic events to the planting of churches to its extensive mission accomplishments. The same is true of many other evangelical churches as well. But what Laura couldn't understand or appreciate is that even more than Christians' passion for evangelism is their passion for the truth. I told her that the Bible, God's Word, declares that Jesus *is* the only way to God (John 14:6), and without him *all* are lost (Acts 4:12). Since that is true according to God, someone had better tell the world while we still can, no matter the cost.

"This is why Christianity is viewed as being so narrow-minded. Christians say they're the only ones who are right, the only ones who have the truth and are going to heaven, and everyone else is wrong. They're right, and the Muslims, Jews, Mormons, Hindus, and anyone else who disagrees with them are toast."

I said, "Laura, you asked, 'Who do they think they are, God or something?'"

"Right," she smirked. I continued, "So what you're saying is that if man says it (like a Christian), then it doesn't mean anything. But if God says it, then it means something. Is that what you're saying?" Laura began to fidget uncomfortably and said, "Okay, if God said it, fine. But not a bunch of overzealous Christians!"

So I replied, "What if God did say it and they're just repeating what he said? Would that make it all right?"

Cornered, Laura reluctantly said, "Okay, if God said it, then I will listen."

I said, "Let's look together to see what God has to say about how to get to heaven."

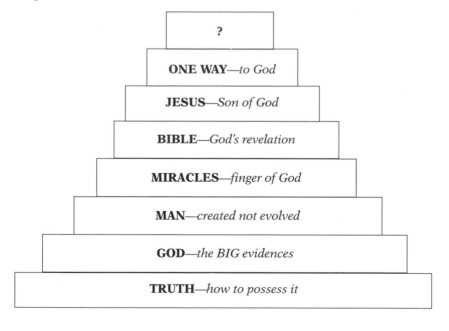

In the course of time, a few hours or many lunches, it will be important to help a person like Laura "connect the dots" of the Bible that will lead to repentance. The "Hot Topics around the Watercooler" section was not assembled randomly but was laid out in a logical succession to show that there is only one way to God, and that way is Jesus Christ.

The chart above illustrates the stair-step progression we made from chapters 5 through 12. The foundation that must be laid first is the matter of truth and who possesses it, as given in chapter 5. The principles of the POSSESSOR acrostic are the ground rules for the discussion and will aid in getting someone to agree that there is truth in this world and help that person to recognize it, especially in reference to other religions.

Once we have agreed on the rules for truth, we move to examining the existence of God as given in chapter 6. A person willing to abide by the laws of truth who examines the BIG evidences will have to concede that God exists and that this is a theistic universe. Establishing in a co-worker's mind the reality of truth and God's existence will be pivotal to everything else. There are three major religious worldviews today: *theism*—God made all (he is the Painter of the painting); *pantheism*—God is all (the Painter is the painting); and *atheism*—there is no God (there is no Painter of the painting). Now we know that only one worldview, theism, is correct and the other two are wrong. So only theistic religions like Judaism, Islam, and Christianity can be right, for they are the only theistic religions. The field has been narrowed in the quest of who has the way to God.

From chapter 6 we learned that God created the universe and put a moral law in human hearts. Thus it follows that since God created the universe, he also created humans, as we saw in chapter 7. This realization throws atheism and evolution out the window and makes us reexamine ourselves as created beings of God who live in his universe. If your friend struggles with suffering and evil as questions of God's existence, chapter 8 will help.

Since God created this world, he can intervene in it to accomplish his will. God's finger intervening in our world is called "miracles," as we saw in chapter 9. So now the miracles of the Bible should no longer be a hindrance to belief.

The three theistic religions cannot all be right, for while they agree in some places, they totally disagree in others. In fact, they hold opposite views, and opposites can't both be true (see chapter 5). Consider the differences between Islam and Christianity.

Islam	Christianity
God: only one person	*God*: three persons in one God
Humanity: good by nature	*Humanity*: sinful by nature
Jesus: merely a man, not God	*Jesus*: more than a man, also God
Death of Christ: he didn't die or rise again	*Death of Christ*: he died and rose again in the same body
Bible: corrupted	*Bible*: not corrupted
Salvation: by works when good deeds outweigh bad ones	*Salvation*: not by works but is a free gift for all who believe

How can we begin to know who is right? Since this is a theistic world, we have to assume that God would want to reveal himself to his creatures. He did this by giving his spokesmen (identified by miracles) his word, which they recorded as sacred writings.

But all three theistic religions have sacred writings, so what do we do now? First, we look for the writers who were verified by God through miracles. This disqualifies Islam, for Muhammad performed no miracles. When challenged to perform miracles to prove he was a prophet from God, he refused and said he was just a man. No clearly defined miracles are in the Qur'an and were only attributed to Muhammad in writings one hundred to two hundred years later. Indeed, while the Qur'an affirms that Jesus did miracles (Sura 5:113), it admits that Muhammad refused to do them (Sura 3:181). Judaism has miracle prophets in the Old Testament, and Christianity has them in the New Testament.

Second, we examine the sacred writings to see if they are trustworthy. The Qur'an is deemed untrustworthy because there is no verification for its accurate transmission from the originals, and what we have is full of errors and inconsistencies.[1] Judaism and Christianity agree that the Old Testament is God's Word, but what about the New Testament? We learned in chapters 10 and 11 that the New Testament has eyewitness accounts that are accurate and were recorded very early. Its events are verified by both archaeology and outside, non-Christian sources. The evidence uncovered reveals that Jesus really existed and that the New Testament writers were accurate in their writings. So the field has now been narrowed down to one in the quest of who has the way to God.

Finally, we come to the central theme of the Bible: Jesus Christ. Since the New Testament is true, we examine what the writers have to say about Jesus. Was he a liar, lunatic, or Lord? After a careful examination using the CROWNED acrostic, we must conclude that Jesus is who he claims to be—the Messiah and God in the flesh.

It was Jesus, not any religious denomination, who said, "I am the way and the truth and the life. No one comes to the Father except through me" (John 14:6). Why do we need salvation, and how is Jesus the only way to God? We use the acrostic ONE WAY to answer these questions. This is an effective way to share the gospel with a person. The ONE WAY acrostic follows three themes: a problem, a solution, and a response.

First, let's look at the *problem*.

O—Offense

We have broken God's law and committed an offense against him. When we break God's law, the Bible calls our actions *sin*. The word for sin in the New Testament means "to miss the mark." Sin is a failure to live up to God's standards. We were created to have fellowship with God, but we chose to go our own way and rebel against God and his rules, laws, and standards. A criminal is someone who breaks the law. All sinners, then, are criminals before him.

Who has sinned? Everyone has sinned and has a black mark against his or her name. "For all have sinned and fall short of the glory of God" (Rom. 3:23). Before we accept Christ's gift of salvation, all of us are sinners and criminals before God. Moreover, since God is a just God, every sinner is also condemned. We committed the crime, the judgment was made, and the sentence carried out.

What is the result of sin? "For the wages of sin is death, but the gift of God is eternal life in Christ Jesus our Lord" (Rom. 6:23). The "wages," or result, of our sin is death. "Death" here means a spiritual separation from God. That is our sentence, our punishment. When Adam first sinned in the Garden of Eden, the immediate result of his sin was separation from God. God searched for Adam, asking, "Adam, where are you?" and Adam hid from God (Gen. 3:9–10). Physical death was the ultimate result. God is holy and humans are sinful. That means that there is this separation, a great gulf between the two.

"Wait! I'm not that bad!" someone exclaims. "For whoever keeps the whole law and yet stumbles at just one point is guilty of breaking all of it" (James 2:10). If you have committed one sin, you are guilty.

If you have broken one of the Ten Commandments, James says here that you have broken them all. Jesus said that if you hate someone in your heart, you are guilty of murdering that person before God (Matt. 5:21–22). Everyone has broken God's law. Everyone has committed an offense. We all are sinners. We all are condemned to an eternity of separation from God.

N — Need

Our situation goes from bad to worse. The need is that we stand condemned before God and are unable to satisfy God's just demands. There is nothing we can do to satisfy God and his standards of justice. Look at the following verses.

- "All of us have become like one who is unclean, and all our righteous acts are like filthy rags; we all shrivel up like a leaf, and like the wind our sins sweep us away" (Isa. 64:6). The best things we can do, even religious activities, are nothing more than filthy rags to a holy God.
- "Therefore no one will be declared righteous in his sight by observing the law; rather, through the law we become conscious of sin" (Rom. 3:20). Keeping the law that was given to the Jews will not make us righteous. Rather, it will make us aware of how destitute we are, for we will constantly fail in the attempt and thus be conscious of our sin.
- "Know that a man is not justified by observing the law, but by faith in Jesus Christ. So we, too, have put our faith in Christ Jesus that we may be justified by faith in Christ and not by observing the law, because by observing the law *no one will be justified*" (Gal. 2:16). No one who tries to observe the law will be justified. No one.
- "Clearly no one is justified before God by the law, because, 'The righteous will live by faith'" (Gal. 3:11). The law will not justify us, for only faith can justify us in the sight of God.
- "For it is by grace you have been saved, through faith—and this not from yourselves, it is the gift of God—not by works, so that no one can boast" (Eph. 2:8–9). All good deeds, all religious activities, are useless in bridging the gap between God

and humans, for the gap is too far for us to overcome. Left to ourselves, our situation is hopeless.

- "The law is only a shadow of the good things that are coming—not the realities themselves. For this reason it can never, by the same sacrifices repeated endlessly year after year, make perfect those who draw near to worship" (Heb. 10:1).

Thankfully, there is a *solution*! Billy Graham once said that religion is man reaching up to God while Christianity is God reaching down to man. Since we could not reach God, God decided to reach down to us and provide the solution.

E—Earn Forgiveness for Us

The Bible reveals that because of our sinful condition, we are in desperate need of a substitute. We need someone who can pay our debt—death (Rom. 6:23)—and clean us so that we can be found blameless according to the Lord's morally perfect standard. The solution would have to do what we could not, and that is earn forgiveness for ourselves. Someone would have to pay our debt. Someone would have to take our punishment. Someone would have to take our place and earn forgiveness. But how could this happen?

In the Old Testament book of Leviticus, animal sacrifices were performed by the Jews to restore broken fellowship with God. When a wrong was committed in Bible times, the person responsible brought an unblemished animal to the altar as an offering for the sin (Lev. 4:1–3). Then the person responsible or the priest laid a hand on the animal's head—an act that symbolized the transfer of guilt from the offender to the innocent animal (v. 4). With this exchange complete, the priest killed the animal, sprinkling some of its blood on one side of the altar and pouring the remainder of its blood at the altar's base (5:5–9).

The emphasis on blood was important, as God revealed: "The life of the flesh is in the blood, and I have given it to you on the altar to make atonement for your souls; for it is the blood by reason of the life that makes atonement" (Lev. 17:11 NASB). The Hebrew word for atonement means "to cover." God was saying that the blood would cover the sin, putting it out of sight and bringing "at-one-ment," or peace, between the sinner and the Lord. Animal sacrifice was a common occurrence in ancient Israel. It was a stark reminder to the people that they were sinners and in continual need of being reconciled to God.

The writer of Hebrews makes three important observations about the animal sacrifices.

1. Sin requires the sacrifice of an animal, and its blood brought forgiveness. Only with the death and blood of the animal would God forgive the person's sinful offense. "But only the high priest entered the inner room, and that only once a year, and never without blood, which he offered for himself and for the sins the people had committed in ignorance" (9:7). "The blood of goats and bulls and the ashes of a heifer sprinkled on those who are ceremonially unclean sanctify them so that they are outwardly clean" (9:13). "When Moses had proclaimed every commandment of the law to all the people, he took the blood of calves, together with water, scarlet wool and branches of hyssop, and sprinkled the scroll and all the people. He said, 'This is the blood of the covenant, which God has commanded you to keep.' In the same way, he sprinkled with the blood both the tabernacle and everything used in its ceremonies. In fact, the law requires that nearly everything be cleansed with blood, and without the shedding of blood there is no forgiveness" (9:19–22).

2. The sacrifices were not permanent. The frequent slaying of animals as sin offerings shows that their blood was insufficient to take away sins permanently. "The law is only a shadow of the good things that are coming—not the realities themselves. For this reason it can never, by the same sacrifices repeated endlessly year after year, make perfect those who draw near to worship. . . . But those sacrifices are an annual reminder of sins, because it is impossible for the blood of bulls and goats to take away sins" (10:1, 3–4).

3. A better sacrifice was needed—a perfect "lamb" who could remove sin from people forever. But who could be worthy enough to be our sacrifice?

W — Worthy

For this sacrifice to be worthy, it would have to have three characteristics. First, the perfect candidate would have to have a body to be sacrificed; he would have to be a man. Second, this candidate would have to be sinless, for God would not accept a blemished offering. Third, this candidate would have to be eternal, or the sacrifice would lose effect over time. Only one person has ever fulfilled these three requirements:

1. He would have to be a *man*. That is, the candidate would have to have a body to be able to die for us. "But when the time had fully come, God sent his Son, born of a woman, born under law, to redeem those under law, that we might receive the full rights of sons" (Gal. 4:4–5). "Therefore, when Christ came into the world, he said: 'Sacrifice and offering you did not desire, but a body you prepared for me; with burnt offerings and sin offerings you were not pleased. Then I said, "Here I am—it is written about me in the scroll—I have come to do your will, O God"''" (Heb. 10:5–7). Jesus Christ was a man: he fulfills the first requirement.

2. He would have to be *sinless*. "How much more, then, will the blood of Christ, who through the eternal Spirit offered himself unblemished to God, cleanse our consciences from acts that lead to death, so that we may serve the living God!" (Heb. 9:14). "For you know that it was not with perishable things such as silver or gold that you were redeemed from the empty way of life handed down to you from your forefathers, but with the precious blood of Christ, a lamb without blemish or defect" (1 Peter 1:18–19). Jesus Christ was not only a man; he lived a sinless life and thus fulfilled the second requirement.

3. He would have to be *eternal* for his sacrifice of himself to apply to all and forever. "Nor did he enter heaven to offer himself again and again, the way the high priest enters the Most Holy Place every year with blood that is not his own. Then Christ would have had to suffer many times since the creation of the world. But now he has appeared once for all at the end of the ages to do away with sin by the sacrifice of himself" (Heb. 9:25–26). "Day after day every priest stands and performs his religious duties; again and again he offers the same sacrifices, which can never take away sins. But when this priest had offered for all time one sacrifice for sins, he sat down at the right hand of God" (Heb. 10:11–12). "Jesus Christ is the same yesterday and

today and forever" (Heb. 13:8). Jesus is a man, he is sinless, and he is eternal. He fulfills all three requirements.

So Jesus, the perfect candidate, came to this earth to be born with a body. That's what Christmas is all about. While on this earth, Jesus was sinless, and his sacrifice was unblemished. Finally, like God, Jesus is eternal, which kept the Old Testament problem of continually having to offer sacrifices from being our problem.

A—Act on Our Behalf

So the perfect candidate for this sacrifice was Jesus Christ. But would he do it? Would he leave the throne room of heaven, be born as a lowly man, and willingly offer himself as the Lamb to be slain for us? The writer of Hebrews answers this question. "Therefore, when Christ came into the world, he said: 'Sacrifice and offering you did not desire, but a body you prepared for me; with burnt offerings and sin offerings you were not pleased. Then I said, "Here I am—it is written about me in the scroll—I have come to do your will, O God"'" (Heb. 10:5–7). One day John the Baptist saw Christ and exclaimed, "Look, the Lamb of God, who takes away the sin of the world!" (John 1:29). Jesus willingly came to this earth to die as a lamb on the altar for us. But why?

In what ways did Christ act on our behalf? The apostle Paul answers this in Philippians 2.

- His *choice.* "Your attitude should be the same as that of Christ Jesus: Who, being in very nature God, did not consider equality with God something to be grasped" (vv. 5–6).
- His *cradle.* ". . . but made himself nothing, taking the very nature of a servant, being made in human likeness" (v. 7).
- His *cross.* "And being found in appearance as a man, he humbled himself and became obedient to death—even death on a cross!" (v. 8).
- His *crown.* "Therefore God exalted him to the highest place and gave him the name that is above every name, that at the name of Jesus every knee should bow, in heaven and on earth and under the earth, and every tongue confess that Jesus Christ is Lord, to the glory of God the Father" (vv. 9–11).

Christ acted on our behalf through his humility, unselfishness, obedience, love, and reward. The results of Christ's redemptive act on our behalf can be seen in the following verses.

- *Redeemed.* "Christ redeemed us from the curse of the law by becoming a curse for us, for it is written: 'Cursed is everyone who is hung on a tree'" (Gal. 3:13). "Who gave himself for us to redeem us from all wickedness and to purify for himself a people that are his very own, eager to do what is good" (Titus 2:14).
- *Justified.* "[We] are justified freely by his grace through the redemption that came by Christ Jesus. God presented him as a sacrifice of atonement, through faith in his blood. He did this to demonstrate his justice, because in his forbearance he had left the sins committed beforehand unpunished—he did it to demonstrate his justice at the present time, so as to be just and the one who justifies those who have faith in Jesus" (Rom. 3:24–26). "He was delivered over to death for our sins and was raised to life for our justification" (Rom. 4:25).
- *Our sin offering.* "For what the law was powerless to do in that it was weakened by the sinful nature, God did by sending his own Son in the likeness of sinful man to be a sin offering. And so he condemned sin in sinful man" (Rom. 8:3). "He himself bore our sins in his body on the tree, so that we might die to sins and live for righteousness; by his wounds you have been healed" (1 Peter 2:24).
- *Bring us to God.* "For Christ died for sins once for all, the righteous for the unrighteous, to bring you to God. He was put to death in the body but made alive by the Spirit" (1 Peter 3:18).

Let's summarize where we have been to this point. Because all of us have sinned and broken God's law, we have committed an *offense* against God. Our *need* is great because we stand condemned before God and are unable to satisfy God's just demands. We need someone who could *earn* forgiveness from God for us—someone who could pay our debt and make us clean. We need a *worthy* member of the human race—a man whose body could be sacrificed, whose life was lived without sin, and whose sacrifice of himself would obtain and perpetuate eternal salvation once for all. More important, we need someone who would actually *act* on our behalf, even if that meant his death. Jesus is that someone. He died that we might live. But how can we get his payment placed on our account?

Y—Yield to Him

Our *response* to Christ is to yield to him. Our yielding to Christ has two aspects: first, repenting, and second, placing our faith in him. The importance of repentance can be seen in the following verses:

- "I have not come to call the righteous, but sinners to repentance" (Luke 5:32).
- "I have declared to both Jews and Greeks that they must turn to God in repentance and have faith in our Lord Jesus" (Acts 20:21).
- "In the past God overlooked such ignorance, but now he commands all people everywhere to repent" (Acts 17:30).
- "The Lord is not slow in keeping his promise, as some understand slowness. He is patient with you, not wanting anyone to perish, but everyone to come to repentance" (2 Peter 3:9).

C. S. Lewis gave us this definition of repentance:

Fallen man is not simply an imperfect creature who needs improvement: he is a rebel who must lay down his arms. Laying down your arms, surrendering, saying you are sorry, realizing that you have been on the wrong track and getting ready to start life over again from the ground floor—that is the only way out of the "hole." This process of surrender—this movement full speed astern—is what Christians call repentance.[2]

Repentance is yielding to Jesus as our Savior and making him Lord of our lives.

True repentance about our sin and the Savior involves faith. Therefore, to be saved, we must place our faith in him. We cannot believe that we can earn our salvation or do any good works that will gain God's justice or forgiveness. Our faith must rest completely in his finished work for us. "God presented him as a sacrifice of atonement, through faith in his blood. He did this to demonstrate his justice, because in his forbearance he had left the sins committed beforehand unpunished—he did it to demonstrate his justice at the present time, so as to be just and the one who justifies those who have faith in Jesus" (Rom. 3:25–26). The key word in these verses is *justified*, which does not mean "just as if I never sinned," for the truth is that we are dead in sin and need a new life. Justification does refer to the act whereby God declares sinning believers righteous while they are still in their sinning state.

To explain this, Billy Graham paints a courtroom scene where God is the judge and he asks us, the accused:

God: John (or) Mary, have you loved Me with all your heart?

John/Mary: No, Your Honor.

God: Have you loved others as you have loved yourself?

John/Mary: No, Your Honor.

God: Do you believe you are a sinner and that Jesus Christ died for your sins?

John/Mary: Yes, Your Honor.

God: Then your penalty has been paid by Jesus Christ on the cross and you are pardoned. Because Christ is righteous and you believe in Christ, I now declare you legally righteous.[3]

What wonderful words of grace fall from God's lips! We can have our sins forgiven and inherit eternal life if we yield to Jesus Christ as our perfect sacrifice. Was Jesus's claim true when he said, "I am the way and the truth and the life. No one comes to the Father except through me" (John 14:6)? Yes, there is only one door to heaven, there is only one way to God, and that is through Jesus Christ alone.

Objections to Jesus Being the Only Way

1. This Is Too Narrow-Minded!

This objection has already been answered in chapter 5. We learned that:

- *Truth corresponds to the facts*. Truth "tells it like it is." If Jesus is the only way to God, then it doesn't matter whether you like it or not. It doesn't matter whether you think it is too narrow-minded. If Jesus is the only way to God (and we have seen this to be true), then it is fact.

- *Opposite ideas cannot both be true at the same time*, such as the earth is round and the earth is flat. If there is a truth, then everything else is false.

- *Most religions make opposite claims*. The Bible says Jesus rose from the dead, but the Qur'an says Jesus did not rise from the dead. One book has to be wrong and the other right. Christianity says that Jesus is the only way to God, while other religions say we have to earn our way to God. Again, someone has to be wrong and the other right.

- *Truth must correspond to reality*. This is how to know who is right. The only religion worth following must point to the truth, to the reality that is evident around us. This book has shown the reality is that this is a theistic universe and that God has sent his Son, Jesus Christ, to die for us. Only those who believe in him will be saved.

2. What about Those Who Are Sincere?

What if someone sincerely believes that stealing your money is okay or that red traffic lights mean "go"? Is it okay if they are sincere? Sincerity in the wrong belief is not okay in the physical world, and it is not okay in the spiritual world either.

Let's sum up some thoughts about sincerity.

Sincerity is not a test for truth. Truth is unchanging even though our beliefs about truth change. People used to believe the world was flat, but they were wrong though sincere. Sincerity cannot change a fact no matter how hard we cling to it.

We can be sincerely wrong. "There is a way that seems right to a man, but in the end it leads to death" (Prov. 14:12). Recall the parable of the blind men and the elephant. Were the six blind men right? No, they *all* were wrong though sincere. The only one who was right was the one with his eyes open to the truth, which was that this was an elephant! Try telling a victim of Hinduism that it doesn't matter what a person believes as long as he or she is sincere. Especially before Christian influence gained momentum in India, millions of Hindus sincerely believed the following:

- Baby girls should be drowned in the Ganges so they could be reincarnated as boys.
- Surviving widows should be cremated alive with their deceased husbands.
- The gross discrimination and prejudice of the Hindu caste system should be enforced.
- It is better not to relieve human suffering, because that would be interfering with people's karma.

Sincerity doesn't save; only Jesus does. In chapter 13, we learned that Jesus is the only way to God.

3. What about Those Who Have Never Heard?

This objection is unfounded, for everyone has heard something about God, and all will be held accountable by God for how they respond to the light they have. Consider the following points.

- *We know that God is loving and wants everyone to be saved.* "This is good, and pleases God our Savior, who wants all men to be saved and to come to a knowledge of the truth" (1 Tim. 2:4). "The Lord is . . . patient with you, not wanting anyone to perish, but everyone to come to repentance" (2 Peter 3:9).
- *Everyone has heard there is a creator God.* "The heavens declare the glory of God; the skies proclaim the work of his hands. . . . There is no speech or language where their voice is not heard" (Ps. 19:1–3). "For since the creation of the world God's invisible qualities . . . have been clearly seen, being understood from what has been made" (Rom. 1:20).
- *Those who reject the light they have are without excuse.* "For since the creation of the world God's invisible qualities . . . have been clearly seen . . . so that men are without excuse" (Rom. 1:20). "All who sin apart from the law will also perish apart from the law . . . since they show that the requirements of the law are written on their hearts" (Rom. 2:12–15).
- *Those who seek the light (of creation) they have get the light (of redemption) they need.* "God does not show favoritism but accepts men from every nation who fear him and do what is right" (Acts 10:34–35). "Anyone who comes to him must believe that

he exists and that he rewards those who earnestly seek him" (Heb. 11:6).

ONE WAY to God Checklist

Problem

O—*Offense*
* We broke God's law and committed an offense against him, which is called sin.
* Everyone has sinned and stands condemned.
* The judgment that has been given is death, separation from God eternally.

N—*Need*
* We are unable to satisfy God's demands and justice.

Solution

E—*Earn* Forgiveness for Us
* We are in desperate need of a substitute who can pay our debt, take our place, and earn forgiveness.
* Initially, God set up a system of animal sacrifices to gain forgiveness for the sinner as that person's sin would be transferred to an animal, its blood would cover the sin, and its death would equal the sentence.
* But this sacrifice was not permanent, and a better one was needed.

W—*Worthy*
* This better sacrifice would have to be a man with a body to be sacrificed.
* This better sacrifice would have to be sinless to be an unblemished sacrifice.
* This better sacrifice would have to be eternal for the sacrifice to apply to all and forever.

A—*Act* on Our Behalf
* Jesus Christ was the perfect sacrifice who acted on our behalf.

• He was born with a body that was sacrificed on the cross and provides eternal salvation, redemption, and forgiveness.

Response

Y—*Yield* to Him

• We need to repent in that we lay down our arms and surrender to him.
• We need to place our faith for salvation wholly in him and not in ourselves.

Digging Deeper on Jesus as the One and Only Way to God

Anderson, J. N. D. *The World's Religions*. London: Inter-Varsity, 1950.

Corduan, Winifred. *Neighboring Faiths*. Downers Grove, IL: Inter-Varsity, 1998.

Geisler, Norman, and Frank Turek. *I Don't Have Enough Faith to Be an Atheist*. Wheaton: Crossway, 2004.

Halverson, Dean. *The Compact Guide to World Religions*. Minneapolis: Bethany House, 1996.

Zacharias, Ravi. *Jesus Among Other Gods*. Nashville: Word, 2000.

Conclusion

Be Ready to Give an Answer

As we began this book, we saw that Jesus said our role in this world is to be salt (to retard the moral corruption of the world) and light (to discuss and defend the gospel). Our arena is the workplace where we spend the majority of our time with a majority of the unchurched. Our approach is not to use our apologetic information as a dagger but rather to engage in dialogue with our questioning co-workers.

In chapter 3, we met Mike who had a bad day when he did not know how to answer Doug's attack on Christianity. Let's review the five things we learned from Mike's bad day.

1. *Unbelievers have good questions.* Some of the questions being asked in the workplace are: "Are all religions true?" "Does God exist?" "Did humans evolve?" "If there is a God, why is there suffering in the world?" "Are miracles possible?" "Can we trust the Bible?" "Are there errors in the Bible?" "Is Jesus the Son of God?" and "Is there only one way to God?" These excellent questions are being asked every day in workplaces across the world.

2. *We have good answers to good questions.* Fortunately, we have good answers! Christianity is a credible faith with credible answers. We gave answers for these questions and put them into an acrostic format that would be easy to understand, remember, and defend.

3. *It is our responsibility to be prepared to give good answers for our faith.* We saw that Mike had some preconceived concepts

about apologetics. For example, he thought that apologetics was all about arguing and being divisive. We have seen that is not true. He thought that apologetics is too difficult to understand and only for the well educated. This book was written to change that idea by handling the tough questions in a way the person on the street could understand. He thought apologetics was unrelated to daily life, but now he was being pummeled every day at work with religious questions! Mike learned that he must be involved in apologetics both for his co-workers and himself.

We are amazed at the few apologetic resources many Christian businesspeople have. Most people think nothing of paying twenty dollars to have a pizza delivered or to get their SUV washed, but they won't pay the same amount to buy a Christian book. In appendix A, we have listed excellent resources that every Christian should have on hand to be prepared apologetically. I guarantee that if you purchase the books we recommend, you won't be disappointed (and the books will last longer than the pizza!).

4. *There are opportune moments for evangelism.* Did you notice the various ways an apologetic topic was raised by unbelievers? The things that stirred the discussion were: a movie (*The Passion of the Christ*), a workplace confrontation, a company policy, two businessmen riding in a car together, lunch meetings, a co-worker's confession, a TV news program, a current book (*The Da Vinci Code*), and a newspaper article.

These opportune moments for evangelism come our way almost every day if we will just look for them. Pray for opportunities, open your eyes, and follow the Holy Spirit's leading when these opportunities arise.

5. *The workplace is a key place for doing apologetics.* The workplace has three elements that make it important in witnessing: diversity, time, and opportunity. The workplace is diverse in that it is a mixed environment of Christians, seekers, and sleepers. We have time to witness in that we spend 60–70 percent of our waking hours with our co-workers. And we have many opportunities to use this time to influence our co-workers for the kingdom.

A few weeks ago, I (Randy) was shoring up a Christian co-worker's faith about the fact that Jesus is the Son of God. I shared with Sarah the CROWNED acrostic of chapter 12 and wrote it down on a napkin. She thanked me for the help and kept the napkin. Last week she asked me for a new napkin with the CROWNED acrostic on it. I asked if she had lost it, but she told me what had happened to it.

"I was having lunch with a friend, and somehow we started to discuss who Jesus really is. My friend wasn't sure Jesus even existed, so I pulled out the napkin you gave me from my business folder and shared the concepts with her point by point.

"When I was done, she frowned thoughtfully for a while. Then she grabbed my napkin, and I said, 'Hey, what are you doing? That's mine!'

"She smiled and asked, 'Sarah, do you mind if I have this? That was some good stuff, and I want to read it again.'

"I told her, 'No, you go ahead and have it. I know where to get another one.' I am so excited about this apologetics stuff!"

May her tribe increase. May her tribe dramatically increase!

Appendix A

Resources for Apologetics

Books

Geisler, Norman. *Baker Encyclopedia of Christian Apologetics*. Grand Rapids: Baker Books, 1999. A one-volume resource that answers a multitude of apologetic questions.

———. *Systematic Theology*. Grand Rapids: Bethany House, 2001, 2002, 2004. A four-volume, comprehensive, and systematic discussion of all the doctrines of the Christian faith.

Geisler, Norman, ed. *Inerrancy*. Grand Rapids: Zondervan, 1979.

Geisler, Norman, and Ron Brooks. *When Skeptics Ask*. Grand Rapids: Baker Books, 1990. Succinct answers to questions about God, other gods, evil, miracles, Jesus, the Bible, science and evolution, truth, and morals.

Geisler, Norman, and Win Corduan. *Philosophy of Religion*. 2nd ed. Grand Rapids: Baker Books, 1988. An in-depth discussion of the main elements of the Christian faith from a philosophical point of view, including religious experience, the existence of God, the problem of evil, and God-talk.

Geisler, Norman, and Thomas Howe. *When Critics Ask*. Grand Rapids: Baker Books, 1992. Answers over 800 difficult questions from every book of the Bible.

Geisler, Norman, and William Nix. *General Introduction to the Bible* Rev. ed. Chicago: Moody, 1986. A comprehensive treatment of the Bible from God to us, including its inspirtation, canonization (collection into 66 books), transmission, and translations.

Geisler, Norman, and Frank Turek. *I Don't Have Enough Faith to Be an Atheist*. Wheaton: Crossway, 2004. Shows that the Christian position is factual, logical, and true while the atheist position is full of holes and demands more faith.

————. *Legislating Morality*. Minneapolis: Bethany, 1998. Deals with the moral decline in America and the solution of legislation to promote good and control evil. Contains fascinating topics to discuss around the watercooler.

Kreeft, Peter, ed. *A Summa of the Summa*. San Francisco: Ignatius, 1990. A summary and explanation of crucial parts of the *Summa Theologica* of Thomas Aquinas, which was one of the greatest works on theology ever written.

Lewis, C. S. *The Abolition of Man*. New York: Macmillan, 1947. An excellent defense of the objective and absolute nature of the moral law by the greatest literary defender of the Christian faith in the 20th century.

————. *Mere Christianity*. New York: Macmillan, 1953. One of the best books ever written defending the essence of the Christian faith beginning with the moral law argument for God's existence.

————. *Miracles: A Preliminary Study*. New York: Macmillan, 1947. A rational defense of the supernatural, including the nature and existence of biblical miracles.

————. *The Problem of Pain*. New York: Macmillan, 1940. One of the best works availible on why God allows suffering by one of the best Christian writers of our time.

McDowell, Josh. *The New Evidence that Demands a Verdict*. Nashville: Nelson, 1999. A classic book on defending the faith and answering questions from today's world.

————. *A Ready Defense*. San Bernardino: Here's Life, 1990. Answers questions about the Bible, Jesus, other religions, and other questions about Christianity.

Sire, James. *The Universe Next Door*. Downers Grove: InterVarsity, 1988. This book opened the door for Christain study of various worldviews and still remains one of the best on the topic.

Strobel, Lee. *The Case for Christ*. Grand Rapids: Zondervan, 1998. Answers the question of credible evidence that Jesus is the Son of God.

———. *The Case for Faith*. Grand Rapids: Zondervan, 2000. Answers the question of whether a person can really believe in God.

Zacharias, Ravi, and Norman Geisler, *Is Your Church Ready? Motivating Leaders to Live an Apologetic Life*. Grand Rapids: Zondervan, 2003. Rightly places the responsibility on the church for equipping and motivating its people to live an apologetic life.

Zacharias, Ravi, and Norman Geisler, eds. *Who Made God? And Answers to Over 100 Other Tough Questions of Faith*. Grand Rapids: Zondervan, 2003. Takes more than one hundred of the top apologetic questions and provides answers in an easily understood approach.

Websites

The following websites are listed to spur you to begin building your own apologetic website library. This is not a complete list, but it is a good start.

Answering Islam (www.answering-islam.org). The top apologetic resource on Islam.

Apologetics.Com (www.apologetics.com). Excellent collection of apologetic articles.

Apologetics Resource Center (www. apologeticsresctr.org). Filled with good apologetic resources.

Christian Answers.Net (www.christiananswers.net). A megasite providing biblical answers to contemporary questions.

Christian Apologetics & Research Ministry (www.carm.org). A great site for equipping Christians in doctrine and apologetics.

The Christian Research Institute (www.equip.org). Hank Hanegraaff as "The Bible Answer Man."

A Christian Thinktank (www.christian-thinktank.com). Hundreds of scholarly articles on apologetic topics.

Dr. Norman Geisler (www.normgeisler.com). Articles by Dr. Geisler as well as tapes and books.

Inerrancy.Com (www.inerrancy.com). The number one place to discuss biblical inerrancy.

Issues that Make Christians Squirm (www.net-burst.net/hot). Deals with thirty-three objections to Christianity in simple terms.

John Ankerberg Theological Research Institute (www.ankerberg.org). Television show host site filled with excellent information.

Marketplace Impact (www.marketplaceimpact.org). Pages of articles by Randy Douglass for Christian in the workplace, which include apologetic questions and answers.

Meekness and Truth (www.meeknessandtruth.org). Hosted by Dave Geisler, Norm's son. Designed to reach skeptical college students.

Probe Ministries (www.probe.org). Has articles, a newsletter, and a radio program for apologetic students.

Ravi Zacharias International Ministries (www.rzim.com). Articles and radio ministry of this great thinker, speaker, and writer.

Ron Rhodes (www.ronrhodes.org). Articles and books from a foremost cult expert.

Soul Device (www.souldevice.org). Articles on basic Christian theology, apologetics, and culture.

Southern Evangelical Seminary (www.ses.edu). This seminary focuses on teaching apologetics in every major. Website has articles as well as information about the school.

Summit Ministries (www.summit.org). Provides worldview materials including conferences, curricula, books, videos, audio, and essays.

Tektonics (www.tektonics.org). Excellent collection of apologetic articles.

Watchman Fellowship (www.watchman.org). Specializes in the cults and New Age.

Worldview Weekend (www.worldviewweekend.com). Excellent resources to help you think and live as a Christian.

Educational Training

Southern Evangelical Seminary (www.ses.edu). Norman Geisler is the president, and I (Randy) was privileged to teach at SES. The seminary focuses on teaching apologetics in every major. SES has just started a Bible college. This website has articles as well as information about the school. If you are serious about learning apologetics, SES is the place to go!

Conferences

Every fall Southern Evangelical Seminary hosts an apologetics conference in Charlotte, North Carolina. For more information, contact the school at www.ses.edu.

Appendix B

Conversational Evangelism Model Outline

Evangelism Training for the New Millennium
"Conversational Evangelism"
Meekness and Truth Ministries (Dave Geisler)
www.meeknessandtruth.org

Introduction: Problems in Doing Evangelism Today

Understanding the times we live in (1 Chron. 12:32) means:

- Redefining what we mean by "evangelism" (1 Cor. 3:6)
- Allowing others to discover the truth for themselves by asking probing questions (2 Tim. 4:3–4)

We also must understand the important role of the Holy Spirit (John 6:63, 65).

The four parts of this model correspond to the four types of conversations we want to have with our non-Christian friends.

Hearing Conversations

This is always the first step where we seek to understand what they actually believe and also detect some of the discrepancies in their viewpoint.

Types of inconsistencies you might hear:

- Belief vs. Behavior (Gal. 2:14–16)
- Belief vs. Belief (Acts 17:22–30)
- Illogical Beliefs

Illuminating Conversations

This is where we ask questions to help people "see" for themselves (without us directly telling them they are wrong) some of the discrepancies in their beliefs. Our goal is to help them question whether their beliefs are a strong enough foundation to build their life on.

- Questions that uncover the meaning of certain unclear terms
- Questions that expose false belief systems or concepts

Uncovering Conversations

This is where we try to uncover the real barriers people have to the gospel (Jer. 17:9).

- Determine whether a person's issue is a legitimate question or concern, or whether it is a smoke screen.
- Formula: If I could answer your question, would that help?
- Determine whether the barrier is mostly an intellectual or emotional question or concern, or a combination of both.
- Uncover the specific emotional baggage a person is carrying.
- Determine whether the barrier requires a more objective or subjective approach (Acts 14:1; Phil. 1:14).
- Find out what a person's biggest barrier to Christianity is.
- Find out what would motivate the person to get answers in these areas.

Building Conversations

This is where we attempt to build a positive case for Christ and look for opportunities to invite them to trust Christ. Our goal is to find common ground with them (1 Cor. 9:22).

- Construct a bridge from those beliefs held in common (even those they are not quite aware of) to a point where they may be open to seriously consider the claims of Christ.

Planks of Common Understanding

1. It matters what you believe!
2. Not all religious viewpoints can be right!
3. Faith must have an object to have merit!
4. Jesus's claims are unique compared to any other major religious leader (John 10:30; 14:6; Acts 4:12; 1 Tim. 2:5).
5. The proof of Christ's claims have no parallel among major religious leaders.
6. Without God, some people find it difficult to find meaning in their lives.

Map out a logical bridge for people to consider.

- Remember the goal.

Has anyone ever shared with you how you can know God personally?

Conversational Evangelism Model in a Nutshell

We want to *hear* people's discrepancies and then *illuminate* them by asking questions that will *clarify* their religious terminology and *expose* the weaknesses of their perspective. Then we want to *uncover* the real barriers and *build* a bridge to help them take one step closer to Jesus Christ (1 Cor. 3:6).

Appendix C

THINK Evangelism Model Outline

Evangelism Training for the New Millennium
The THINK Method of Evangelism
Meekness and Truth Ministries (Dave Geisler)
www.meeknessandtruth.org

Introduction
(Clarifying Misconceptions that Affect Our Witness)

Evangelism is a process (1 Cor. 3:6).

Being ready means to eagerly anticipate their objection (1 Peter 3:15).

Biblical faith must have an object to be valid (1 Cor. 15:14).

Important distinction between "belief that" and "belief in."

Trust in the Holy Spirit

- To empower us to speak in a way that makes a difference (Acts 14:1)

    * Remember that we are just an instrument (1 Cor. 2:14).

    * Evidence can persuade one to "believe that" but not "believe in" Christ (James 2:19).

- To empower us to live godly lives (Phil 1:14)

Hear the Discrepancies/Contradictions

- The contradiction can be between what they say they believe and how they live (Gal. 2:14–16).
- The contradiction can be between two mutually contradictory beliefs they hold (Acts 17:22–30).

Examples:

Jesus is my Savior. / I can measure up.
The Bible is reliable. / I must do good works to be saved.

- The contradiction can be in the statement itself.

Examples:

You should be skeptical about everything.
Always avoid making absolute statements.
God is so far beyond us that we cannot really know anything about him.
There really is no absolute truth.

Illuminate Discrepancies by Asking Questions

- Questions that uncover the meaning of certain unclear terms

Examples:

Terms like: *good*, *Savior*, *died for us*, *Son of God*

- Questions that expose false belief systems

Examples:

Does it matter what we believe?
Can all religious views be right?
Why don't you believe that the Bible is reliable?
Do you think people will be held accountable for how they live?
    If so, what is the standard (Matt. 5:48; James 2:10)?

Navigate around Barriers

- Find the right balance in your approach between objective and subjective evidence (Acts 14:1; Phil. 1:14).
- Determine whether the barrier is an intellectual or emotional question or concern.
- Uncover the emotional baggage that they are carrying.
- Determine whether their issue is a legitimate question or a smoke screen.

    Formula: If I could answer your question, would that help?

- Find out what their biggest barrier to Christianity is.
- Find out what would motivate them to get answers in these areas.

Examples of Barriers:

Believing all religious views are equally valid.
Response: Show them that Jesus is unique (John 10:30; 14:6; Acts 4:12).
Being unwilling to commit to a religious perspective.

Response: Ask them if it were possible to know the truth, would they want to know it?

- Construct a bridge from those beliefs held in common (even those they are not quite aware of) to a point where someone may be open to seriously consider the claims of Christ.
- Map out a logical bridge from God's existence to Jesus, proving he is the only way to God (see our website under "Defense of Christianity Outline").

Building Blocks to Construct the Bridge

1. It matters what you believe.
2. Not all religious viewpoints can be right.
3. Faith must have an object to have merit.
4. Jesus made unique claims compared to any other major religious leader (John 10:30; 14:6; Acts 4:12; 1 Tim. 2:5).
5. The proof of Christ's claims has no parallel among major religious leaders.
6. Without God, some people find it difficult to find meaning in their life.

Keep the Door Open for Sharing the Gospel (2 Tim. 4:2)

- Remember the goal.
- Look for opportunities to transition to spiritual discussions.

Example:

In talking about evil you could say:

You know _____, there is a lot about the problem of evil that I don't know. But I do know that there will come a day when God will hold people accountable for the evil acts they have committed and the suffering they have caused (2 Cor. 5:10; Heb. 9:27). That is why it is important that we have a right relationship with God! Has anyone ever shared with you how you can know God personally?

Appendix D

Non-Christian Sources within 150 Years of Jesus

The primary sources for the life of Christ are the four Gospels, but there is significant evidence for the existence of Jesus from sources outside the Bible that supplement and confirm the New Testament account. These sources come largely from ancient historians, government officials, and Jewish and Gentile sources from the first century. All the quotes are taken from the Norman Geisler, *Baker Encyclopedia of Christian Apologetics* (Grand Rapids: Baker Academic, 1999), s.v. "Jesus, Non-Christian Sources."

Ancient Historians

Cornelius Tacitus (ca. AD 55–120) was a Roman historian who lived through the reigns of over a half dozen Roman emperors. He has been called the "greatest historian" of ancient Rome (in the *Annals* and the *Histories*). Tacitus recorded at least one reference to Christ and two references to early Christianity:

Consequently, to get rid of the report, Nero fastened the guilt and inflicted the most exquisite tortures of a class hated for

239

their abominations, called Christians by the populace. Christus, from whom the name had its origin, suffered the extreme
penalty during the reign of Tiberius at the hands of one of our
procurators, Pontius Pilatus, and a most mischievous superstition, thus checked for the moment, again broke out not only in
Judea, the first source of the evil, but even in Rome, where all
things hideous and shameful from every part of the world find
their center and become popular. (*Annals*, 15.44)

He affirms that a man named Christ existed and refers to Christians
who were named after Christus (Latin for *Christ*), who "suffered the
extreme penalty" (was put to death) under Pontius Pilate during the
reign of Tiberius, and he mentioned that the "superstition" (belief in
the resurrection) started in Judea, and made its way even to Rome.

Suetonius was chief secretary to Emperor Hadrian (reign, AD
117–138). He made two references to Christians:

Because the Jews at Rome caused continuous disturbances
at the instigation of Chrestus, he expelled them from the city.
(*Claudius*, 25)

After the great fire at Rome. . . . Punishments were also inflicted
on the Christians, a sect professing a new and mischievous
religious belief. (*Nero*, 16)

He says there was a man named *Chrestus* (or Christ), certain Jews
caused disturbances related to Christ (unknown to him whether
these disturbances were caused by Christ or antagonistic Jews), and
Claudius became annoyed and threw the Jews out of Rome (including Paul's associates Aquila and Priscilla) in AD 49. Christians were
persecuted after the fire, and they professed a "new religious belief"
(belief in the resurrection).

Flavius Josephus (AD 37/38–97) was the Jewish historian under
Emperor Vespasian. Josephus had two passages of interest in his
Antiquities, written in early 90s. The first refers to James, "the brother
of Jesus, who was called Christ." The second reference is the most
important and the most debated. The Josephus quote most authors
have cited has been accused of having some Christian interpola-
tions in it, some Christian additions introduced over time, and thus

is not credible to many. Because of this, we will examine an Arabic manuscript containing Josephus' statement about Jesus, which is a different and briefer rendering than the normal rendering:

> At this time there was a wise man named Jesus. His conduct was good and [he] was known to be virtuous. And many people from among the Jews and the other nations became his disciples. Pilate condemned him to be crucified and to die. But those who became his disciples did not abandon his discipleship. They reported that he had appeared to them three days after his crucifixion, and that he was alive; accordingly he was perhaps the Messiah, concerning whom the prophets have recounted wonders. (cited in Habermas, *The Historical Jesus*, 186)

Even this Arabic rendering of Josephus's text is an extraordinary witness to the life, death, and influence of Jesus. It states that Jesus existed and was known to be a wise and virtuous man who had Jewish and Gentile disciples. Pilate condemned him to be crucified. The disciples reported that he had risen from the dead on the third day. This idea had been attached to his proclamation that he was the Messiah.

Thallus (AD 52) wrote about Jesus, earlier than anyone else, in the early AD 50s. Though none of his works survived, a few citations of his are preserved by other writers. One of these writers was Julius Africanus in about AD 221, who quotes Thallus in a discussion of the darkness which followed the crucifixion of Christ:

> On the whole world there pressed a most fearful darkness; and the rocks were rent by an earthquake, and many places in Judea and other districts were thrown down. This darkness Thallus, in the third book of his *History* calls, as appears to me without reason, an eclipse of the sun. (*Extant Writings*, 18 in the *Ante-Nicene Fathers*)

Africanus identifies the darkness which Thallus explained as a solar eclipse with the darkness at the crucifixion described in Luke 23:44–45.

Government Officials

Pliny the Younger (AD 112) was a Roman author and administrator who served the governor of Bithynia in Asia Minor. Ten books of Pliny's correspondence are extant today. The tenth book, written around AD 112, speaks about Christianity in the province of Bithynia and also provides some facts about Jesus. Governor Pliny was taking action against the Christians but was unsure of how far he should go. So he wrote to Emperor Trajan to explain his strategy and ask for advice, describing the early Christian worship practices:

> They [the Christians] were in the habit of meeting on a certain fixed day before it was light, when they sang in alternate verses a hymn to Christ, as to a god, and bound themselves by a solemn oath, not to any wicked deeds, but never to commit any fraud, theft or adultery, never to falsify their word, nor deny a trust when they should be called upon to deliver it up; after which it was their custom to separate, and then reassemble to partake food—but food of an ordinary and innocent kind. (*Letters*, 10:96)

From Pliny's letter, we find that he affirms Jesus lived, early Christians worshiped Jesus as God, probably met to worship on Sundays, Jesus had disciples who followed his ethical teachings such as the Lord's Supper, and that they were persecuted for their faith. Later in the same letter, Pliny calls the teaching of Jesus and his followers "excessive superstition" and "contagious superstition," which may refer to Christian belief and proclamation of the resurrection of Jesus.

Emperor Trajan (AD 112?) in his reply to Pliny's letter gives the following guidelines for persecuting Christians:

> No search should be made for these people; when they are denounced and found guilty they must be punished; with the restriction, however, that when the party denies himself to be a Christian, and shall give proof that he is not (that is, by adoring our gods) he shall be pardoned on the ground of repentance, even though he may have formerly incurred suspicion. (*Letters*, 10:97)

Trajan affirms that Jesus lived, he was worshiped by his disciples, that this worship spread, and his followers were to be persecuted for not worshiping the Roman gods, yet this persecution was not without restrictions.

Emperor Hadrian (AD 117–138) wrote concerning the persecution of Christians and those who would accuse Christians falsely:

> I do not wish, therefore, that the matter should be passed by without examination, so that these men may neither be harassed, nor opportunity of malicious proceedings be offered to inform-ers. If, therefore, the provincials can clearly evince their charges against the Christians, so as to answer before the tribunal, let them pursue this course only, but not by mere petitions, and mere outcries against the Christians. For it is far more proper, if anyone would bring an accusation, that you should examine it. (*Ecclesiastical History*, 4:9)

Hadrian affirms that Jesus existed, he had disciples, Christianity spread far, and that these followers were persecuted for their faith.

Jewish Sources

The **Talmud** (AD 70–200) was written between 70 and 200 during the so-called Tannaitic period. The most significant text is Sanhedrin 43a:

> On the eve of Passover Yeshu was hanged. For forty days before the execution took place, a herald went forth and cried, "He is going forth to be stoned because he has practiced sorcery and enticed Israel to apostasy. Any one who can say anything in his favour, let him come forward and plead on his behalf." But since nothing was brought forward in his favour he was hanged on the eve of the Passover! (*Babylonian Talmud*)

This passage confirms that Jesus actually existed, was crucified on the eve of Passover, and was preceded by a herald, plus another reference in this section mentions five disciples of Jesus.

Toledoth Jesu (fifth century) is a late, anti-Christian document that says that the body of Jesus was secretly moved to a second grave because the disciples were planning to steal the body. When the disciples found the original tomb of Jesus empty, they concluded that he had risen from the dead. But the Jewish authorities were informed of the true location of the body of Jesus. This document reflects the first antagonistic explanation as found in Matthew 18:11–15. This document affirms that Jesus existed and that his tomb was empty.

Gentile Sources

Lucian (second century) of Samosata was a second-century Greek writer whose works contain sarcastic critiques of Christianity:

> The Christians, you know, worship a man to this day—the distinguished personage who introduced their novel rites, and was crucified on that account. . . . You see, these misguided creatures start with the general conviction that they are immortal for all time, which explains the contempt for death and voluntary self-devotion which are so common among them; and then it was impressed on them by their original lawgiver that they are all brothers, from the moment that they are converted, and deny the gods of Greece, and worship the crucified sage, and live after his laws. All this they take quite on faith, with the result that they despise all worldly goods alike, regarding them merely as common property. (*Death of Pelegrine*, 11–13)

From Lucian we learn that Jesus existed, was worshiped, introduced new teachings, and was crucified for these teachings. These teachings included the brotherhood of believers, the importance of conversion, and the denying of other gods. The followers of Jesus believed themselves immortal and had contempt for death, voluntary self-devotion, and renunciation of material goods. Though Lucian was a critic, he gives an informative account of Jesus and early Christianity outside of the New Testament.

Mara Bar-Serapion (first through third century) wrote to his son Serapion sometime between the late first and early third centuries. The letter contains an apparent reference to Jesus:

> What advantage did the Athenians gain from putting Socrates to death? Famine and plague came upon them as a judgment for their crime. What advantage did the men of Samon gain from

burning Pythagoras? In a moment their land was covered with sand. What advantage did the Jews gain from executing their wise King? It was just after that their kingdom was abolished. God justly avenged these three wise men: the Athenians died of hunger; the Samians were overwhelmed by the sea; the Jews, ruined and driven from the land, live in complete dispersion. But Socrates did not die for good; he lived on in the statue of Hera. Nor did the wise king die for good; he lived on in the teaching which he had given. (British Museum, Syriac, ms, add. 14, 658; cited in Habermas, *The Historical Jesus*, 200)

This passage confirms that Jesus existed, was thought to be a wise and virtuous man, was considered by many to be the king of Israel, and that the Jews put him to death, but Jesus lived on in the teachings of his followers.

Phlegon (b. ca. AD 80) was a freed slave of Emperor Hadrian. None of Phlegon's works are in existence today, but he is mentioned several times by later writers. Origen, who cites Phlegon, mentions that Jesus made predictions about future events that had been fulfilled.

Now Phlegon, in the thirteenth or fourteenth book, I think, of his Chronicles, not only ascribed to Jesus a knowledge of future events (although falling into confusion about some things which refer to Peter, as if they referred to Jesus), but also testified that the result corresponded to His predictions. (Origen, *Contra Celsum* XIV in the *Ante-Nicene Fathers*)

Origin adds another comment about Phlegon:

And with regard to the eclipse in the time of Tiberius Caesar, in whose reign Jesus appears to have been crucified, and the great earthquakes which then took place, Phlegon too, I think, has written in the thirteenth or fourteenth book of his Chronicles. (Origen, *Contra Celsum* XXXIII in the *Ante-Nicene Fathers*)

Julius Africanus agrees on the last reference to Phlegon, adding a bit more information:

Phlegon records that, in the time of Tiberius Caesar, at full moon, there was a full eclipse of the sun from the sixth to the ninth hour. [Julius Africanus, XVIII]

In a final reference, Origen quotes Phlegon on the subject of the resurrection:

Jesus, while alive, was of no assistance to himself, but that he arose after death, and exhibited the marks of his punishment, and showed how his hands had been pierced by nails. (Origen, LIX)

From Phlegon, we see that Jesus existed, he predicted the future, that there was an eclipse at the time of the crucifixion, and that this eclipse occurred during the reign of Tiberius. After his resurrection, Jesus appeared and showed his wounds, especially the nail marks from the crucifixion.

Presented in chart form, the evidence cited earlier from extrabiblical, non-Christian sources that either explicitly mentions or at least implies an acknowledgement of Jesus's resurrection from the dead stacks up quite impressively, corroborating the resurrection accounts in the New Testament.

What this sometimes hostile, non-Christian evidence suggests about Jesus can be summarized by the following words:

- *Existed*—every witness confirms that a man named Jesus actually existed, some by statement, others by inference
- *Virtuous*—Jesus was seen as a righteous man
- *Worshiped*—Jesus was thought of as a god by his followers and to be worshiped as such
- *Disciples*—Jesus had followers who practiced his teachings
- *Teacher*—Jesus was a great teacher
- *Crucified*—Jesus was crucified on a cross
- *Empty Tomb*—three days later the tomb of Jesus was empty
- *Early Belief in Jesus's Resurrection*—the earliest disciples believed that Jesus rose from the dead.
- *Spread*—the teachings and worship of Jesus spread across the known world
- *Persecution*—the disciples of Jesus suffered greatly for their faith in Jesus as the Christ

Non-Christian sources within 150 years of Jesus

Source	AD	Existed	Virtuous	Worship	Disciples	Teacher	Crucified	Empty Tomb	Disciples' Belief in Resurrection	Spread	Persecution
Tacitus	115	X			X		X	X*		X	X
Suetonius	117–138	X		X	X			X*		X	X
Josephus	90–95	X	X	X	X	X	X	X	X	X	
Thallus	52	X					X*				
Pliny	112	X		X	X	X		X*		X	X
Trajan	112?	X*		X	X					X	X
Hadrian	117–138	X*			X					X	X
Talmud	70–200	X					X				X
Toledoth Jesu	fifth century	X						X			
Lucian	second century	X		X	X	X	X				X
Mara Bar-Serapion	first through third century	X	X	X		X	X	X*			
Phlegon	80?	X					X	X	X		

*implied

Sources

Babylonian Talmud
Toledoth Jesu
Eusebius, *Ecclesiastical History*, C. F. Cruse, trans.
Flavius Josephus, *Antiquities of the Jews*
G. Habermas, *The Historical Jesus*, chapter 9
Lucian of Samosata, *The Works of Lucian of Samosata*
Origen, *Contra Celsus*
Pliny the Younger, *Letters*, W. Melmoth, trans.
A. Roberts and J. Donaldson, eds., *The Ante-Nicene Fathers*
Suetonius, *Life of Claudius*
Suetonius, *Life of Nero*
Tacitus, *Annals*

Notes

Chapter 1: Our Role

1. Haddon Robinson, *The Christian Salt and Light Company* (Grand Rapids: Discovery House, 1988), 99.
2. Ibid., 105.
3. John MacArthur, *The John MacArthur New Testament Commentary, Matthew 1–7* (Chicago: Moody, 1985), 239.
4. Ibid., 240.
5. Robinson, *Christian Salt and Light Company,* 106–7.

Chapter 2: Our Arena

1. Lee Strobel, *Inside the Mind of Unchurched Harry and Mary* (Grand Rapids: Zondervan, 1993), 85.
2. Dr. Randy Douglass shares these six key business success principles in his Impact Your Marketplace seminar. For more information, see his website at www.market placeimpact.org.
3. Os Hillman, "Faith and Work Facts and Quotes," International Coalition of Workplace Ministries, www.icwm.net, www.marketplaceleaders.org/pages. asp?pageid-7892.
4. For more information, go to the American Center for Law and Justice (ACLJ) website at www.aclj.org and check out Workplace Rights under the Issues Spotlight.
5. See this at www.aclj.org, Issues Spotlight, Workplace Rights, Witnessing Resources.
6. For more information, visit Larry Moyer, EvanTell, Inc., www.evantell.org. Flash animation of the Bad News/Good News presentation can be seen at this website.
7. Robinson, *Christian Salt and Light Company,* 106.

Chapter 3: Why Apologetics?

1. Norman Geisler and Ron Brooks, *When Skeptics Ask* (Grand Rapids: Baker Books, 1990), 11.
2. Ibid.

3. Ravi Zacharias and Norman Geisler, *Is Your Church Ready? Motivating Leaders to Live an Apologetic Life* (Grand Rapids: Zondervan, 2003), 91–94.

4. Geisler and Brooks, *When Skeptics Ask*, 11.

5. Zacharias and Geisler, *Is Your Church Ready?* 104–7.

Chapter 4: How Should We Do Apologetics?

1. Psalm 14:1; 53:1 KJV.

2. For more information on the Office Zoo seminar, see www.marketplaceimpact. org.

3. Gary Smalley, *Making Love Last Forever* (Dallas: Word, 1996), 153–55.

4. Ibid.

5. Dave Geisler of Meekness and Truth Ministries has developed the THINK method of evangelism, which can be found at www.meeknessandtruth.org/tools/THINK. See also appendix C.

6. Dale Carnegie, *How to Win Friends and Influence People* (New York: Pocket Books, 1940), 144.

7. Ibid.

8. Zacharias and Geisler, *Is Your Church Ready?* 37.

9. Smalley, *Making Love Last Forever*, 144–47.

10. This evidence is covered in chapter 12.

Chapter 5: Are All Religions True?

1. Norman Geisler and Frank Turek, *I Don't Have Enough Faith to Be an Atheist* (Wheaton: Crossway, 2004), 57.

2. Ibid., 39.

3. Ibid., 54.

Chapter 6: Does God Exist?

1. Geisler and Turek, *I Don't Have Enough Faith to Be an Atheist*, 65–66.

2. Gregory Koukl, "Objection Overruled," *Stand to Reason Commentary* (1996), www.str.org.

3. George Will, "The Gospel from Science," *Newsweek*, November 8, 1998.

4. For a deeper treatment of the SURGE discoveries, see Geisler and Turek, *I Don't Have Enough Faith to Be an Atheist*, 74–86.

5. Ravi Zacharias and Norman Geisler, eds. *Who Made God? And Answers to Over 100 Other Tough Questions of Faith* (Grand Rapids: Zondervan, 2003), 54–55.

6. Quoted in Fred Heeren, *Show Me God* (Wheeling, IL: Daystar, 2000), 168.

7. Robert Jastrow, *God and the Astronomers* (New York: Norton, 1978), 14.

8. "A Scientist Caught between Two Faiths: Interview with Robert Jastrow," *Christianity Today*, August 6, 1982, emphasis added.

9. Geisler and Turek, *I Don't Have Enough Faith to Be an Atheist*, 92.

10. Hugh Ross, *Creator and the Cosmos* (Colorado Springs: NavPress, 1995), 111–45.

11. As quoted in Lee Strobel, *The Case for Faith* (Grand Rapids: Zondervan, 2000), 77.

12. Geisler and Brooks, *When Skeptics Ask*, 21.

13. Richard Dawkins, *The Blind Watchmaker* (New York: W. W. Norton, 1987), 1.

14. Sue Bohlin, "Evidence for God's Existence," *Probe Ministry Commentary* (1999), http://www.probe.org/docs/evidence.htm.

15. Geisler and Brooks, *When Skeptics Ask*, 23.

16. C. S. Lewis, *Mere Christianity* (New York: Macmillan, 1952), 45.

17. Gregory Koukl, "Guilt and God," *Stand to Reason Commentary* (1994), http://www.str.org.

18. Geisler and Turek, *I Don't Have Enough Faith to Be an Atheist*, 171.

Chapter 7: Did Humans Evolve?

1. Michael Behe, *Darwin's Black Box* (New York: Free Press, 1996), 232, 191, 251, 243 (emphasis in original).

2. Francis Darwin, *The Life and Letters of Charles Darwin* (New York: D. Appleton, 1887), 202.

3. This is taken from the title of chapter 6 of Geisler and Turek, *I Don't Have Enough Faith to Be an Atheist*, 137.

4. Dawkins, *Blind Watchmaker*, 17–18, 116.

5. Strobel, *Case for Faith*, 110.

6. Charles B. Thaxton, Walter L. Bradley, and Roger L. Olsen, *The Mystery of Life's Origin* (Dallas: Lewis and Stanley, 1984), back cover.

7. George Johnson, "Science and Religion: Bridging the Great Divide," *New York Times*, June 30, 1998.

8. Francis Crick, *Life Itself* (New York: Simon and Schuster, 1981) 88.

9. See Thaxton, Bradley, and Olsen, *Mystery of Life's Origin*, 194.

10. Strobel, *Case for Faith*, 110.

11. Charles Darwin, *On the Origin of Species* (New York: Penguin, 1958), 280.

12. David M. Raup, "Conflicts between Darwin and Paleontology," *Bulletin, Field Museum of Natural History*, January 1979, 22, quoted in Paul S. Taylor, *The Illustrated Origins Answer Book*, 4th ed. (Meda, AZ: Eden, 1993), 108.

13. Phillip E. Johnson, *Darwin on Trial*, 2nd ed. (Downers Grove: InterVarsity, 1993), 126–27.

14. Hank Hanegraaff, *The Face that Demonstrates the Farce of Evolution* (Nashville: W, 1998), 34.

15. Stephen J. Gould, "Evolution's Erratic Pace," *Natural History* 86 (1977): 13–14. More recently Robert B. Carroll, curator of vertebrate paleontology at the Redpath Museum at McGill University, affirmed Gould's assessment when he wrote, "What is missing are the many intermediate forms hypothesized by Darwin" ("Towards a New Evolutionary Synthesis," *Trends in Ecology and Evolution* 15 (2000): 27–32.

16. Jonathan Wells, *Icons of Evolution: Science or Myth? Why Much of What We Teach about Evolution Is Wrong* (Washington, DC: Regnery, 2000), 178.

17. Michael Denton, *Evolution: A Theory in Crisis* (Bethesda, MD: Adler & Adler, 1985), 286.

18. Wells, *Icons of Evolution*, 219.

19. Geisler and Turek, *I Don't Have Enough Faith to Be an Atheist*, 154–55.

20. Go to http://www.gallup.com/content/login.aspx?ci=1942.

21. Dawkins, *Blind Watchmaker*, 1987.

22. Johnson, *Darwin on Trial*, 19.

23. Charles Darwin, *Origin of Species*, 6th ed. (New York: New York University Press, 1988), 154.

24. See "Riker Finds Bigger Gap in Chimp, Human Genes," *Japan Times*, July 12, 2003, http://japantimes.co.jp/cgi-bin/getarticle.pl5?nn20030712b6.htm.

25. Mouse Genome Sequencing Consortium, "Initial Sequencing and Comparative Analysis of the Mouse Genome," *Nature* 420 (December 5, 2002): 520–62.

26. Steve Jones, interviewed at the Australian Museum on *The Science Show*, ABC Radio, January 12, 2002.

27. Denton, *Evolution*, 67.

28. Ibid.

29. Alvin Plantinga, "Two Dozen (or So) Theistic Arguments" (lecture, 33rd Annual Philosophy Conference, Wheaton College, Wheaton, IL, October 23–25, 1986).

30. Strobel, *Case for Faith*, 108–9.

31. Richard Lewontin, "Billions and Billions of Demons," *New York Review of Books*, January 9, 1997, 317.

32. Geisler and Turek, *I Don't Have Enough Faith to Be an Atheist*, 162.

Chapter 8: If There Is a God, Why Is There Suffering in the World?

1. Strobel, *Case for Faith*, 29.

2. Geisler and Brooks, *When Skeptics Ask*, 63.

3. For example, Psalms 10:1; 22:1; 42:9; 43:2; 44:23–24; 74:1, 11; 88:14.

4. C. S. Lewis, *The Problem of Pain* (New York: Macmillan, 1962), 93.

5. Paul Brand and Philip Yancey, *Fearfully and Wonderfully Made* (Grand Rapids: Zondervan, 1980), 37–38.

6. Geisler and Brooks, *When Skeptics Ask*, 63.

7. Harold S. Kushner, *When Bad Things Happen to Good People* (New York: Schocken Books, 1981).

8. Charles R. Swindoll, *For Those Who Hurt* (Grand Rapids: Zondervan 1977).

9. Dan Story, *Defending Your Faith* (Nashville: Nelson, 1992), 176–77.

10. Geisler and Brooks, *When Skeptics Ask*, 64–65.

Chapter 9: Are Miracles Possible?

1. C. S. Lewis, *Miracles* (New York: Macmillan, 1947), 106.

2. Geisler and Turek, *I Don't Have Enough Faith to Be an Atheist*, 201.

3. Ibid., 212.

4. Ibid., 210.

5. Ibid., 216.

Chapter 10: Can We Trust the Bible?

1. "Was Jesus Married?" *ABC Prime Time Monday*, November 3, 2003.

2. Some excellent books about *The Da Vinci Code* are Darrell Brock, *Breaking the Da Vinci Code* (Nashville: Nelson, 2004); Hank Hanegraaff, *Da Vinci Code: Fact or Fiction?* (Wheaton: Tyndale, 2004); and Erwin Lutzer, *The Da Vinci Deception* (Wheaton: Tyndale, 2004).

3. Geisler and Turek's book *I Don't Have Enough Faith to Be an Atheist* lists ten reasons (pp. 275–97).

4. Colin J. Hemer, *The Book of Acts in the Setting of Hellenistic History* (Winona Lake, IN: Eisenbrauns, 1990), 376—82.

5. Geisler and Turek, *I Don't Have Enough Faith to Be an Atheist*, 263–68.

6. Ibid., 269.

7. Charles Colson, "An Unholy Hoax?" *Breakpoint* commentary, March 29, 2002 (no. 020329), http://www.epem.org/UnholyHoax.htm.

8. From a speech delivered at the Mississippi College School of Law, reported at http://tmatt.gospelcom.net/column/1996/04/24/.

9. Dr. Norman Geisler, quoted in Lee Strobel, *The Case for Faith* (Grand Rapids: Zondervan, 2000), 131.

10. J. Barton Payne, *Encyclopedia of Biblical Prophecy* (London: Hodder & Stoughton, 1973), 674–75.

11. Geisler and Turek, *I Don't Have Enough Faith to Be an Atheist*, 229.

12. To see the John Rylands fragment in person, visit the John Rylands University Library of Manchester. To view pictures of this fragment, visit http://rylibweb.man/ac.uk/.

13. Norman Geisler, *Baker Encyclopedia of Christian Apologetics* (Grand Rapids: Baker Books, 1999), 532.

14. William F. Albright, *Archaeology and the Religion of Israel* (Baltimore: Johns Hopkins University Press, 1953), 176.

15. Colin J. Hemer, *The Book of Acts in the Setting of Hellenistic History* (Winona Lake, IN: Eisenbrauns, 1990), 381.

16. William Lane Craig, *The Son Rises* (Eugene, OR: Wipf & Stock, 2001), 101.

17. Paul Barnett, *Is the New Testament Reliable?* (Downers Grove: InterVarsity Press, 1986), 38–40.

18. Paul Barnett, *Jesus and the Rise of Early Christianity* (Downers Grove: InterVarsity Press, 1999), 343.

19. Geisler and Turek, *I Don't Have Enough Faith to Be an Atheist*, 241.

20. Most scholars date this creed prior to AD 40. See Gary Habermas, *The Historical Jesus* (Joplin, MO: College Press, 1996), 152–57.

21. For a breakdown of these quotations, see Norman Geisler and William Nix, *General Introduction to the Bible* (Chicago: Moody, 1986), 431.

Chapter 11: Are There Errors in the Bible?

1. Augustine, *Reply to Faustus the Manichaean*, 11.5 in 14 vols., Series 1, ed. Philip Schaff, *A Select Library of the Nicene and Ante-Nicene Fathers of the Christian Church*, 1886-1894; repr., (Grand Rapids: Eerdmans, 1956).

2. The biblical authors include a lawgiver (Moses), a general (Joshua), prophets (Samuel, Isaiah, et al.), kings (David and Solomon), a musician (Asaph), a herdsman (Amos), a prince and statesman (Daniel), a priest (Ezra), a tax collector (Matthew), a physician (Luke), a scholar (Paul), and fishermen (Peter and John). With such a variety of occupations represented by biblical writers, it is only natural that their personal interests and differences should be reflected in their writings.

3. Norman Geisler and Thomas Howe, *When Critics Ask* (Grand Rapids: Baker Books, 1992).

4. Ibid., 37.

5. Ibid., 42.

6. Ibid., 140.

7. Ibid., 167–68.

8. Ibid., 183–84.

9. Ibid., 191–92.

10. Ibid., 220.

11. Ibid., 307–8.

12. Ibid., 326–27.

13. Ibid., 328–29.

14. Ibid., 335.

15. Ibid., 343; Lee Strobel, *The Case for Christ* (Grand Rapids: Zondervan, 1998), 217.

16. Geisler and Howe, *When Critics Ask*, 352.

17. Ibid., 361.

18. Ibid., 364–65.

19. Ibid., 365.

20. Ibid., 367.

21. Ibid., 383–84.

22. Several online sources attribute this poem to John Clifford (1836–1923), one of which identified him as a Baptist minister and social reformer.

Chapter 12: Is Jesus the Son of God?

1. Strobel, *Inside the Mind of Unchurched Harry and Mary*, 46.

2. Tim LaHaye, *Jesus: Who Is He?* (Sisters, OR: Multnomah, 1996), 59.

3. John Ankerberg and John Weldon, *Everything You Ever Wanted to Know about Mormonism* (Eugene, OR: Harvest House, 1992), 134.

4. "*Let God Be True*," 2nd ed., The Watch Tower Bible & Tract Society (1952), 33.

5. "*Make Sure of All Things*," The Watch Tower Bible & Tract Society (1953), 207.

6. Sun Myung Moon, *Divine Principle*, 2nd ed. (The Holy Spirit Association for the Unification of World Christianity, 1973), 258.

7. Victor Wierwille, *The Word's Way Studies in Abundant Living*, vol. 3 (American Christian Press, Way International, 1971), 37.

8. Bertrand Russell, *Why I Am Not a Christian* (New York: Touchstone, 1957), 19.

9. From an ordination sermon William Channing preached for the Reverend Jared Sparks in the First Independent Church of Baltimore on May 5, 1819. To read the sermon, go to http://www.transcendentalists.com/unitarian_christianity.htm.

10. Taken from Dave Branon, *Who Is This Man Who Says He's God?* (Grand Rapids: RBC Ministries, 1988), http://www.discoveryseries.org/q0205/.

11. Josephus, *Antiquities of the Jews*, 20.9.1.

12. Vice-presidential debate, Omaha, NE, October 5, 1988, www.thehistorychannel.com/speeches/archive/speech_222.html.

13. Lewis, *Mere Christianity*, 55–56.

14. Geisler and Brooks, *When Skeptics Ask*, 115.

15. S. R. Driver, *The Fifty-Third Chapter of Isaiah according to the Jewish Interpreters* (New York: KTAV, 1969), 1876–77.

16. Strobel, *Case for Christ*, 183.

17. Ibid, 184.

18. Geisler and Turek, *I Don't Have Enough Faith to Be an Atheist*, 222.

19. Ibid., 223.

20. Norman Geisler and Abdul Saleeb, *Answering Islam* (Grand Rapids: Baker Books, 1993), 64–65.

21. Ian Wilson, *Jesus: The Evidence* (1984; reprint, San Francisco: HarperSan-Francisco, 1988), 140.

22. Geisler, *Baker Encyclopedia of Apologetics*, 713.

23. Ibid., 48.

24. William D. Edwards, M.D., et al. "On the Physical Death of Jesus Christ," *Journal of the American Medical Association* 255, no. 11 (March 21, 1986): 1463.

25. Strobel, *Case for Christ*, 203.

26. Ibid., 205.

27. Geisler, *Baker Encyclopedia of Christian Apologetics*, 655.

28. Ibid., 381–85; Gary Habermas, *The Historical Jesus* (Joplin, MO: College Press, 1996), chapter 9.

29. Josh McDowell, *The Resurrection Factor* (San Bernardino, CA: Here's Life, 1981), 84.

30. Geisler and Turek, *I Don't Have Enough Faith to Be an Atheist*, 312.

31. See Edwin Yamauchi, "Easter—Myth, Hallucination or History?" *Christianity Today*, March 15, 1974, March 29, 1974.

32. Geisler and Brooks, *When Skeptics Ask*, 123-25.

33. Kenneth Scott Latourette, *American Historical Review* 54 (January 1949): 272.

34. Martin J. Scott, *Jesus as Men Saw Him* (New York: P. J. Kennedy and Sons, 1940), 29.

35. Philip Schaff, *History of the Christian Church* (repr.; Grand Rapids: Eerdmans, 1962), 103.

36. Charles Babington and Alan Cooperman, "The Rev. Moon Honored at Hill Reception; Lawmakers Say They Were Misled," *Washington Post*, June 23, 2004, A.01.

37. Schaff, *History of the Christian Church*, 103.

38. Geisler and Turek, *I Don't Have Enough Faith to Be an Atheist*, 290–91.

39. This essay was adapted from a sermon titled "Arise, Sir Knight!" by Dr. James Allan Francis in *The Real Jesus and Other Sermons* (Philadelphia: Judson, 1926), 123–24.

Chapter 13: Is There Only One Way to God?

1. Geisler and Saleeb, *Answering Islam*, 178–204.

2. Lewis, *Mere Christianity*, 59.

3. Billy Graham, *How to Be Born Again* (Waco: Word, 1977), 118–19.

Norman L. Geisler is the president of Southern Evangelical Seminary and one of the world's leading Christian apologists. He has authored over sixty books and defended the cause of Christ throughout the United States and internationally.

For more information about Dr. Geisler or Southern Evangelical Seminary, see www.normgeisler.com or www.ses.edu.

Randy Douglass is president of Marketplace Impact, a ministry equipping Christians in the workplace. He has served as pastor, seminary professor, and business consultant.

For more information about Dr. Douglass and Marketplace Impact, see www.marketplaceimpact.org.